VEGETARIANS *and* VEGANS *in* AMERICA TODAY

VEGETARIANS *and* VEGANS *in* AMERICA TODAY

Karen Iacobbo
and
Michael Iacobbo

Foreword by Jeffrey Moussaieff Masson
and Leila Masson

AMERICAN SUBCULTURES
Bruce Jackson, Series Editor

Westport, Connecticut
London

Library of Congress Cataloging-in-Publication Data

Iacobbo, Karen.
  Vegetarians and vegans in America today / Karen Iacobbo and
Michael Iacobbo ; foreword by Jeffrey Moussaieff Masson and Leila Masson.
     p. cm. — (American subcultures, ISSN 1559-2375)
  Includes bibliographical references and index.
  ISBN 0–275–99016–8 (alk. paper)
  1. Vegetarianism—United States. 2. Vegetarians—United States.
3. Vegans—United States. I. Iacobbo, Michael. II. Title. III. Series.
  TX392.I234 2006
  613.2'620973—dc22   2006004353

British Library Cataloging in Publication Data is available.

Library of Congress Catalog Card Number: 2006004353
ISBN: 0–275–99016–8
ISSN: 1559-2375

First published in 2006

Praeger Publishers, 88 Post Road West, Westport, CT 06881
An imprint of Greenwood Publishing Group, Inc.
www.praeger.com

Printed in the United States of America

The paper used in this book complies with the
Permanent Paper Standard issued by the National
Information Standards Organization (Z39.48–1984).

10 9 8 7 6 5 4 3 2 1

We dedicate this book to Ludovico and Gloria Tomasso. Thank you both for your love, encouragement, and support throughout our long vegetarian and writing journey. We also dedicate this book to Guido and Carol Iacobbo. Thank you both for your love and support, and we thank Guido for taking over at PP whenever asked.

This book would not have been possible without the people who generously, courageously, honestly, and eagerly shared their thoughts about vegetarianism. We thank you all and dedicate this book to you, too.

CONTENTS

FOREWORD

Can we imagine a world without meat? It will have to be an imaginative activity, because in fact during the last fifty years the world's meat production has quadrupled. But even if you are not a vegetarian, it is worth thinking about what kind of world we would live in if eating meat were eliminated.

First, how many fewer animals would die? Well, something close to 50 billion animals are killed every year for food. At least 10 billion of those animals are slaughtered in the United States alone. Each and every one of those deaths is a personal tragedy for the animal who undergoes it.

Don't we have enough human tragedies to consider, without having to stop to think about animals? Well, we would have fewer human tragedies too: 6 million children under age five die every year as a result of hunger and malnutrition. How many people, right now, feel hungry every day? Close to a billion—that is, one in every six people on earth.

How would the disappearance of animal-based foods help these people? One-third of all the land on earth is used to raise livestock. In the United States, 60 percent of all grain is fed to livestock. Suppose we were using the earth's land to grow fruits and vegetables, or all that grain in the United States were fed to people instead of animals destined for slaughter (and who meanwhile need to use most of what they eat to keep warm and survive until they are killed). All right, animals would benefit from not being killed, anyone can see that. How about our earth? Would the earth benefit too? Who can doubt it? Almost

65 percent of Central America has been cleared to create pasture land for grazing cattle. Who benefits? Not the cattle; not the people who inhabit these forests, whose average daily income is less than a dollar; and not, you can be certain, people across the world who are suffering from hunger. If 30 percent of the world's forested areas have already been converted to animal use, the only people benefiting are those who need it least. Orwell famously warned that the future might be a jackboot forever stomping the human face. Our ecological footprint is like that unforgettable image forever pressing into the face of the earth and causing untold suffering.

We all know that the purity of our water is threatened by runoff from the waste of animals raised for food. We all know, too, how much of it is needed. More than half the water used in North America goes to irrigate land used to feed cattle.

Human health is threatened as well. Meat is intimately associated with heart attacks, strokes, cancer, and high blood pressure. The list is actually endless. Few doctors any longer would dispute the deleterious influence of meat and related products on human health. It has been calculated that the average person would live ten years longer if he or she gave up meat.

The question is, are people beginning to get this message? Yes and no.

Jeffrey explains: When I first went to primary school in America, in 1946, I was the only vegetarian in my class. When I was in high school in Switzerland in 1957, I was the only vegetarian in my class. When I went to Harvard in 1961, I was the only vegetarian in my class. When I went to teach Sanskrit at the University of Toronto in 1971, I was the only vegetarian in my department. And finally, when I went to Berkeley in 1979 as a psychoanalyst, I was the only Freudian analyst in the Bay Area who was a vegetarian.

What a sea change has taken place. Vegetarians are so commonplace in America that even McDonald's has to cater to them. It is hip to be vegan, and vegans are sprouting everywhere. Of course, the health concerns are clear, as one can see from reading Colin Campbell's *The China Study* (Benbella Books, 2005). One need not be a vegetarian to recognize that something strange is going on with American food. Witness the popularity of *Fast Food Nation*. Even university presses are aware of the change. See Steven Striffer's *Chicken: The Dangerous Transformation of America's Favorite Food* (Yale University Press, 2005).

Karen and Michael Iacobbo, authors of the popular *Vegetarian America: A History*, explain why in this new and exciting book. Vegetarianism and veganism are no longer for the elite, and the reasons a person becomes vegetarian are as diverse as the people themselves. It is now nearly mainstream to avoid meat. Those of us who must struggle on a daily basis with people who cannot believe this will be pleased to have such a spirited ally as this new book. We highly recommend it.

Jeffrey Moussaieff Masson
Leila Masson

Jeffrey Moussaieff Masson, PhD, is the author of the New York Times best-sellers *When Elephants Weep* and *Dogs Never Lie About Love*. He has also written a book about the emotional lives of farm animals, *The Pig Who Sang to the Moon*.

Leila Masson, MD, MPH, has a medical degree from Germany, did her pediatric specialty at the University of California at San Francisco, and has a Master of Public Health degree from Harvard and a diploma in Tropical Medicine from London. She is also an international lactation consultant with a particular interest in human nutrition.

SERIES FOREWORD

The guiding spirit for American Subcultures is not an anthropologist or sociologist or social scientist or a theorist of any kind. Rather, it is the greatest American poet of them all, Walt Whitman, proclaiming in "Song of Myself":

> Do I contradict myself?
> Very well then I contradict myself,
> (I am large, I contain multitudes.)

As do we all. No one belongs to and is fully identified or explained by membership in only one subculture, though at a particular moment in time one subculture may be dominant in any of us.

When we're traveling abroad, we may think of ourselves (and be identified by others) as Americans, but most of the time that category is too gross to be of any use for anything but caricature. It covers too many things that are not us, and it omits too many things that are. We are, in the course of our days, people who live in this town or that city, people who are gay or straight, people who work at this trade or that profession. We are bowlers, machinists, dancers, lawyers, ballplayers, students, teachers, cooks, eaters, lovers, bikers, cross-dressers, Vietnam vets, Gulf War (I) vets, Gulf War (II) vets, cops, crooks, bodybuilders, surfers, novelists, nudists, Buddhists, Muslims, Jews, Christians, born-agains, drug addicts, Internet addicts, street people ...

A subculture is part of a larger culture. In ordinary scholarly or popular discourse, the meaning of *subculture* depends on who is talking and what he or she is talking about. If the subject is North

America, a subculture could be anything from local Little League team players and their parents to lawyers or Jews or Yankees or Westerners. But even those categories are often too broad to be of use. If the subject is Westerners, then further subcultures are coastal, mountain, high plains, water-rich, water-poor, farming, or ranching Westerners. You can slice the apple a hundred ways, nearly all of them valid.

An African American musician from New York who went to Harvard and who is on active duty in the reserves in Iraq is at once a member of several distinct subcultures. Army reservists in Iraq are most obviously members of the subculture of the American military, but they are also members of such more specific military subcultures as Special Forces or the medical corps or helicopter pilots or the infantry. They are also as much members of the subcultures of Tennessee farmers or Los Angeles bus drivers or New York schoolteachers as they were when they left home. A man serving a prison sentence is most obviously and immediately a member of the subculture of convicts, but he is also a white or black or Hispanic or Native American or Asian. Neither the reservists nor the convicts leave those other parts of their experience and knowledge at home with their civilian clothes.

An interest or a behavior is not enough to define a subculture. Everyone eats and most people run sometimes, but eaters don't constitute a subculture on the basis of that fact alone and neither do people who run only to catch the bus. But vegetarians who are part of the community of information of other vegetarians are members of a subculture, as are runners who take part in serious running events. Likewise oenophiles and professional cooks and artisan bakers.

Which is to say, every one of us is not only a resident of this or that geographical place but also a member of this or that community of interest, concern, ethnicity, behavior: our lives are in our subcultures, several of them, simultaneously or alternatively.

And that is what the books in American Subcultures, each of them written by experts in a particular field or area, are about. Each explores a specific piece of the great range of interest and behavior that in sum comprise the essence of American life.

Bruce Jackson
Series Editor

PREFACE

What is a vegetarian? The Rochester Area Vegetarian Society of New York defines *vegetarian* as "the practice of living without the use of flesh, fish or fowl, and the ideal of complete independence from animal products."*

Who are American vegetarians? Why did they become vegetarians? What are their opinions of controversies of concern to people who eat no meat or animal products? Is there a vegetarian subculture?

The oldest and truest meaning of *vegetarian* is a person who practices the philosophy of nonviolence toward animals, a philosophy Albert Schweitzer termed "reverence for life"; vegetarians, therefore, believe eating the flesh of animals is ethically wrong. Originally the word *vegetarian* seems to have meant *vegan*: vegans are vegetarians who strive to consistently express their philosophy through eating only foods from the plant kingdom, and choosing to avoid services and products that involve exploitation, abuse, or killing of animals.

Today, for whatever reasons, a person who consistently avoids eating meat is classified as a vegetarian, although dispute exists as to the validity of the label when one eats no meat only for health or aesthetic reasons rather than to respect animals.

A person who eats meat on occasion, even if a few times a year, is not a vegetarian. Therefore, a semivegetarian, pesco-vegetarian, flexitarian, or whatever new term might be in vogue that means someone who occasionally eats meat, is not a vegetarian.

*Throughout this book, we refer to vegans as vegetarians, unless otherwise specified.

Vegetarians are a minority, and it follows that, no matter how typical of modern Americans their other practices and philosophies are, they perceive the world a little differently than do their meat-eating friends, relatives, coworkers, and classmates. To most meat-eating people, a hamburger is a juicy taste treat. To vegetarians, a hamburger is the remains of a painfully slaughtered, terrified cow.

This book explores the vegetarian world in the United States from the vegetarians' point of view. It also provides a glimpse of what it is like to be a vegetarian living amid meat eaters who might or might not tolerate such a difference.

Before writing this book, we knew perhaps a dozen of the people we interviewed because we had interviewed them previously. We found the interviewees using the Internet, vegetarian periodicals and books, and from recommendations. We even met a few vegetarians after first observing them picketing at a restaurant in downtown Boston, or enjoying a backyard veggie barbecue or picnic at a farm sanctuary in rural Massachusetts, attending a vegetarian festival in Maine, and at the Power of One, the twentieth annual Compassionate Living Festival in North Carolina.

Although we thought we knew what to expect when we began conducting interviews for the book, we have discovered that in other contemporary writings on vegetarianism particular perspectives have been overemphasized or not included, perhaps because these points of view are not well known or not publicized by those who hold them.

Unlike other writings today on vegetarianism, this book does not focus on one particular perspective but instead showcases the myriad ideas, opinions, philosophies, and lifestyles found in the loose-knit American vegetarian community. We did not set out to uncover or favor any particular point of view. The people interviewed do not fit into a monolithic group of political, religious, or any other beliefs or practices. Vegetarians and vegans cannot be placed into any category except one: they eat no flesh of any animal or eat nothing derived from animals. We wish we had the time and space to include all of the vegetarians who want to be heard, who want their perspectives to be known.

Here is a sample taken from two brief interviews conducted for this book. Vegetarians will likely hear a ring of familiarity in the stories two women share, yet these remarks are unique—like each person in this book, and each vegetarian in the United States.

Erica Jurgensen is a woman in her twenties from Massachusetts who assisted us with compiling the interviews. Her mother, a vegetarian, allowed Erica to make her own choice whether or not to eat meat. Not until Erica was a college student did she decide to go vegetarian, and she went straight to veganism, largely for health and aesthetic reasons, but also out of empathy for animals used for milk, eggs, and flesh. She writes,

> While eating, I think about the nutritional aspects of food, and the question "Where did these beets come from?" is answered by their earthy taste; never again will I sit in front of a piece of pork asking, "Where did this come from?" . . . I used to work as a waitress at an upscale catering facility. It was really difficult to do—my rent was paid by my circling the room making sure everyone had their fill of baby lamb chops.
>
> When I first became a vegetarian, I felt like I was going through some test. People were drawn to me, but not in the good way. Everyone wanted to start fights; and everywhere I went people would comment to me on my not eating meat: "This is the circle of life," they said, and "Would you like some?" offering me some smelly meaty dish, and "Oh I forgot you don't eat [meat]." Since I am the type who wears her heart on her sleeve, I defended myself. Now that I am older, I couldn't care less what people feel about my lifestyle, and like most issues I stand strong on, a lot of thought goes into my actions. My activism is shown by where I put my money.

The second young woman dedicates a large part of her life to spreading the word. Elana Kirshenbaum, a teacher and founder of Rhode Island Vegan Awareness, lives just outside Providence, Rhode Island.

> I grew up in a typical suburban neighborhood in Rhode Island. As a child, I loved other animals but my behavior often innocently expressed the opposite. If I saw a cow on a farm, I'd want to visit with her, but on the dinner plate, my fork was ready to eat her flesh. I never really considered that the food on my plate was once a living, breathing animal. Classic children's stories, drawings, and songs about pigs complacently going to the market, cows grazing amidst an idyllic pasture, and roosters greeting the morning, all peacefully euphemized a brutal reality of enormous suffering. In addition, television shows, commercials, and advertisements reinforced these myths. Fortunately, I had a strong sense that animals did matter and their lives were valuable in and of themselves.

After learning how animals were raised for food, Elana, while still in her teens, eliminated most animal products from her diet. She recalls her experience at a weekend visit to an animal sanctuary that convinced her to stop eating any animal products. "I looked into the large, beautiful eyes of cows. I stroked a turkey as she closed her eyes and relaxed in contentment. I learned about the dairy industry and was horrified. I knew the animal suffering was far worse than any nightmare I could have dreamt. I knew that it was morally wrong to raise animals in captivity and kill them for my food. From that experience, I instantly stopped eating all products from animals and now enjoy a wide variety of delicious foods."

LIST OF INTERVIEWEES

All interviews conducted by e-mail unless otherwise noted.

Adams, Carol, telephone interview, August 2005
Aftosmes, Alyssa, September 2005, Massachusetts
Ahuv Ben Rahm, telephone interview, September 2005,
    South Carolina
Akers, Keith, June 10, 2005, Colorado
Allan, Sterling, June 2005, Utah
Allen, Zel and Reuben, 2005, California
Aloisio, Elizabeth, May 2001, Rhode Island
Amato, Paul, August 31, 2005, Pennsylvania
Ankerberg-Nobis, Truly, February 2006
Anthony, Piers, September 3, 2005, Florida
Baer, Steve, August 3, 2005, Massachusetts
Baker, Karen, October 16, 2005, Washington
Baker-Kinney, Jasmin, August 16, 2005, Washington
Ball, Matt, August 5, 2005
Ballard, Jill, July 1, 2005
Barman, Dilip, July 25, 2005, North Carolina
Barnard, Neal, June 2005, Washington, DC
Bartell, Stephen, August 9, 2005
Beckley, Chris, August 27, 2005, Colorado
Bennett, Beverly Lynn, July 2005, Oregon
Bergeron, Ken, September 2, 2005, Connecticut
Bessette, Linda, October, December 2005, Rhode Island
Binge, Eleni and Rob, July 13, 2005, North Carolina

Bisanti, Katrina, July 2005, Rhode Island
Blizzard, Amy, June 20, 2005, Indiana
Bowlby, Rex, August 11, 2005, California
Branford, Suzanne, September 21, 2005, Nevada
Braunstein, Mark, August 11, 2005, Connecticut
Brigish, Dina, September 19, 2005, Virginia
Bullock, Carol, August 16, 2005, Washington
Burtt, Melanie, August, September, 2005, Rhode Island
Campbell, T. Colin, August 2005, New York
Carman, Judy, August 3, 2005, Kansas
Carr, Diane, July 21, 2005, Vermont
Carroll, Ellouise, July 27, 2005, Washington
Chase, Al, August 29, 2005, Oregon
Chase, Heather, June 13, 2005, Arizona
Church, Jill Howard, September 25, 2005, Georgia
Cirivello, Jill, July 28, 2005, Iowa
Clement, Brian, Florida
Coffey, Gerry, July 2005, Alabama
Cohen, Robert, August 2005, New York
Colletti, Rod, August 7, 2005, Louisiana
Connelly, Joe, October 14, 2005, California
Corcoran, Miriam and Jim, August 15, 2005, Michigan
Cousens, Arielle, July 30, 2005, Maine
Cousens, Jadrien, July 30, 2005, Maine
Cousens, Linda, July 30, 2005, Maine
Croce, Shakira, October 6, 2005, Georgia
Curry, David, September 3, 2005, Indiana
Cuthbert, Cathy, July 14, 2005, California
Cwyner, Elaine, August 1, 2005, Massachusetts
DeRose, Chris, August 25, 2005, California
Davis, Brenda, July 16, 2005
Davis, Gail, July 16, 2005, Indiana
Dear, Father John, June 20, 2005, New Mexico
Deneen, Eric, October 2005, Massachusetts
Dennis, Ann and Dave, August 19, 2005, Massachusetts
Dennis, Dash, August 2, 2005, Oklahoma
Duffel, Dewey Ross, August 12, 2005, Montana
Duggan, Amy, August 4, 2005, New Mexico
Duprey, Brian, August 6, 2005, New York
Eisenberg, Caitlin, September 4, 2005, Massachusetts
Eisenberg, Mark, September 4, September 24, 2005, Massachusetts
Embar, Wanda, August 17, 2005, Wisconsin
Ezell-Vandersluis, Cheri, Massachusetts
Finch, Mary, September 19, 2005, Arkansas

Finley, Alissa, August 9, 2005, Oklahoma
Fisher, Ollie, October 15, 2005, Missouri
Fisher, Perdita, October 15, 2005, Missouri
Foster, Christopher, October 17, 2005, Utah
Frederick, Dew, September, 2005, Florida
Fredericks, Jan, September 2005, New Jersey
Friedrich, Bruce, August 4, 2005, Virginia
Fuchs, Michael Stephen, August 24, 2005, California
Garcia, Caroline, August 8, 2005, Louisiana
Goodwin, Derek, August 16, 2005, Massachusetts
Graham, Doug, August 9, 2005, Florida
Hall, Lee, August 29, 2005, Connecticut
Harris, William, July 2, 2005, Hawaii
Hartglass, Caryn, June 21, 2005, New York
Heatley, Kathy, August 4, 2005, Vermont
Heidrich, Ruth, July 2005, Hawaii
Heinrich, Chris, September 18, 2005, Idaho
Heller, Meria, June 2005, September 26, 2005
Herzstein, Lisa, August 23, 2005, California
Hobbs, Suzanne Havala, October 2005, North Carolina
Hooten, Josh, June 24, 2005, Oregon
Huebner, Linda, August 2, 2005, Vermont
Hyland, Rev. J. R.
Jones, Pattrice, September 1, 2005
Jones, Susan Smith, September 2005, Los Angeles
Joy, Melanie, August 31, 2005, Massachusetts
Jurek, Scott, September 7, 2005, Washington
Jurgensen, Erica, September 2005, Massachusetts
Kahn, Richard, September 17, 2005, California
Kalina, Shari, May 23, 2005, Pangea, Maryland
Kelly, Jill, July 2005, Massachusetts
Kelly, Matt and Mary, July 15, 2005, Massachusetts
Kidd, David, August 2005, Ohio
Killian, Earl, August 24, 2005, California
Kingsbury, Judy, 2005, Indiana
Kirshenbaum, Elana, September 29, 2005, Rhode Island
Klaper, Michael, September 27, 2005, California
Kubersky, Erica, July 15, 2005, New York
LaFleur, Michelle, October 15, 2005, Florida
Lehmkuhl, Vance, October 16, 2005, Pennsylvania
Lewis, Noah, August 31, 2005, Pennsylvania
Lyman, Howard, August 2005
Lynn, Crescent, September 29, 2005, Texas
Mackey, Jim, October 10, 2005, Texas

MacNair, Rachel, August 2005, Missouri
Malanga, Sally, August 2005, New Jersey
Malkmus, Rev. George, August 2005, North Carolina
Marcus, Erik, August 2005, New York
Margison, Mary, July 14, 2005, Rhode Island
Marino, Danielle, August 29, 2005, Illinois
Mason, Laura, September 29, 2005, Maryland
Maurer, Donna, August 2, 2005, Massachusetts
McCarthy, Colman, October 12, 2005, Washington, DC
McCloy, Johanna, June 29, 2005, California
McCormack, Karaena, October 11, 2005, Washington
McHenry, Keith, August 2005, Arizona
Meier, Erica, October 17, 2005, Maryland
Mertz, Rachel, August 25, 2005, North Dakota
Mickens, Leah, September 3, 2005, Georgia
Miner, Judy, July 2005, Vermont
Monson, Shaun, August 9, 2005, California
Murphy, Melissa, September 26, 2005, Wyoming
Murti, Vasu, July 31, 2005, California
Nelson, Jeff, September 24, 2005, California
Newkirk, Ingrid, August 4, 2005, Virginia
Nguyen, Hoai, November 5, 2005, Massachusetts
Nunez, Dick, August 11, 2005, South Dakota
Patton, Jody, August 15, 2005, Minnesota
Pavlina, Erin, June 14, 2005, Nevada
Payne, Diana, October 1, 2005, Delaware
Pearson, Marcia, September and October, 2005, Washington
Pedan, James, September 24, 2005, Montana
Perry, Tricia, October 9, 2005, Massachusetts
Pickarski, Ron, August, September, 2005, Colorado
Pierson, Bob, August 24, 2005, New Mexico
Piraro, Dan, October 16, 2005
Pizzirusso, James, August 1, 2005, Washington, DC
Portalatin-Berrien, Corey, October 17, 2005, Washington, DC
Potts, Don, September 2005, Missisippi
Powers, Alyson, August 5, 2005, Iowa
Pyle, Bob, telephone interview, October 2005, Maryland
Rahm, Ahuv Ben, telephone interview, South Carolina
Regan, Tom, September 28, 2005, North Carolina
Regenstein, Lewis, September 2, 2005, Georgia
Renideo, Delisa, July 18, July 25, 2005, Alaska
Rense, Jeff, September 24, 2005
Rice, Pamela, July 7, 2005, New York

Rice, Stacy, July 12, 2005, Pennsylvania
Richardson, Shakela, July, September, 2005
Rodgers, Thomas, September 2005, Utah
Roghair, Susan, August 17, 2005, Florida
Rose, Stewart, July, August 2005, Washington
Rosenberg, Howard, August 2005, California
Rowe, Martin, October 13, 2005, New York
Rubenstein, Jennifer, August 15, 2005, Kentucky
Salamone, Connie, January 2006, New Hampshire
Samfield, Emily, September 6, 2005, Georgia
Sapon, Stanley, October, 2005, Florida
Saunders, Kerrie, July 21, 2005, Michigan
Sargent, Sukie, July 21, 2005, Texas
Saul, Bradley, July 2005
Schroeder, Kurt, August 10, 2005, Indiana
Schwartz, Gil, August 10, 2005, Minnesota
Schwartz, Richard, August 8 and 21, 2005, New York
Sephton, Kaz, November 6, 2005, Texas
Shriver, Saiom, July 2005, Ohio
Shurtleff, Bill, July 2005, California
Smith, Jeffrey, July 2005, Iowa
Smith, Roslyn Abramovitch, August 25, 2005, North Dakota
Southarn, Rhys, July 1, 2005, New York
Stahler, Charles, July 15, 2005, Maryland
Stuntebeck, Dan, June 22, 2005, Wisconsin
Svoboda, Alexanda, September 26, 2005, Nebraska
Talifero, Jinjee, August 16, 2005, California
Taylor, Jeanine, August 16, 2005, Massachusetts
Taylor, Jim, August 20, 2005, West Virginia
Tinsley, Hope, August 24, 2005, Illinois
Torres, Jenna and Bob, August 28, 2005
Tuttle, Will, July 28, 2005
Vandenberg, Krissi, July 29, 2005, Virginia
Walden, Shelton, October 2, 2005, New York
Weaver, Anne, July 30, 2005, North Carolina
Weaver, Val, August 11, 2005, California
Weers, Gloria, July 15, 2005, Texas
Weill, Lige, September 2005, Tennessee
Wieland, Susan, August 2, 2005, Maryland
Wilson, Melanie, June 13, 2005
Winters, Craig, June 2005, Washington
Wise, Heather, July 28, 2005, New York
Wolfe, David, July 4, 2005, California, Hawaii

Wood, Jessica, July 30, 2005, Maine
Zagorsky, Kim, August 2005, Rhode Island
Zakarian, Joy, August 20, 2005, California
Zezima, Mickey, August 27, 2005, New York
Ziegler, Scott, August 2005, Louisiana

ACKNOWLEDGMENTS

It is our pleasure to offer a heartfelt thank you to each vegetarian interviewed for this book. Each one of you has presented a glimpse of your vegetarian experience, and we are delighted to share this with our readers.

We are also grateful to our editor, Hilary Claggett, for her encouragement, patience, and belief in us and this book. It might not have been published without her support and that of our outstanding assistants. We also thank the other individuals whose work has made this book a reality: Linda Ellis-Stiewing, Senior Project Manager, and Marcia Goldstein, Permissions Coordinator.

Our assistant Elana Kirshenbaum's diligence, patience, and organizational ability kept us on track. Erica Jurgensen, who assisted us on our last book, *Vegetarian America: A History* (Praeger, 2004) came through for us once again. Her good humor and willingness to help kept us from feeling overwhelmed.

Our special thank you is offered to Jeffrey Moussaieff Masson and Leila Masson for kindly and generously writing the excellent and original foreword. The ideas expressed by the Massons no doubt speak for many vegetarians.

We would also like to thank Judy Carman, Dr. Melanie Joy, Vance Lemkuhl, Bob Pyle, Rachel Kalina, Cheri Ezell-Vandersluis and Jim Vandersluis, Connie Salamone, Saiom Shriver, and Stanley Sapon for allowing us to publish their poetry, lyrics, art, writings, or photography. It is our pleasure to thank David Koesher for his legal expertise.

The following people kindly allowed us to attend their events, thoughtfully suggested people to interview, or graciously shared contact information: Beth Gallie, Steve and Helen Rayschick, Cheri Ezell-Vandersluis and Jim Vandersluis, Mary Margison, Marcia Pearson, Lige Weill, James Leveck, Saiom Shriver, Chris Beckley, and Tom Regan.

We would like to thank the following people for their love, support, and especially their patience during those times when we had to miss opportunities because we were busy conducting research, e-mailing, interviewing yet another person, or writing and revising the manuscript: John and Diane Wenckelium; Eric, Diane, Erica, and Tayla King; Al, Donna, Angelo, Anthony, and Haley Nardolillo; Elizabeth Aloisio and Robert Arruda; Jim and Cindy Fiedler; and Gil Gordon and Carol Kennedy.

INTRODUCTION

Especially should those who apprehend the deepest wisdom and
preserve through life the relish for elegant studies and pursuits,
abstain from flesh, cherishing justice which animals claim at man's
hands, nor slaughtering them for food or profit.

A. Bronson Alcott, Tablets, 1879

THE MAIDEN VOYAGE OF A VEGETARIAN FOOD FESTIVAL

On the last Saturday of July 2005, inside the gothic wonder called the
State Street Church, David Marley spent the late morning preparing
for the crowd. The World War II navy veteran was helping Beth Gallie,
head of the Maine Animal Coalition, set up tables in the church's ad-
jacent hall. Gallie, noting the sunny and steamy summer weather that
normally coaxes people to the beaches, wondered how many people
would show for her group's first-ever vegetarian food festival.

Before long, the parking spaces in front of the church in the heart of
Portland, Maine, were scarce. The caterer arrived, then the vendors,
and the musicians, then the first attendees, most dressed as if they
were going to a picnic or the beach. People wasted no time in heading
for the table covered with steel trays brimming with basmati rice,
curried chickpeas, a vegetable mixed with tempeh, and desserts such
as chocolate and blueberry pie.

A woman looked at one tray tentatively, as if she was ready to go for
a swim but wasn't sure if the water would be too cold. "It's Indian," said

a man, as he scooped some rice into a bowl and topped it off with the chickpea concoction. The woman took the bowl and sat at one of the tables near the hall's stage, where a husband-and-wife violinist duo played classical music.

Most attendees couldn't resist a peek at a table with the sign "Woody's Goodie's," aptly featuring sugar cookies, chocolate cake slices, and other desserts for sale at one dollar each. Jessica Wood, a resident of the nearby town of Biddeford, had baked the treats at home the previous night. She wanted to demonstrate that vegetarian food was more than just applesauce, rice cakes, and tofu. Wood also wanted to dispel the myth that being a vegan is difficult. "The thought of being a vegan is much worse than actually being one," she said.

As the afternoon wore on, people continued to pour in. One pair, arriving late from Boston, spent about four hours in traffic. About half of the attendees were middle-aged, and about a dozen children and teens attended. At one table, two teens—twins, in fact—were jabbing their forks into their plates of sauce-covered rice as they discussed the reaction from their peers to their preferences for a plant-based diet.

"They always ask a lot of questions. Do you eat eggs or fish? Why are you a vegetarian?" said Jadrien Cousens, fourteen. "You don't get teased. They are more curious than anything else." His sister Arielle explained that her meat-free diet was fairly easy to maintain. While out with her friends, she orders pizza instead of hamburgers.

The twins, both athletes, were raised vegetarian. Their mother, Linda Cousens, quit eating meat twenty years ago after realizing that a plant-based diet was healthy and that eating animals was hypocritical because she loved them. Cousens glanced around the room, smiled, and called the food festival a very supportive event that could raise interest in vegetarianism in the Portland area.

The gathering featured speeches by Beth Gallie and Sean Faircloth, a Maine state Democrat representative and a vegetarian. The politician stated that the government subsidizes the meat and dairy industry and urged attendees to rediscover "true conservative values" by fighting for healthy school lunch options. He said that banning junk food like soda doesn't clash with freedom of choice because it's readily available elsewhere. Gallie, a lawyer by profession, alerted attendees that existing animal welfare laws fail to include farm animals and called on attendees to lobby the legislature since the "government is not looking after animals."

At the end of the festival, David Marley, not a vegetarian, looked around and said, "They can come back anytime. It's good, clean fun. Maybe this can help with the obesity problem." The success of the Portland event seems to ensure it will return as an annual event.

It was the maiden voyage of a vegetarian food festival, but not the first time that meat abstainers had ties to Portland. In the 1850s, Jeremiah Hacker, a reformer and Quaker, published the *Portland Pleasure Boat*, a newspaper advocating abolition, animal rights, and Grahamism (vegetarian natural living), as described in our book, *Vegetarian America*.

A NIGHT OF ACTIVISM IN AN EASTERN CITY

A few weeks prior to the Portland event, in Boston, Massachusetts, not far from the "Cradle of Liberty"—Faneuil Hall—on a sweltering July day when the temperature flirted with the 100-degree mark, and whiffs of a garbage smell swirled out of street grates, about two dozen demonstrators who eat no meat marched in an elliptical pattern outside a chain steak restaurant on Boylston Street, one of Boston's most bustling spots. As patrons dined on a patio, some of them occasionally turned to give a quick glance at normal-looking men and women—demonstrators—belonging to the Massachusetts Animal Rights Coalition. Some of the demonstrators held placards and signs. One activist carried a flat-screen monitor showing footage of gaunt, crippled baby cows in crates—footage meant to show restaurant patrons who eat veal exactly where their dinner came from. A few cops were looking at the protest, occasionally joking, but sometimes glaring as if to say, "Keep in line or there is going to be trouble." Steve and Helen Rayschick, who founded the coalition, belie the mass media–created stereotypes of animal rights activists—and vegans. Helen retired early from her career as a scientist and technical writer/editor to work for animals, and Steve is a community college professor. Gracious, cordial, down-to-earth, and new grandparents, they are two typical Americans who care about animals, but who are untypical in that their empathy is extended to farm animals, and they put their caring into action by taking to the busy Boston streets and handing passersby leaflets showing the reality of life for animals on factory farms.

Across the street at Hynes Convention Center, unknown to many of the protestors and perhaps with a touch of synchronicity, the Boston International Film Festival was premiering *Earthlings* by filmmaker, actor, and vegetarian Shaun Monson. The animal rights documentary includes disturbing footage shot in a slaughterhouse. Several blocks from the convention center is a mansion where nearly a century earlier, Boston socialite M.R.L. Freshel of the Millennium Guild, an animal rights group, presented a film documenting animal suffering in slaughterhouses.

Helen and Steve Rayschick, founders of the Massachusetts Animal Rights Coalition. Courtesy Helen and Steve Rayschick.

A few days later, on a sweltering and drizzly day, some of the steak house protestors, along with some sixty other vegetarians from Massachusetts, New Hampshire, Vermont, and Rhode Island traveled through a state forest and a picturesque New England town to gather at the Rayshicks' home set amid wildflowers in a field. In the company of others who share their values, the partygoers drank beer or lemonade, barbecued veggie burgers and soy hotdogs, ate nondairy chocolate desserts, and toasted vegan marshmallows. Several dogs ran loose, including one rescued from a lonely basement and another saved after an automobile accident. A three-legged dog rolled on his back to have his belly rubbed, something his wagging tail and happy face revealed he enjoys. Several of the guests gravitated to the kitchen, which was nearly covered with desserts like chocolate cake and brownies, and discussed threats to activists' freedom of speech, media bias, and Infowars.com, the Web site of investigative journalist Alex Jones.

THANKSGIVING

Activism for animal rights started early in America. Laws were even passed to protect animals in the eighteenth century. Vegetarian food festivals date at least as early as the 1840s, when abolitionist and animal liberationist John Grimes, MD, held Christmas dinners, free of charge, for the people of Boonton, New Jersey. But it is the celebration of meat-free Thanksgiving that has become a cornerstone of vegetarian culture. The popular annual gatherings date to at least 1895, when members of the Vegetarian Eating Club gathered at the University of Chicago to feast on chestnut soup, pasta d'Italia, mushroom rissoles, pumpkin pie, angel food cake, and many other treats.

Today, such celebrations are usually held in church basements or halls on the weekend preceding the holiday. One 2004 feast, held in Providence and put on by Rhode Island Vegan Awareness (RIVA), drew a capacity crowd of two hundred people, some of them arriving with family members who were not vegetarians. The feast featured quinoa mushroom loaf, garlic mashed potatoes, roasted sweet potatoes, cranberry pecan sauce, sautéed kale, sweet potatoes, corn bread, and desserts such as vanilla maple cake, vegan whipped cream, and apple crisp. Coffee, often absent at such events or replaced by herbal or root-based brews, was steaming from steel dispensers, and books and literature espousing plant-based diets or animal rights, usually plentiful at such events, covered several banquet tables at one end of the hall.

The Thanksgiving feast, prepared by Katrina Bisanti, a Rhode Island caterer of vegetarian-only food, won over meat eaters, who joined their fellow diners and headed back for seconds. Comments ranged from, "I didn't miss the turkey" to "I'm glad there was no tofu."

CELEBRATING VALENTINE'S DAY

A few months before the RIVA feast, on a chilly Saturday before Valentine's Day, several young activists gathered in front of a mall in downtown Providence holding posters painted with the words, "Be Sweet, Don't Eat Meat," "Have a Heart, Go Veg.," and "Meat Stops a Beating Heart." Some shoppers whisked hastily by the activists as if they were panhandlers, but others stopped and sampled the nondairy chocolates on the tray held by Laura Barlow. One well-dressed woman took a chocolate, bit into it delicately, and said, "Hmm . . . very good. No milk, eh?" Some motorists tooted their horns and gave the thumbs-up sign, and others slowed to a crawl to read the signs, but most of them just ignored the group.

HAS VEGETARIANISM ARRIVED?

Like the demonstrations advocating vegan chocolate for Valentine's Day, American vegetarians, whether or not they drink cow's milk or eat hens' eggs, may be accepted or rejected because they do not eat animal flesh. Most of the time, they are likely to experience degrees of acceptance and rejection in their lives from people who eat meat.

Rachel Kalina published an essay about this subject in *Pipe Dream*, a newspaper of Binghamton University in New York:

> When I began to shift from a vegetarian to a vegan, people started noticing that I wasn't having the cheesecake, but rather the vegan pumpkin pie. "Don't just order that because it's vegan!" they would say, as if I was committing some kind of crime or encroaching on their personal beliefs.
>
> Maybe it's a lack of self-control that others have, or maybe they feel threatened that I just don't follow the same rules as they do. Do I care? Of course not. I'm not budging an inch from what I enjoy doing....
>
> A huge misconception is that being a vegan will automatically result in a personal calendar full of PETA events. I barely know any vegetarians, let alone any other vegans. I feel that in this area of my life I'm making a small individual difference for the betterment of animal-kind.

People who never eat meat are not monolithic in their opinion of whether vegetarianism has finally gained acceptance by the dominant meat-eating culture. Some "veggies," observing that many restaurant chains offer meat-free food, or that their college cafeterias offer a daily vegan option, say yes. Others, who may be the only vegetarian at their workplace or even in their neighborhood, are inclined to say no.

Very little doubt exists that more people are cutting all forms of flesh foods from their diets. Polls reveal that the number of vegetarians and vegans in the United States is a small minority, but this minority appears to be growing slowly but steadily. A 2003 Vegetarian Resource Group Harris survey of adults over age eighteen reported that 2.8 percent of those surveyed said they never eat meat, poultry, fish, or seafood. A Zogby poll in 2000 reported the percentage at 2.5 percent.

What's more, the growth in the number of vegans has outdistanced the growth of vegetarians. Charles Stahler, cofounder of the Maryland-based Vegetarian Resource Group, estimates the number of vegans—people who never eat meat, poultry, fish, and dairy—could be as high as one-third to one-half of the total number of vegetarians.

"This is truly amazing in our culture, which was so dominated by the economics and habits of meat consumption. It's even more amazing that vegans were almost nonexistent and now could be one-third to one-half of vegetarians. The growth in vegetarians and vegans is totally incredible. I never would have imagined this twenty-five years ago," said Stahler.

Other numbers reported by the 2003 poll show that a higher percentage of women, 3.6 percent compared to 2 percent for men, said they don't eat meat, poultry, or fish and seafood. Middle-aged Americans show slightly higher numbers—3 percent of those ages forty-five to fifty-four are true vegetarians. Broken down by region, the western United States features the highest concentration of people who identify themselves as vegetarian, with 4 percent of both the general population and college graduates taking that label.

As previously mentioned, grassroots advocates have different opinions on the subject. Linda Huebner, who works for the Humane Society of the United States, relates her personal opinion: "Veg*nism is still such a 'fringe' way of life in the USA—we're probably the smallest recognized minority in the country." On the other hand, Wanda Embar, founder of Veganpeace.com, believes vegetarianism "has definitely entered mainstream society. Vegetarians are more respected now then I believe they ever have been. Most restaurants have vegetarian options and more people are willing to accommodate their vegetarian guests."

Some advocates of dinner without meat acknowledge the rising popularity of vegetarianism but also recognize that the numbers are still diminutive. The perspective of Professor Richard Schwartz, PhD, president of the Jewish Vegetarians of North America and author of *Judaism and Vegetarianism* is that "there has been significant progress toward vegetarianism and veganism in recent years, but I do not believe that it can be said that it has 'arrived.' The fastest-growing segments of the food industry are soy products and organic foods, but when my wife and I attend a wedding, bar mitzvah, or other celebration, we are often the only ones who order special vegetarian meals, or we are among a very small group that does so. While there have been many recent articles about vegetarianism in the media, and many young people, especially females, are becoming vegetarians, the percentage of people who are vegetarian is still relatively small."

Vegetarian culture in the United States thrives in some areas while it is barely visible or downright absent from other areas. Finding a vegan restaurant in North Dakota can be a challenge, while New Yorkers and Seattle residents have dozens to choose from. The more metropolitan the locale, the greater the chance of finding restaurants, cafes, and stores that sell food and other products made without animal ingredients.

New Yorker Caryn Hartglass, executive director of EarthSave, believes that the metropolis where she resides offers the most for non–

meat eaters. "NYC is the best place in the world for vegetarians to eat! We have the greatest number of restaurants and a very varied selection of cuisines. There are many health food stores as well offering up a wonderful variety of food to go."

When it comes to the herbivore diet, New York City reigns supreme in some areas but lags in others. Pamela Rice, author of *101 Reasons Why I Am a Vegetarian*, explained,

> As for vegetarian restaurants, New York City is a mecca. There is no doubt about that. Throughout Manhattan and into the burroughs, you have great places to enjoy meat-free dining. NYC vegetarians can't get enough presentations about raw vegetarian cooking and health.... The vegetarian scene in New York City: To be honest, it is a little bit pathetic. There are pockets of life, but without a healthy volunteer spirit (something this town seriously lacks), any viable activist presence is rare indeed. If you're a vegan, and you seek the singles scene, you may have some company. But as for people working together to build vegetarian culture, you'll probably only find it in the commercial sphere. The most successful vegetarian endeavors are tied to commercial enterprises: restaurants primarily.

New York, Seattle, and San Francisco might arguably be the best cities for those who never put meat on their plates, but other cities can pose a legitimate challenge. The twin cities of Minneapolis and St. Paul, for example, boast several animal rights organizations, including the nationally renowned nonprofit Compassionate Action for Animals, over two hundred vegetarian-friendly restaurants, a variety of food co-ops, and several organizations promoting the meat-free lifestyle. "With all this pro-veg activity in Minnesota, awareness and acceptability of vegetarianism have been steadily increasing," says Gil Schwartz, campaign coordinator for Compassionate Action for Animals.

South of Portland, the city of Eugene, Oregon, features a vegetarian presence. After living in Ohio, chef and *VegNews* columnist Beverly Lynn Bennet, a vegan, says Eugene

> certainly seems like a vegetarian paradise! There are a few all-vegetarian restaurants, amazing organic farmer's markets, loads of locally owned natural foods stores, and lots and lots of fellow vegans and vegetarians. Is Eugene some sort of vegan utopia? Not really. In many ways it's similar to most other small cities in the country in terms of the pervasiveness of the SAD [standard American diet] diet and the national food grid controlled by a handful of multinational corporations interested only in the bottom line. But there are many more options for vegans and vegetarians here that make it very livable, and very easy to eat and live as

a vegan. We [vegans and vegetarians] are still in the minority here in Eugene as we are anywhere else, but it's a lot easier for us to find good organic vegan food and like-minded people to share it with. Just about any restaurant in town will at least be familiar with what veganism is, and they may already have vegetarian selections on the menu that can be made vegan.

Most of America's metropolitan areas feature a sizable vegetarian community. But people who don't want to eat meat and organizations that support them are just about everywhere, even in locales that rely heavily on animal agriculture. Take Oklahoma, where cattle and steak barbecues are part of everyday life. But according to Dash Dennis, the state has a small, thriving vegetarian scene, particularly in college towns like Stillwater, with two organizations—Vegetarian Society of Stillwater and a statewide organization called the Vegetarians of Oklahoma. As an advocate, Dennis spreads the word.

Another Oklahoma resident, Alissa Finley, reports that awareness of vegetarianism in her home state has increased greatly in recent years.

Now, that is different than acceptance and understanding, but awareness is certainly a necessary step. Growing up in Oklahoma, I never even heard of vegetarianism, much less ever met a vegetarian. When I went to a restaurant and tried to order something "vegan," the servers had never heard this word before and became even more confused, so I usually refrained from using it. I began just describing what I wanted my food to be like: no meat, no dairy, and no eggs. Now, many times if I'm ordering food in that manner, the server might stop me and say, "Oh, are you vegan?" I love that feeling! Just the fact of more and more people knowing what veganism is, and that vegans and vegetarians are really all around them—not just some "hippies in California."

Finley says that people are surprised to learn that vegetarianism exists in her state.

The number one statement I get when meeting new people as a VegOK representative is, "Really? I didn't know there was a vegetarian group in Oklahoma. Are there many of you? Isn't it hard to be a vegetarian in Oklahoma?" There is a strong perception that Oklahoma is decidely veg-*un*friendly. I've lived in other areas of the country and in general, I don't think people are more anti-vegetarian than most other areas around the country. I've encountered hostility towards vegism in many states.

However, Oklahoma does have a higher than average number of traditionally conservative-minded people, backed by generations of family-run animal agribusinesses. And we do not have a single all-vegetarian restaurant in all of the Oklahoma City area and surrounding suburbs. All this together may give the impression of daunting difficulty for being veg*n in Oklahoma, but I believe that it just appears that way from the "outside." Once a person makes that decision to look into vegism, there are certainly strong resources here in Oklahoma in the form of information and great friends to be found just within VegOK.

On the other hand, it seems like it would be easier to find a puddle in the Mojave Desert than to find a fellow vegetarian in some areas of the United States. Delisa Renideo, who lives outside Anchorage, Alaska, says vegetarians and vegans in her area are scarce, except for members of Rays of Hope, a group she cofounded in 2002. "Though there are no dedicated vegetarian restaurants, grocery stores do sell tofu, whole grains, nuts, and meat and dairy analogs."

"Vegetarianism hasn't arrived in Alaska," observes Renideo, who notes that the state, and the United States as a whole, remain "very carnivorous country." Renideo, who became a vegetarian a quarter century ago because of concerns about world hunger after reading *Diet for a Small Planet* by Francis Moore Lappé, hosts monthly vegan dinners, cooking classes, and showings of documentaries.

Vegetarianism might have arrived in the United States, but not everyone has laid out the welcome mat. Judy Carman, cofounder of Animal Outreach of Kansas and author of *Peace to All Beings: Veggie Soup for the Chicken's Soul*, agrees: "Well, if it were a person, we could say it has arrived and been introduced to just about everyone in the room. But has our fellow been accepted or understood? Certainly, many more people have accepted vegetarianism than ever before in the U.S., but we are still a long way from helping the majority understand the many benefits."

That an inconsistency exists in the level of acceptance and understanding of vegetarianism is problematic. More than that, it is a part of a paradox. In this book, we explore the vegetarian world and the complexities of being vegetarian within a meat-eating society.

PART

I

VEGETARIAN WORLD

1

TRANSFORMATION: FORMER MEAT EATERS TELL THEIR STORIES

I hereby declare that I have abstained from the flesh of animals for one month and upwards; and that I desire to become a member of the Vegetarian Society; and to cooperate with that Body in promulgating the knowledge of the advantages of a Vegetarian Diet.

Pledge at first annual meeting of the American
Vegetarian Society, New York City, September, 1850

Like the meat abstainers of the nineteenth century, today's vegetarians agree on one point: They do not eat animals. Beyond this classification, the population of vegetarians consists of people with virtually every point of view and background. The vast majority of vegetarians are not raised in families that abstain from meat. This chapter features a selection of stories of change from meat eater to meat abstainer.

The first story of conversion is a cowboy's epiphany. Thomas L. Rodgers's transformation to one who eschews animal flesh began in 1990, just days before "serious cancer detection, surgery and treatment work began." Rodgers, a former rancher who lives in Utah, and who ran in 2004 for state senate as a member of the Constitutional Party of Utah, recalls his horrific experience:

[F]ar exceeding 250 pounds (I stopped getting on the scales out of self embarrassment and denial) and no longer feeling like I was the invincible, unstoppable, independent entrepreneur and functional man I had labored to be for decades. As my own boss in my sometimes animal

Vegan cowboy Tom Rodgers. Courtesy
Tom Rodgers.

husbandry and all-the-time mechanical responsibility and business, I
was never short on exercise. My work was always physically demanding
and strenuous. I could "throw" a cow, "drop" a cantankerous horse, pull
wire or break thread on the largest rusty pipe or bolt without difficulty.
I did unfortunately believe—as I had been thoroughly taught—that I
needed to "sufficiently" consume—for the "good" of my health, teeth and
bones—the products of my own past dairy and animal husbandry
industry. I had no shortage of milk! eggs! or flesh! I should have been as
healthy as my old horse, "Frisky." But it was not so!

Rodgers recalls that he suffered several strokes while undergoing
cancer treatment and surgery. "My life declined and its limits became no
larger than the hospital ward or my own imprisoning bedroom. All else
in my life's dreams and efforts collapsed, vanished or were taken away."
   In June of 1990, the strokes took their toll on the cowboy, who is also
a scientist. His sight and speech were diminished, and his motor
functions were severely impaired on his left side. Endless headaches,
pain, and perpetual nausea followed.

   Depressed with my dysfunction overwhelmed, as therapy (additional cancer cleanup surgeries) and treatment continued! My world
no longer fully visible, workable and for the most part communicable, nor
rational, crumbled about me. So unannounced to me, as my oncologist,
neurologists and internal physicians labored with my body, a team of

psychiatrists were quietly adding to my cabinet full of practitioners and beneficiaries. And their tiny pills further disconnected me from logic and life. By November 1990, continually sedated, irrational, and without help, my business and finances crumbled. Creditors in the path, not understanding, nor able to go another way, began their "legal" yet ruthlessly inevitable cancer-and-stroke-victim's crush.

Rodgers's health continued to decline as his heart began to fail. He recalls that in the summer of 1991 he nearly died as he spent time either in the "old familiar emergency bed in the VA for an encounter now with another cold steel table" or in his bedroom in the care of his family, especially his daughter Nina.

Passing near death!—I understood nature's wisdom—and my foolish errors! I had to make and so did make compassionate intelligent change! Prior to June 29 1991, I would have consumed most anything placed before me. But on June 30, my struggled, and strangely out of character words, to the hospital dietitian—who I surprisingly requested to come to my side—immediately as I was salvaged from death in that emergency room was: "Nothing need die, that I might live!" Sensing her and everyone's disbelief from this old once rancher's request, struggling again to speak, I restated "Nothing is to lose its life, so that I may have mine!"

That wonderful lady of the kitchen facilities understood. And from that day forward—as my "angel" in the hospital kitchen—she made sure that my hospital menu was only of gentle foods!—that nothing more was to suffer for me!—or my appetite! As a former dairyman/rancher this new way of thinking was unusual, uncomfortable, even offensive to many of my friends and family; most—like me—with our dairy ranching roots, *profits* and *pride* set firm in the long honored (—and lucrative) "traditions of our fathers!"

The Utah man recovered as he stuck to a plant-based diet. By mid-1993, he was well enough to run in a twenty-six-mile marathon in the desert. Escaping the jaws of death acts as a mighty motivator that will rapidly transform even lifelong meat eaters like Thomas L. Rodgers into plant eaters. Now known as the publisher of VeganCowboy.com, he changed from one who ate a typical American diet to an advocate of veganism whose words are read around the world over the Internet.

In the past a few leading advocates of vegetarianism quit eating meat after developing illnesses they attributed to the American meat-laden diet. William Andrus Alcott, MD, James Caleb Jackson, MD, and Rev. Sylvester Graham (who we designated Father of American Vegetarianism in our last book, *Vegetarian America: A History*) changed their diets and went down in history. The decision to eliminate meat might come slowly, or it might be spontaneous, as was the case for one young woman from the South.

Mary Finch describes herself as a young mother and wife first, and then a certified nursing assistant and doula. Finch, from the area of Fayetteville, Arkansas, has two children. She recalls her awakening to vegetarianism: "It was in 1997, I was newly married and had just read a book on the health benefits of eating a mostly raw diet and we decided to give it a try. That day I got rid of everything in the house that was not vegan. We ate 80 percent raw vegan foods for three years and then gradually started adding more cooked foods into our diets. We still eat a lot of raw but also enjoy cooking and baking."

People unfamiliar with vegetarian cuisine, and especially with vegan cuisine—raw or cooked—might believe that those who do not eat meat or drink cow's milk spend their days deprived of gustatory pleasures, choosing an austere existence of chewing cellulose-dense vegetables. Shakela Richardson learned otherwise. President of the Campus Vegetarian Society at the University of Illinois in Chicago, she unexpectedly discovered the taste pleasures of plant-based cuisine. "I was born and raised in Chicago, Illinois. I became a vegan at age fifteen. I was a sophomore in high school when I was invited to the Soul Vegetarian Restaurant in Chicago. I tasted the food there once and just loved it. Mind you, I didn't know anything about vegetarianism and I had many diet-related health problems. I was even on the verge of diabetes and high blood pressure at fifteen! I had received much information on vegetarianism and health, and decided to give it a try. I have been in great health ever since."

Like Richardson, others who would never have thought of quitting meat eating under normal circumstances did so when faced with health woes, or they turned to vegetarianism after realizing that meat eating was a detrimental factor contributing to the health troubles of a friend or family member. Earl Killian, a retired microprocessor design professional who lives in the San Francisco Bay Area, recalls such an awakening on Killian.com:

> In 1990 a friend of mine underwent surgery to clean out an artery that had become nearly completely blocked. It was caused by high cholesterol. This prompted me to have my own blood test in early 1991 where I found that I too had high cholesterol (though not as high as my friend). I received the standard medical advice to cut down on saturated fat and cholesterol intake. I began to do so (I cut out eggs, shellfish, butter and other fats) and also began reading more on the subject. The more I read the less enticing meat became. I had never smoked; it seemed so stupid to engage in an activity so bad for your health. My reading made me realize that eating meat is just as unhealthy as smoking tobacco. In 1992 I

became a lacto-vegetarian. I have remained lacto-vegetarian ever since. I am inclined toward a vegan diet, and generally I am vegan at home, but I am not yet prepared to give up restaurant dining just yet. However, I do avoid leather and fur.

Ollie Fisher, DMD, a holistic health practitioner and dentist from St. Louis, Missouri, recalls why he became a meat abstainer:

> My mother died from cancer. My father died from cancer. My step-mother died from cancer. My older sister has ovarian cancer. My younger brother had a heart attack in his forties. My grandfather died from heart disease. My uncle died from lung cancer and heart disease. Both of his wives died from cancer. I was told that the disease was hereditary. So when I discovered that a group of African Americans had returned to Israel, changed to a vegan diet, and eliminated most of the diseases plaguing this country, I eagerly changed my diet. That was in 1993.

Jinjee Talifero of the Ekaya Institute of Living Food Education in California switched to a meat-free and plant-based diet after experiencing health woes. Talifero, coauthor of *The Garden Diet* with her husband Storm, a raw food vegan for thirty years, writes, "I was only twenty-six but in poor health and badly overweight. I tried every diet fad available and totally dedicated myself to improving my health but failed miserably! I became completely upset with myself and depressed. Then I found the raw vegan diet and within a few weeks I was experiencing levels of health I never knew existed. I'm now thirty-eight and feeling better and better all the time." The Taliferos, who appear younger than their years, are the subject of *Breakthrough—A Raw Film Documentary*, and the family follows the raw diet from *The Essene Gospel of Peace*.

Health draws many to eschew meat. In 1999, Miriam and Jim Corcoran of Michigan founded Veggies in Motion (VIM) to find more like-minded people to help them educate the public on plant-based nutrition. Miriam explains why she crossed meat off her grocery list: "Doctors using conventional medicine have never helped me with any chronic conditions; the general prescription was a choice of pills or operations. Doctors need education on nutrition, quickly. Our children are dying from overprocessed foods, too much fat, and in general poor diets. In 1992, I watched the video *Diet for a New America* and it changed my life. I educated myself about plant-based nutrition and cured myself from 'family history' ailments." Her husband, Jim, "went veg" in 1989 after reading about it in EarthSave literature. The Corcorans say the acronym for their organization, VIM, "ties in with vigor! Giving us the dual meaning that we are a thriving and effective organization."

Also initially motivated by health concerns, Rev. George Malkmus put himself on a raw food diet after he was diagnosed with colon cancer in 1976. After recovering, the Baptist minister began researching all aspects of vegetarianism, worked with Ann Wigmore in Boston, and spent two years learning natural hygiene at the Shangri-La Health resort in Florida. In 1986, Malkmus founded his Hallelujah Acres ministry on a farm in Edison, Tennessee, and a couple years later released his book, *Why Christians Get Sick*. In 1992 he opened a restaurant and soon had to relocate it to meet demand. The Tennessee preacher and his wife, Rhonda, began holding seminars, releasing audio and videotapes, publishing a newsletter, and making radio and television appearances to promote his Hallelujah Diet, a vegan and mostly raw food eating plan. Hallelujah Acres soon outgrew their base, and Malkmus relocated it to Shelby, North Carolina, in 1997. Two years later, he founded Hallelujah Acres Canada in Ontario.

"I have personally been following this Genesis 1:29 diet for nearly thirty years after having followed the Standard American Diet (SAD) for forty-two years. I have personally experienced both the world's diet and the Genesis 1:29 diet, and know what each of the diets has done in my own physical body. I have been there and done that! . . . Christians have neglected such a diet for too long, despite God's mandates as outlined in Genesis." Malkmus believes that people must break the addiction of the standard American diet, which the nutritional community has strengthened by "programming" people. "About 90 percent of all physical sickness is caused by animal products, which is an addiction akin to alcoholism," says Malkmus, noting that about two million people worldwide follow his Hallelujah Diet.

Michelle LaFleur, of New Port Richey, Florida, broke away from the meat habit. The fitness show competitor, who works as a caregiver to the elderly, recalls that she was "always told, 'If you don't eat your meat you will not maintain or develop muscle.' I listened to my instincts and seventeen years ago I stopped eating red meat because someone told me it rots in our colon. Yuck! Fourteen years ago, I stopped eating all meat. Six years ago I went vegan and could not be happier to have removed all animal products from my diet. Yes, even cheese."

LaFleur at first was a "very quiet vegetarian. If anyone asked me, 'Why don't you eat meat?' I would meekly say, 'Oh, I don't like it.'" Her quietness ended after viewing the films *Peaceable Kingdom* and *Factory Farms*, and she went on to start two nonprofit organizations: Save Innocent Lives Foundation and Food for Life.

A. Dew Frederick, PhD, historian and film documentarian who says she resides in the "tropics of south Texas," was inspired to change her way of eating upon learning about African American centenarian sisters who were vegetarians, Bessie Delany, who died in 1995 at age 104, and Sadie Delany, who died in 1999 at 109. Sadie's book, *Reflections on Life without Bessie* deeply influenced Frederick:

> To my surprise, I learned that they were never married (and they never dated; it seems their lives were dedicated to academics and each other in a healthy way) and strictly devoted to being vegetarians and yoga, and they shunned all medical services until one of them fell at home and broke her hip. They were heterosexual and not in the closet about anything, much like myself. They are an inspiration to me because we as Afro-Americans do not have many long-livers, healthy, Afro-American women. So many women of color who live to an advanced age live in poverty, unsafe neighbors, eating bad foods and addicted to the TV and organized religion, as well as having custody of grandchildren living in their homes, and they are bitter about life and worn out!

Up north, Stewart Rose of Vegetarians of Washington and his spouse were inspired to leap from meat eating to veganism.

> My wife, Susan, and I are Orthodox Jews. It is the custom of our marriage to read the Bible together every Sabbath morning. We became vegans after experiencing a biblical inspiration while reading the Bible. For some time we practiced veganism privately and had no interest in public education and advocacy. One day I found myself in need of some surgery and while recovering in the hospital I was sent one meat meal after the other. When the nurse came in, she asked why I wouldn't eat the food. I told her that I was a vegan. She said, "That's funny, we thought you were Jewish!" I knew at that moment that I had to do something to further the vegetarian movement. I have been working in the movement ever since.

Nearly thirty years ago, Richard Schwartz, PhD, professor emeritus, mathematics, College of Staten Island and author of *Judaism and Vegetarianism* was a meat-and-potatoes person. "My mother was sure to prepare my favorite dish, pot roast, whenever I came to visit with my wife and children. It was a family tradition that I would be served a turkey drumstick every Thanksgiving. Yet, I have not only become a vegetarian, but I now devote a major part of my time to writing, speaking, and teaching about the benefits of vegetarianism." Schwartz first eliminated red meat from his diet after becoming aware of the "tremendous waste of grain associated with the production of beef" while reviewing literature related to world hunger that he used in teaching a course on mathematics and the environment. After reading about the health benefits of vegetarianism and how animals are treated on factory farms, Schwartz in 1978 decided to join the International Jewish Vegetarian Society as a practicing vegetarian.

Kim Zagorsky, manager of FoodWorks. Courtesy the authors.

Spiritual beliefs that lead to rejecting meat may be orthodox or out of the ordinary. Jill Kelly, PhD, a resident of the Sirius Community in Shutesbury, Massachusetts, reports becoming a vegetarian when she began to do "energy work," and "became sensitive to energies—whenever I ate meat, the energy of the animals' last memory opened and I could see and feel their slaughter. I decided I didn't wish to participate in violence like that anymore. It was Good Friday 1996."

A person might value kindness to animals, even working to help cats and dogs or wildlife, and yet eat chickens, cows, and pigs. Eventually such a person might awaken and decide to extend compassion to farmed animals and forsake meat, or meat, milk, and eggs.

Roslyn Abramovitch Smith of West Fargo, North Dakota, explains, "My spouse, Howard, had stopped eating meat twenty years ago for health reasons, and I ate meat in moderation. With serious consideration more than four years ago of the fact that I am an outspoken animal rights advocate and activist, I could no longer consume animals with a clear conscience and a calm heart. My decision was finalized after having researched factory [farming] . . . after viewing a few videos and reading various articles, I decided then and there that I would never eat meat again."

Sometimes a person rejects meat for animal rights reasons and then explores how vegetarianism benefits health. This was what happened to one young adult, Kim Zagorsky, a vegan from Rhode Island:

I went vegetarian when I was twelve (on Thanksgiving day actually). At first it was for animal rights reasons, but then I started reading about the health benefits of a veg diet. I went vegan when I was seventeen. I'm twenty-nine now and since I run a health food store I don't find it hard to eat well at all. Also, I love to cook. My mother didn't know what to make for me when I was younger and veg so I just learned to cook for myself and I'm glad I did. Working in the health food industry, I also feel it's one of the absolute best things you can do for your health. It doesn't require you to buy any fancy, expensive pills or follow some ridiculous diet, yet if you just stick to the basic principles you'll be in better shape than most.

For other people, eschewing meat for health reasons leads to also avoiding it because of modern factory farming practices. Hope Tinsley, a young seminary student in Evanston, Illinois, writes, "I became a vegetarian for health and taste reasons originally, but the longer I am one, the more I do it as a moral choice. I do not believe we should be torturing animals before we eat them. I think if more people met their meat... they would oppose the way we treat animals. If more people met their meat, perhaps we would change the way we raise our meat and I could go back to eating it."

David Curry, an engineer who lives in Indiana, decided to stop eating meat in 1986. "The main reason," explains Curry, "was our discon-nection with modern-day food production techniques and our food and the devastation that is having on the ecosystem. Later it was health and animal welfare as well." Curry learned reasons for rejecting meat from reading *Diet for a New America* by John Robbins.

A meat eater might not seriously consider the vegetarian question until meeting a person who eats no animal flesh. Krissi Vandenberg, executive director of Vegan Action, a nationwide advocacy organiza-tion based in Virginia, recalls her transformation: "When I was in high school, I knew only one vegetarian. I was curious about his diet choice and after talking with him I went to a large animal rights march in DC (I think it was 1989 or 1990). There I picked up a lot of information about the ethical and humane reasons for being vegetarian and de-cided right then that I could no longer eat animals."

Thirty-year-old Bostonian Eric Deneen, writer and lead singer of the rock band BabyStrange, wants America to "put the buffalo wings down and eat some broccoli." He easily changed his diet after discovering that meat-free food is tasty:

I became a vegetarian when I was seventeen. I'd never really thought about it before and then our auto mechanic quit and went into business making veggie burgers. He gave us some and I realized that I could live with meat alternatives.... It was hard not having the convenience of fast-food places but my high school girlfriend became a vegetarian around the same time and we sort of just made it work. It was satisfying because at that age I hadn't really made any big life decisions and stuck to them for very long. There was some name calling—I think "fag" was a pretty common one—but that comes with the territory when you are doing something different. There is also a lot of questions, "Why do you wear leather blah blah blah?" . . . I just heard about Veggiedates.com and I was surprised that we're doing that now. I usually mention that I'm a vegetarian early on when I'm dating someone but only because it seems to come up. I don't think I could get serious with a girl that isn't a vegetarian because it's such a big part of your lifestyle at a certain point. . . . I'm going to raise my children vegetarian as well as Buddhist, so I need to be with a woman that's on the same page.

People who eat meat are aware that animals are slaughtered for human beings to dine on lobster flesh, pork bellies, and turkey wings. However, this awareness burns dim at best, since the dominant culture considers discussion of the reality of meat production as a social taboo. Exceptions to this rule of unawareness that meat was once an animal do exist, as when people childishly or callously joke about dining upon Tom Turkey for Thanksgiving dinner, when they choose a turkey from a farm flock for slaughter, or when they pick out a live lobster at the store from the cramped aquarium to bring home to boil. When people go fishing, they witness the suffocation of a fish that is soon transformed into an entrée slathered in lemon, butter, and breadcrumbs, and when they go hunting they might bring home the deer they have killed that is transformed into a freezer full of venison.

These are exceptions to the usual mindlessness of meat eating. Most often people do not even refer to the fact that meat was an animal. Carol J. Adams, author of *The Sexual Politics of Meat*, coined the term *absent referent*. Thus, people will discuss whether the meat on their plate is fresh, tasty, tender or tough, rare or well done, but never that it is actually flesh from an individual animal, who might have been befriended by a human being and suffered for the sake of someone's taste buds.

When a person breaks through the concrete wall of cultural denial of the reality of meat, the consequences can be so unsettling or enlightening that a person's life changes forever, even if not immediately. Therefore, one path to vegetarianism winds through pain—the sudden, powerful emotional punch to the soul that people who have empathy, love, or just respect for animals feel upon discovering the details of the origin of meat. For some, that blow to the psyche hurts mightily because the meat on the table was part of a friend.

Kansan Judy Carman, author of *Peace to All Beings: Veggie Soup for the Chicken's Soul*, tells us her story:

Judy Carman. Courtesy Judy M.
Carman.

When I was ten years old (1954), we lived on a seven-acre property, and my parents bought some lambs. They had babies; I named them all; and, of course, I loved them. They were my dear, sweet friends. One day I came home from school to find them missing. Mom told me they had sold them. I had not had a chance to say good-bye, and I was inconsolable. I missed them so much, I thought I would die without them. Well, by now you have probably already guessed what happened at the dinner table that evening.

I sat down for the usual meat, potatoes, peas, etc. when someone mentioned how good the "lamb" was. The sudden rush of realization that the meat on my table was one of my friends hit me like a lightning bolt. They weren't just gone; they were all dead; and we were eating them. I was horrified and confused. I looked at my plate, and there was a piece of flesh that had been cut out of my friend. This was a funeral, not a meal, and all I could do was cry. Yet everyone else was exclaiming with pleasure how tasty it was. In a sense, I was experiencing culture shock, as I took my first steps back from the culture I was born into and wondered if I really belonged in it. It had never dawned on me until then that meat was actually dead animals just like the adorable ones in the storybooks and like my friends, the lambs.

I had never heard the word "vegetarian" at that time. My uncles worked at the Kansas City stockyards, and meat had this aura of wealth and status about it. Everyone I knew ate meat. There were certainly no veg options at school. So, ignorant as I was, my first attempt at going veg involved secretly feeding my meat to the dogs under the table and living on cream-filled cupcakes, frosted flakes, and white Wonder bread which I liked to roll up into little balls.

Can anyone say "malnourished"? Anyway, I ended up eating meat again, because I thought I had to, but I felt bad about it. It just seemed wrong to me. I knew I was eating my friends. It wasn't until the 1970s that I began to learn about the veg life. Books were coming out about it, many animal rights groups had formed, and a restaurant opened up in Kansas City called the Golden Temple that was vegetarian. A small group of like-minded folks and I began learning how to change the way we ate. I did not hear the word "vegan" until some years later. It took some time for me to make all the shocking discoveries about modern American food, but gradually the pieces all came together, and the big picture emerged. I realized that my original motivation for not wanting to eat animals was an ethical one.

Like Carman, cofounder of Lawrence-based Animal Outreach of Kansas, Suzanne Branford's path away from meat eating began at a young age. The cardiac technician and Vegetarian Society of Nevada founder remembers: "I was only six years old when I thought that killing and eating animals was not right. I realized to my dismay that the animals placed under my care were for food. A bullet or club to the head, a slashed or severed throat, scalded in boiling water was the sad destiny for the animals I cared for, the animals so similar to me, the animals I loved."

Branford learned early in life that a meat-eating culture does not encourage vegetarianism. "I remember pushing my friends aside on my plate and eating my veggies first. At thirteen years old I stopped eating red meat. My parents expressed grave concerns for my meatless lifestyle. After years of awareness and enlightenment, I eliminated all animals and their by-products from my lifestyle and am now a vegan going on seventeen years. I feel that all animals have a right to life and it's unnecessary, cruel and inhumane to kill and consume animals to satisfy our violent palates."

Whether or not one is encouraged to reject meat when as a child, ethical principles usually are a determining factor for a person to remain a true vegetarian, or, for those like Branford who take that principle to the furthest reach, a vegan.

Linda Anne Bessette's spiritual and ethical beliefs caused her not to consume or use any animal products. Brought up in Rhode Island by parents who taught her to give to others, as a child, Bessette raised money for charities and rescued animals. While in college, she volunteered at an orphanage, which led to a career in social services that would span three decades. She became a vegetarian almost thirty years ago, and tells us:

Before graduating from the University of South Carolina, during an environmental science class, we were required to watch a particular movie on the Mississippi River which demonstrated specific industries that were polluting it on a daily basis. They showed a slaughterhouse with animals in line, and then hanging upside down, soon to be put to a horrific death. After graphic scenes of bloody water and animal carcasses, I swore never to touch animal meat again. That was twenty-eight years ago and I have never placed a living thing on my tongue since. I only use products that are not derived from animals.

In 2005, Bessette was moved by scenes of Hurricane Katrina, so she organized a relief effort to collect supplies for the victims. Bessette, a social worker, took in homeless animals through her newly founded Flower Dogs Sanctuary.

My basic belief is that we have become a throwaway society. In addition, I feel it has become too prevalent in American society. A little bit of power, I always say . . . is a dangerous thing. We as human beings must let go of the need to exert power to feel good, and allow only God . . . whatever we conceive him to be, to determine when a life will end, whether it be an animal, unborn baby, prisoner, or living person needing machines to sustain life. . . . I will continue to practice respect for all living things throughout my days and try to help those in most need, and it is my hope that I will have made a small impact on all living creatures and society as a whole.

Bessette passed on her vegetarian reverence for life to her daughter, Tara Jane. "I vowed to raise her vegetarian and taught her at an early age to accept the differences of others. She has been raised in a household that places a low value on external riches and I encourage a simple lifestyle with an emphasis on the intrinsic rewards of caring for others."

American writer Michael Stephen Fuchs, author of *The Manuscript*, a novel, who currently resides in Europe, witnessed the suffering of animals here at home, which led him to stop eating meat:

Full of cow flesh from one last lunch at T-Bell [Taco Bell], I was bouncing through the mountainous stretches of Highway 81 west of Charlottesville [Virginia]. On the steep incline, I went to pass a slow-moving truck; it was actually a large pickup, towing a trailer. Inside the trailer were five cows (though there was really only room for four). They all had their necks bent at near 90-degree angles to fit into the cramped space. One was craning my way, and as I made eye contact with her, I realized she was terrified, in addition to crowded. As the truck bounced over the road, she struggled to keep her feet under her, and her eyes were wide with drawn-out fear and discomfort.

All I could think at that moment was that they were taking this poor gal, and her friends, off to the Taco Bell factory, to replace the tacos I had eaten earlier that day. And, at that moment, I called an end to the carnivorous madness. I had looked into the eyes of the folks I had been eating, and I couldn't have them killed for my lunch any more.

Another young adult, Alissa Finley, of Oklahoma City, Oklahoma, broke away from meat eating and took up the cause of helping farmed animals. "Growing up, I always felt a great deal of compassion and empathy towards animals. I wanted to take in every stray I saw. However, I never once connected my love of animals to the fact that I was eating them. I never heard the word vegetarianism; I didn't know anyone who was a vegetarian." But Finley had an awakening when she attended a summer camp in the late 1980s when she was eighteen. During her first day, the counselors explained that vegetarian options were available.

But first, they needed a count. I will never forget the face of the counselor that asked those of us who wanted vegetarian meals to raise our hands. It was as if all the sound traveled out of his mouth and slammed me right on my chest. Gears turned. Lights flashed. And I said to myself, "I have an option?! Of course! How can I possibly eat animals?! It sounds ludicrous now—how have I not seen this before?" Other students around me raised their hands, maybe about eight out of one hundred attendees. They were vegetarians—they looked just fine....I never ate another piece of an animal's body again. I could no longer justify it once I had this knowledge. And knowledge came strikingly and terrifyingly fast.

Finley fortified her dietary choices when she attended Cornell University and joined Cornell Students for the Ethical Treatment of Animals and began to learn not only about the lives of farm animals but every other facet of animal abuse. Members of the group spend many weekends volunteering at Farm Sanctuary in Watkins Glen, New York. One day she asked another volunteer that "very naive, very common question, 'But, why don't you drink milk or use eggs? I mean, you're not killing the animal to get those, right?'" After the volunteer showed her the cows rescued from the dairy and veal industry, and the laying hens and the battery cages they were forced to live in, Finley became a vegan that very afternoon. "How does a person understand how these industries function and *not* become vegan—that's the hard part for me to wrap my head around. But over the years, I have seen the defenses and the habits and the ignorance in people, and I try to remember that once upon a time, I was not a vegan either."

Sometimes the shocking realization that meat was once an animal triggers a reawakening. Jim Taylor, president of the National Humane Education Society in West Virginia, had such an awakening:

> From my infancy, I was reared a vegetarian. From the age of six—when I entered grade school—my parents permitted me to choose whether or not I would continue with a vegetarian diet. Despite being the only vegetarian in my rural elementary school, I chose to continue eating a vegetarian diet until I was fifteen years of age, at which time I began eating meat. Regretfully, I continued eating meat until I was thirty-five years of age, at which time I returned to eating a vegetarian diet. The impetus for returning to a vegetarian diet was as follows: In October of 1994, during my drive from Colorado to Virginia where I had accepted a position with the National Humane Education Society, I stopped during the night to purchase some gasoline and just happened to see a tractor pulling a two-tiered trailer that was packed full of cows and calves. It was a very cold night, and I could see the cows/calves' foggy breath eminating from between the slats of the trailer. It was just such a sad sight, as were the sounds of the calves calling for their mothers. And at that moment, I simply said to myself, I can no longer eat meat. I never want any animal to suffer in order for me to fill my stomach.

Taylor's grandmother is a legendary figure in the humane education movement: Anna C. Briggs, beloved founder of the National Humane Education Society. At age ninety-five, Mrs. Briggs is the eldest vegetarian featured in this book. She also was a founder of the Vegetarian Society of D.C., an organization dating to the 1920s, and thought to be the oldest vegetarian group in the United States. (Her grandson says until a few months ago, she worked five days a week. Unfortunately, Mrs. Briggs suffered a stroke just before this book went to print.)

In the 1930s, Briggs's husband managed an animal shelter in Maryland. Mrs. Briggs's account of her transformation to vegetarian, written several years ago, exemplifies the sentiments of countless vegetarians who are horrified into eschewing meat.

> His animals had good care, but lacked the human touch, so I spent many hours there. One day, my husband asked me to go to the abattoir (the local slaughterhouse) to fetch some food for the dogs. I would do anything for those dogs, but I didn't know what I was getting myself into.
>
> To buy the meat, I had to observe a lot of awful things. I could hardly stay; it was nerve-wracking to hear the cows bleating in their fear. They knew where they were going. They sensed it as surely as anything. I could hear them in their death throes as well, screaming and squealing. . . . I've never regretted my choice in diet, and have enjoyed much better health

because of it. In rethinking our position on the food chain, I remember my mother.

She fed me and my brothers meat because everyone said to do so. "They need meat for good health," the doctor told her. Then when I announced my vegetarianism, my brothers couldn't understand it. Our mother defended my position with a phrase that has stuck with me ever since: "I never did think that meat was fit for human consumption."

It's easy to see the benefits of a vegetarian diet. But many of us don't want to see the other side of the coin, the ethical question. Living a meat-free life equals erasing cruelty on a daily basis. Every time I choose an apple instead of an animal's carcass, I feel good about eating it. An apple tree drops its fruit naturally; steak is stolen from a cow by harsh human violence.

You have only to look into an animal's eyes to know that it has a soul or listen to its cries to realize that it has feelings, too. I made my pledge of compassion seventy years ago, and have never been tempted to change it.

American culture considers such compassion childish or sentimental. Yet a child led Diane Carr of Lexington, Massachusetts, to vegetarianism.

When my daughter Vanessa was 12, she announced she would stop eating meat. At the time she wanted to be a veterinarian and she had always had a keen sense of fairness and never felt superior to other people or animals. She had also just seen the movie *Babe* (1995). I also saw the movie and swore immediately off pork myself, but continued to think other meats were acceptable. (In fact her older brother had already been a vegetarian a few years earlier, but for health reasons, and I remember I used to coax him to eat it when he visited me.) But with my daughter's broader view of respect for animals, I felt her determination, and started cooking vegetarian to be sure she got enough protein. Though I had phased out buying meat to cook at home, I continued to eat meat when I went to a restaurant.

Over the next two years, as an environmentalist, I expanded my philanthropic net to join PETA, but used to throw away their magazine because I could not bear to face the possible cruel pictures inside. Then I opened an article about chickens. I faced the graphic photos of chickens on a factory farm and read the article. I said, "Something has to be done about these farming methods." I began to stop *all meat*, regardless of the social context, the dearth of vegetarian alternatives, or the fact that it was Thanksgiving and all my relatives were upset. I stopped dairy and became vegan a couple of years later...as a result of talking to other animal rights activists. In the end, it was a child's integrity, *Babe*, PETA, and other activists who changed me.

Wisconsin resident Wanda Embar, publisher of Veganpeace.com, was led by a sibling to vegetarianism.

> I became a vegetarian because my sister was vegetarian. I was fifteen years old and started out by simply following my big sister's lead. But soon after, I started reading a lot of books and became interested in all aspects of vegetarianism. Especially the animal cruelty aspects became very important to me. When I was twenty, I read a book which included a chapter about the cruelty in the dairy industry. It talked about how the dairy cows are constantly kept pregnant and about how their calves are removed from them soon after they are born. That day I became vegan (February 27th, 1990). I didn't even know whether there were any other vegans where I lived.

For a vegetarian to be well-informed about vegetarianism is common. Seventeen-year-old Jasmin Rhiannon Baker-Kinney of Redmond, Washington, tells us:

> The first is for the animals. I don't think that it's right for us to kill innocent animals and eat them just because they "taste good" and because it brings in large profits. I don't believe that eating animals is right, even when they aren't in slaughterhouses. I have been vegetarian my entire life and I'm one of the healthiest kids I know. This stated, being vegetarian is much better for you than eating meat. Our bodies were built like herbivores, not carnivores. Many of the diseases that people die from today, such as heart attacks and strokes, could be avoided by becoming vegetarian. Many people think that vegetarians don't get enough protein, but that's not an issue if you eat a wide variety of things. Soy and legumes have all the protein you need and many other things such as spinach supply some protein as well. I also think that being vegetarian is better for the environment. A lot of the pollution that we have today is due to meat production factories both where the animals are stored before their cruel deaths and the factories that they are murdered in.

Jasmin Baker-Kinney's parents are vegetarians as well; her mother, Karen Baker, abstains from meat, "first and foremost for the animals. Later I also added environmental and health to my reasons for being veg."

Gil Schwartz, campaign coordinator of Compassionate Action for Animals of Minneapolis, Minnesota, became a vegetarian nine years ago at the age of twelve. "I decided to go vegetarian off a whim. As I looked into proper vegetarian nutrition, I started reading about factory farming and its problems. With the knowledge that suffering was inextricably linked to eating meat, I decided to confirm my commitment to the diet. After being challenged by my omnivorous friends in high school regarding the suffering that went into the eggs and dairy I consumed, I decided to go vegan to remain consistent with my ethics."

Caroline Garcia, a studio art major specializing in printmaking from Jeanerette, Louisiana, a tiny town in the middle of Cajun country, became a vegan at age nineteen.

> I met someone who ended up becoming my best friend, and he was vegan. I had thought about vegetarianism for a while—I never really liked meat that much. It was just what was always for dinner. It's pretty hard to get away from meat in Louisiana. . . . Anyway, one day I was eating an omelet that had bacon in it. I was thinking about how much I liked bacon, and then realized all the pain and suffering at least one animal went through because I liked the way it tasted. It's not like bacon is something that has any nutritional value, and I felt it was awfully selfish of me to cause so much misery for that sort of reason. So that was it, and I applied that to eggs and dairy as well, and went straight from a bacon omelet to being vegan.

Mary Margison of upstate New York, who attends the University of Rhode Island, recalls how she became vegetarian:

> My sister was quite persistent when she told me she had something to show me, yet she wouldn't tell me what it was. I drove over to her apartment, eating what was to be my last bacon, egg, and cheese bagel from Dunkin' Donuts. I arrived at her apartment and watched a ten-minute version of PETA's *Meet Your Meat* DVD on her computer. I spent the next ten minutes dry-heaving over her toilet and vowed never to condone that sort of abuse again. I went vegan pretty quickly after learning about all the blood and pus in dairy products, as well as milk's link to veal, ground beef, growth hormones, pesticides, and antibiotics. That was just over three years ago.

Like many other teens, Caitlin Eisenberg of Massachusetts was profoundly affected after learning of the fate of animals. "I became a vegetarian in the summer of 2004 after I went to Best Friends Animal Sanctuary in Kanab, Utah, and I met a pig. I realized that eating them was horrible, so I stopped. Then I went vegan in April 2005 after attending the Grassroots Animal Rights Conference in NYC and read some materials and realized I needed to take the extra step and go vegan."

Just prior to Caitlin's conversion, her dad, Mark Eisenberg, set an example for her by dumping meat from his diet after a visit to a well-known Web site. "About three years ago, I was reviewing some information on the PETA site regarding legislation to extend the humane slaughter act. The accounts and video/images of cruelty in the factory farming system pushed me to stop participating in the system."

Young and naive or older and wiser, people awaken to vegetarianism in their own time. Anne Weaver, eighty-four, from Winston-Salem, North Carolina, became a vegan in 1989, "after hearing Dr. Michael Klaper and Dr. John McDougall at North American Vegetarian Summerfest." What they said convinced Weaver veganism "was the healthy way to go. I also thought it was best for the environment and animals. In 1990, soon after Summerfest, my husband and I started our Very Vegetarian Society here and are still meeting monthly with a program and potluck."

Like Weaver's vocation, Cheri Ezell-Vandersluis's work benefits animals. Her journey to vegetarianism and the cofounding of Maple Farm Sanctuary in Mendon, Massachusetts, began in a place antithetical to animal liberation. She reveals that when she was employed by a drug manufacturer as an autopsy and histology technician, she thought she would help animals. Ezell-Vandersluis told us she worked on the bodies of beagles that had been "dosed with experimental compounds." The dogs lived in cages, and she had petted and comforted them until pathologists and veterinarians stopped her, saying that if the animals had a will to live then the experiments would fail.

Ezell-Vandersluis recounts this experience on her farm's Web site, along with her next place of employment—an aquarium, where she witnessed a dolphin isolated from his fellows and accidentally trapped in netting. She and other people dove into the water, trying to untangle him, but he perished while his dolphin mates, helpless to rescue him, screamed. Eventually, Ezell-Vandersluis and her spouse operated a goat milk farm, but then became disturbed at having to sell the kids for slaughter. "Jim and I stood at the gate too many times listenting to baby goats cry as they were driven away," she confesses. Determined to change their ways, the couple sent the remaining goats to no-kill sanctuaries, and then over time established Maple Farm Sanctuary. "Jim and I are vegetarians and do as much sanctuary work as our finances will allow," she explains. Ezell-Vandersluis, who is now a vegan, teaches the public about the lives of farm animals along with her husband.

Part of the American culture, yet also apart from it, vegetarians are creating their own thriving subculture, which we will now explore.

2

FOOD, HOSPITALITY, AND BUSINESS

Reforms can never be brought into effect by parliaments, prohibitive laws, and peace-commissions, they must begin in the home, in the school, in the office, in the workshop, as it is here where the false notions of human nature have ruled so long.

Otto Carque, *The Foundation of All Reform*, 1904

Veteran vegetarians can recount horror stories about dining at restaurants or cafeterias, or attending weddings, barbecues, retirement dinners, and other events. These stories run the gamut from sitting in front of a plate of soggy vegetables to some oily concoction seemingly prepared in hell. All too many vegetarians can recall when the only edible items available were salad and a dinner roll, or french fries (that is, if they weren't cooked using beef stock). They also had to call the chef in advance to make sure there were no surprises lurking in the pasta sauce or the pizza crust. In some cases, it was a roll of the dice—the chef couldn't guarantee that the ingredients were free of meat or dairy.

Out on the road, fast-food restaurants remain a meat eater's dream, but many of them have now seen beyond the butcher's knife to the light of a profitable market and have added meat-free fare. Burger King now offers the BK Veggie Burger, although vegans can't have it their way since it includes dairy ingredients. The burger behemoth McDonald's offers a meat-free burger called the McVeggie at certain locales in California, Canada, and New York City. Other chain restaurants, including Wendy's and Subway, also feature meatless sandwiches, and several of the smaller, regional chains even offer vegan fare.

On the whole, vegetarian food sales reached $1.6 billion in 2003, double the amount posted for 1998, according to Mintel, a research firm. And the increase will continue unabated for years to come. In 2008, the number will increase by 61 percent, predicts Mintel. Though consumers who aren't vegetarians but are looking for healthier foods have fueled this rise, the availability of meat-free foods will make it easier for people to switch to a plant-based diet.

VEGETARIANS AND FOOD SERVICE

In recent years, the media have reported on the rise of obesity, particularly among school-age children. Health advocates decry fatty foods offered in school cafeterias as one of the culprits, and school systems across the United States, in a knee-jerk approach to the problem, either have banned or are in the process of banning soda, candy bars, and other foods deemed junk food. Vegetarian advocates have jumped into the debate by demonizing meat and dairy as equal or worse contributors to obesity than junk food. Neal Barnard, MD, head of the Physicians Committee on Responsible Medicine, puts much of the blame on government and big business. "The U.S. Department of Agriculture continues to use the National School Lunch Program as a dumping ground for excess pork, beef, cheese, chicken and other high-cholesterol, low-fiber, fatty animal products. Three out of every four dollars spent on government food assistance programs go toward the purchase of these unhealthful foods."

However, most vegetarian advocates are now trying to convince school systems not so much to outlaw certain foods as to offer healthy plant-based meal options. Susan Wieland, director of Consumers for Healthy Options in Children's Education, helped local advocates in three states—California, Hawaii, and New York—to persuade their legislatures to pass resolutions to study the possibility of offering vegetarian food options for school lunches. At first, food service executives were hesitant.

They saw the vegetarian community as an "outside" interest whose needs were not as important as other demands they face on a more regular basis. The resolutions helped clarify, across the state, that bringing veggie options into the schools not only [serves] a substantial segment of the school population who had very little, if anything, that they could eat (vegetarians, vegans, children of different religions and ethnicity, plus students with medical needs) but was also a viable and healthy option for all students. Whereas previously we had problems getting audiences with food service directors, now they tend to readily accept our involvement.

Vegetarian advocates have long tried to persuade food vendors such as airlines and ballpark concession stands to add meat-free food to their bill of fare. Sometimes the adage "One person can make a difference" comes true, particularly in the case of an actress who was galvanized into action after being disappointed at a ballpark.

While attending a baseball game in Dodger Stadium in April 2000, Johanna McCloy searched the halls of the stadium for vegetarian food other than a bag of peanuts or popcorn. After coming up empty, McCloy called the stadium's concession manager the following day, suggesting that concession stands add veggie subs and soy hotdogs to the sandwich menu, while reinforcing her argument with statistics on the rise in demand for meat substitutes and an offer to act as a broker between manufacturers and food managers. Shortly after, Dodger Stadium began selling veggie subs.

The actress, who portrayed Ensign Calloway on *Star Trek: The Next Generation* and starred in beer commercials, knew she was onto something good. McCloy contacted every Major League Baseball stadium to work as a consultant for concession managers, manufacturers, and distributors. Her efforts caught the attention of the media, and celebrities like St. Louis Cardinals manager Tony LaRussa, a longtime vegetarian, offered to make endorsements. The California food consultant founded Soyhappy.org to help her efforts.

But decisions to add meat-free food arise more from business concerns than to satisfy the demands of vegetarians, says McCloy. "What's important to remember is that we are dealing with a food *business*, so it isn't as much the matter of cultural receptivity that hinders the progress at this point, but the logistics of food service." McCloy's business savvy has yielded results: ten ballparks added vegetarian food by 2005. The latest success occurred at the concessions at RFK Stadium in spring 2005 after McCloy convinced Aramark Corp., the Philadelphia food services company that runs the concessions, to add soy hotdogs to the menu. Even fans who eat meat want healthier food, a vital fact that plays a key role in persuading food service managers to add meatless burgers, soy hotdogs, and other plant-based items.

The culture is becoming better informed about health and vegetarian alternatives are increasing in sales in retail markets all the time. Think about Gardenburger. It's no longer considered "weird" to the public. It's almost expected on a menu. Think about soy milk. It's offered at every

Starbucks. Times are changing. Vendors are aware that this is not just a "vegetarian" issue. It's an issue that covers health and culture and real demand. Soy Happy always offers statistics on consumer demand to prove that this is not about a small percentage of the population that is strictly vegetarian. In fact, most sales are to individuals that are *not* vegetarian. It's an important fact.

The same logic applies to grocery stores, restaurants, and other food service areas.

At the Cafeteria

A 2004 study of 100,000 college students conducted by Aramark, a Philadelphia-based food service and facility management company, reported that one in four students want vegan meals on campus. Aramark didn't become one of *Forbes* magazine's Most Admired Companies by ignoring such potential. Soon after the report was released, the food giant began developing meals for the hordes of vegans eager to sink their forks into something besides limp legumes, potatoes, or any other uninspired dishes sans animal ingredients.

"Aramark introduced Just4U in June 2004, and has since added more than 220 vegan and vegetarian recipes to the lineup," said Mike Crane, senior director of culinary development in a press release. "We've created vegan items such as Sweet Thai Tofu Stir-Fry, Broccoli Teriyaki, Eggless 'Egg' Salad, and Vegan 'Cheese' Burgers to name a few."

The same year, Veg Advantage began offering free consultation services to institutions and restaurants on menu development, recipes, and product research and distribution. Spokesman Corey Portalatin-Berrien says the company, which lists chefs with training from the Natural Gourmet Cookery School and the Culinary Institute of America, adapts vegetarian food to the style of cuisine offered. "With an Italian restaurant we recently worked with, we helped them create a vegan version of the chicken marsala they serve using seitan and a roasted vegetable stock as the base for the sauce to create a vegan version. That seems to be doing very well. It also works well for the restaurant since they use many shared ingredients and the same process."

Sysco, another giant food services provider, has jumped into the market by introducing meals aimed at vegans. under the name MoonRose. These include soy-based plant proteins, whole grains, legumes, and comfort foods such as chili, pizza, burgers, soups, and desserts.

The Chefs

Chef Ron Pickarski, known affectionately by many in the vegetarian community as Brother Ron for the years he spent as a Franciscan brother, helped formulate some MoonRose products. His company, Eco-Cuisine, aided the marketing efforts and developed several dry mixes for brownies, muffins, cookies, pancakes, and other desserts, and mixes for entrées such as seitan sausage and vegan-style chicken.

Sysco made the right choice. Pickarski did for vegetarian cuisine what Julia Child did for French cooking, elevating it to heights never seen before. The executive chef founded and directs the American Natural Foods Team, which competes at the quadrennial International Culinary Olympics in Germany. In the 1980s and 1990s, he won seven gold, silver, and bronze medals with plant-based foods and was the first chef in the history of that prestigious event to do so. The Colorado resident also appeared on many television shows, produced a video and wrote the book *As You Like It* (2001), and has been featured in *Vegetarian Times*, *Art Culinaire*, *The National Culinary Review*, *Denver Post*, *USA Today Weekend*, *Boston Globe*, *Miami Herald*, and other publications.

Pickarski founded Eco-Cuisine in 1986 as a consulting company before it evolved into a vegan product development company. Realizing that the market for plant-based cuisine was on the rise, he started

Award-winning chef Ron Pickarski. Courtesy Ron Pickarski.

working on a line of vegan food service products in 1996. The effort has paid off. In 2004, sales at least doubled from the previous year, and Eco-Cuisine landed several major accounts, including two national food service accounts.

Boulder, Colorado–based Eco-Cuisine features products that are tantalizing to anyone who prepares plant-based food for the public—particularly when it comes to economics. Ready-to-cook seitan costs about $6 a pound, while Eco-Cuisine's dry seitan mix costs about $1.30 a pound. Chefs can easily "plug the mix into the menu," says Pickarski. "It's almost seamless with minimum labor. Our ground beef mix, for example, can be plugged into their recipes for chili, sloppy joes, meatloaf, Salisbury steak, etc. And the chefs tell me that they can pass this off as meat. It's a good selling point because food service establishments are driven by price. They have to make the numbers work."

Connecticut chef Ken Bergeron believes that chefs in the United States are waking up to the fact that plant-based diets are here to stay and will increase in popularity. Bergeron, as a member of the Southern Natural Foods Team, won the first gold medal ever awarded to an all-vegetarian menu at the Culinary Olympics in Frankfurt, Germany, in 1992. His book is *Professional Vegetarian Cooking*.

> The world of food has been affected by the vegetarian trend mostly because of the demand. Professional chefs and cooks realize the importance [of] serv[ing] meals that are free of animal products to their vegetarian dining public and have sharpened their skills in this area. Of note too is the fact that some of the nation's top chefs create all-vegetable tasting menus, and there has been great interest in the raw foods restaurants that have opened throughout the country. The culinary achievements of vegetarian chefs, through their restaurants, books and culinary competitions, have helped vegetarianism gain respect. Resistance disappears when chefs realize the financial benefit gained from serving vegetarian food, especially to large groups.

Such resistance continues to fade among top gourmet chefs as they add separate vegetarian menus or at least offer plant-based choices, says chef Al Chase, founder of the Institute for Culinary Awakening with marketing director Donna Benjamin. "But the resistance is from chefs who think they cannot bake successfully without eggs, milk, [or] cream or cook without animal products. Many chefs still are not aware of the health and environmental benefits, cost effectiveness and ever-growing popularity of an organic, plant-based menu, not only for their vegan and vegetarian customers but also for their health-aware clientele."

Chase, the first vegan chef to present dishes at venues such as the Culinary Institute of America and Omega Institute for Holistic Studies, and who has recipes on the back of Rapunzel Pure Organics Chocolate Baking Products, believes that ultimately the chef's customers will drive the change. "Food awareness is growing as more and more veg-friendly classes and programs are being offered. There is still a perception that vegetarian/vegan food is boring and bland and only revolves around salad, tofu, rice and beans. Delicious, inviting organic, vegan cuisine can be utilized as a 'healthy hook' to get vegetarian advocacy issues out on the table—literally and figuratively."

Like Chase, Pickarski predicts that vegetarianism will make significant inroads into the meat-eating mainstream only with tasty food. "The vegetarian movement is exploding through health-conscious consumers. That pushes people to try it. But the food has to be tasty so they can get by the poor taste perception. Once that is done, and they become comfortable with the food, they will be the gateway to staunch meat eaters."

Chef Beverly Lynn Bennett, author of *The Complete Idiot's Guide to Vegan Living*, agrees that tasty and readily available vegan food will win over meat eaters:

> Absolutely, tasty vegan food can really help open minds to the possibility of a life without animal products. It can be a good way to open up the door to changing people's perceptions and misconceptions about what it's like to not have meat and all sorts of other animal foods on their plate, and that's an important step toward stopping a lot of animal suffering. I have heard many non-veggie people make the statement that "I could stop eating meat, but I would have no idea what to eat in its place. I don't want to eat beans and seaweed for three meals a day!" or "I could give up dairy, but I can *not* live without ice cream and cheese!"

For the general mainstream population, vegetarian has become a taste option, rather than a dedicated dietary choice. People might say, "Let's eat vegetarian tonight," just as they say, "How about Chinese today?" But Bennett sees this as a positive sign for the future.

> I think that any time a person chooses to eliminate animal products from their lives is a good thing, and certainly better than if they didn't include a "vegetarian night" into the mix to begin with. In a way, vegetarianism *has* become just another taste option for some people, but compared to the alternative of "meat seven nights a week," it's a step in the right direction and may actually serve as a regular reminder that they could eliminate meat from their meals and it wouldn't be the end of the world. As more people hear about the health effects of avoiding animal ingredients, the more that "vegetarian night" might be expanded to two,

three, four, or more nights per week. For a long time, vegetarianism was a fringe thing, and now it has become mainstream enough to become an often-considered taste option.

Chef Elaine Cwyner, who teaches a course on vegetarian cuisine at Johnson and Wales University, warns that chefs need proper training. "The danger is that if the chef is not adept at creating real vegetarian food, there is the likelihood that meat products, like beef base, or gelatin, could find their way into a vegetarian selection." Cwyner's course covers the basics of vegetarianism, nutrition, food products used, and history, and concentrates on vegan, lacto-ovo, and macrobiotic diets. For their final project, the students research and create recipes for a grand buffet served to over fifty invited guests, and they showcase their production and service skills, she says.

But Cwyner says convincing conventional chefs poses a challenge. "I've been endearingly called 'Lightweight' and 'Tofu Tilly' by chefs at school, but as health problems have stricken my fellow chefs, they have changed their tune and become more accepting of the alternative foods that are available. Most have been classically trained and will never give up duck or foie gras, but that is their prerogative. I just keep the doors open and if they need information, our department provides what we can to answer their questions."

The Restaurants

There are hundreds, if not thousands, of restaurants, cafés, and bistros that serve only plant-based foods. Very few of them fall into the gourmet dining category. But Millennium Restaurant in San Francisco breaks out of the pack by offering an animal product-free menu in surroundings that can compare with most gourmet meat-based establishments.

Millennium, located on Geary Street in the city's historic district, features entrées ranging from truffled white bean cassoulet (a concoction of wild rice and parsnip griddle cake, sautéed broccoli di cicco, and shaved Himalayan truffles) to pecan-crusted polenta (creamy roasted garlic polenta with a sauté of mixed chicories and black olive-leek confit). Desserts include chocolate almond midnight (almond cashew crust, mocha chocolate filling, raspberry sauce, white chocolate mousse) and sorbets and cookies made in-house. The restaurant also reserves dates for special events. On the second Wednesday of each month, patrons who bring in a meat-eating friend for Convert a Carnivore Day receive 25 percent off their total bill, and each Sunday closest to the full moon features an Aphrodisiac Dinner. In 2004, respondents to *VegNews* magazine's annual Veggie Awards survey voted

Millennium as their favorite restaurant, and their chef, Eric Tucker, took honors for favorite chef.

San Francisco's Lisa Herzstein, who has eaten at the restaurant about a hundred times in its decade of existence, offers a review:

> Most of the time I've eaten there with omnivores, and all of them have enjoyed the restaurant, including those who are accustomed to dining at fine restaurants. The dishes are creative with unique mixes of ingredients for unusual and delicious flavors, and the presentation is beautiful of all their foods. The service is friendly and responsive and the atmosphere is that of a gourmet restaurant. Most people would not even notice the lack of animal products on the menu. There is an all-organic fine wine list also.

On the other end of the spectrum are the more typical restaurants, cafés, and bistros that serve food free from animal products—small and casual establishments where the owner often works in the kitchen, waits on tables, and might help out with the cleanup.

On an early September evening in Melanie's Vegan Eden, tucked into a street corner in the Fox Point neighborhood of Providence, Rhode Island, several college students occupy three of the five tables, digging their forks into their delights. They are dressed in frumpy clothing, but on closer inspection, the clothes more than likely originate from boutiques rather than bargain-basement stores. An older couple sits at another table, playing one of the dozen or so games that sit on the shelf that runs along the perimeter of the seating area, while waiting for a Boy Named Sue, a dish featuring sautéed mock chicken.

In the kitchen, owner Melanie Burtt, her mom Kimberly, and others are busy baking, blending, tossing, mixing, whipping, dicing, and slicing the food that will end up at the tables. The staff prepares everything on the spot—there is no precooked food on the premises, or cake that might have been chilling in the refrigerator for weeks. Burtt says,

> At the restaurant, I try to keep the profit on everything really low to encourage more people to eat vegan food more frequently. The problem with this is that I make everything from scratch, which is super labor intensive. The food becomes more expensive when I am making everything from scratch with quality ingredients, as opposed to a restaurant selling a frozen four-month-old cheesecake that they bought for $6 (for the entire thing) to people for $8 a slice. Moreover, organic foods are more expensive because it costs a great deal for a little farm to get official organic approval. This will change when more people buy organic and every produce supplier eventually will want to switch over because of the demand.

As closing time approaches, a waitress places a banana split with Melanie's homemade fudge syrup in front of a customer, who looks at it like a cat first spotting a mouse. The banana split was completely devoured by the time the waitress came back with a fresh glass of water. The restaurant's most popular items, says Burtt, include oven-baked macaroni and cheese, Philly cheesesteaks stuffed into home-made rolls, turkey clubs, lemon and herb sautéed chicken, sausage pizzas, grilled polenta, barbecued drumsticks, caramel apple crumble cheesecake, cookies and cream cheesecake, white chocolate and milk chocolate cheesecakes, pink and lime green swirled cupcakes, gooey cinnamon buns, banana splits with extra homemade fudge syrup, and "anything with whipped cream on it and all of it is 100 percent vegan, of course." The twenty-four-year-old woman says her plant-based foods have an added benefit: "Well, pound for pound, I'd have to say that tofu, or any other vegetable or grain meat alternative, is far cheaper than any meat. Try getting a pound of steak for a dollar and change."

Burtt, who became a vegetarian when she was nine years old because she didn't "see a difference between my dog and any other animal," was at first pessimistic about the prospects of a vegan restaurant in Providence but was pleasantly surprised once the business was up and running.

> Before I opened, I was concerned that there were less than a handful of vegans or vegetarians in Rhode Island. I thought I was going to have absolutely no business. Basically no one I dealt with in the Fire Department, and maybe one person in the Health Department, knew what the word vegan meant. I hope I am changing that and am presenting a healthy paradigm. I was surprised at how many people were vegan or veggie or whatever in RI. There are a lot of people that come into the restaurant that I previously never knew were vegan—most likely because I don't run around with a scarlet V on my chest screaming "I'm vegan!" from the top of my lungs.

Other restaurants, similar to Melanie's Vegan Eden, are dotted across the United States. Some of them are located in areas not normally associated with vegetarianism. Take the Sweet Melissa Vegetarian Café, which was opened by Melissa Murphy in 1999 in Laramie, Wyoming.

> Laramie is surprisingly open to the idea of vegetarianism for a small town in Wyoming. Being a college town helps, not only because of the students, but also the kind of people attracted to the university atmosphere. We are the only strictly vegetarian restaurant in the area, but

there are several other veg-friendly establishments. We are about 50/50 vegan and ovo and/or lacto. No fish; no chicken. I'd guess at least 75 percent of our customers are not vegetarian. They seem pleasantly surprised by what we offer. I've seen a little bit of hostility or closed-mindedness, but not much. The vegetarians seem thrilled to find a place where they can order anything off the menu and don't even have to ask if there's chicken broth in the soup. Our most popular menu items are portobello fajitas, falafel pita, lentil loaf with mashed potatoes and gravy, and our soup of the day. However, the favorites change from day to day and season to season.

Other restaurants that serve no meat are owned by members of a particular religion or organization. There are several Country Life Vegetarian Restaurants located in the United States and abroad, each owned by a member of the Seventh-Day Adventist Church. They feature buffet-style dining with dishes ranging from lasagna and seitan stew to pot pie and macaroni and cheese, and desserts like chocolate pie and a variety of vegan whipped crème toppings. The Country Life restaurant in Boston, which closed in 2004, was a favorite meeting place for lectures held by the Boston Vegetarian Society.

The Hare Krishnas also have members with restaurants—each one bears the name Govinda's. The first one opened in Haight-Ashbury, but now there are over a dozen, including one in Tucson, Arizona. The restaurant features a salad bar with twenty items, make-your-own dressings, several varieties of soup including vegetable and bean, seitan shish kebab, and Indian cuisine.

Similarly, Hoai Nguyen, thirty-one, owner of Grasshopper, a vegan restaurant in Allston, Massachusetts, serves food that fits the ancient Buddhist spirit of nonviolence. Nguyen, whose parents cooked for a Buddhist temple in Vietnam, lists sweet and sour veggie "chicken," curried coconut noodles, and black veggie "beef" as some of his popular dishes.

Perhaps the largest vegan restaurant chain in the world belongs to the African Hebrews of Israel, which considers itself a nation and not a religion. There are several Soul Vegetarian Restaurants, as they are called, located throughout America, including Washington, DC, Chicago, and Charleston, South Carolina. Ahuv Ben Rahm, manager of the Soul Vegetarian in Charleston, says his restaurant offers vegan and raw vegan delights, with macaroni and cheese, barbecued tofu, sweet potato pie, and carrot cake as favorites among customers. "We are the largest chain of vegan restaurants in the world. We wanted to provide healthy food that also tasted good for the people in the communities that knew nothing of vegetarianism. Everything we serve is one hundred percent vegan," says Rahm.

Some vegetarians who like to prepare food have opted to open catering businesses. While working as a computer consultant, Katrina Bisanti came to the realization that vegetarian food was the one thing she was passionate about. She enrolled at the Natural Gourmet Cookery School in New York, took night classes while working in Rhode Island, and graduated in 2003. She quit her computer job and began offering her services as a personal chef, and was delighted to discover that there was a demand for meals without meat.

> I started out doing personal chef services. I originally thought that I would have a hard time finding clients who would want vegetarian cooking. I was definitely wrong. It took me a year to develop my clientele, but I have had up to nine weekly clients during that time. The majority of them choose a vegetarian personal chef to incorporate more health-supportive dishes into their week. I'd say the majority of my clients are non-vegetarians who have had health issues, and are seeking a healthier option.

Bisanti says vegetarians are relieved to find a caterer like her. "Usually, they've already spoken with 'traditional' caterers, who don't have knowledge of vegan/vegetarian cooking. I recently received an e-mail from a woman who was interested in having a vegan wedding. She summed it up well; when she spoke with a traditional caterer about having a vegan wedding, the caterer recommended the cheese ravioli."

HOSPITALITY

So much of vegetarian culture revolves around food. Whether people eliminate animal products from their diet for health, spiritual, or other reasons, they will patronize institutions that offer food that satisfies them. An ever-increasing number of hotels, cafeterias, airlines, and others in the hospitality industry are making efforts to accommodate them, but change comes slowly.

Some vegetarians are filling the vacuum with bed-and-breakfast inns that serve food free from animal products. Ron and Kathy Heatley opened up the Sweet Onion Inn in Vermont over a decade ago, and it has since become a magnet for vacationing vegetarians. Here's their story, as told by Kathy:

> We have been doing this for eleven years now and before this Ron was a health food store owner for ten years. He has a lot of knowledge that he brings to this lifestyle and this work. . . . I met him in search of my health

by shopping in his store. I found that he was helping me to get well so I married him. Today our marriage is stronger than ever and that is a lot to say of two people who operate a labor-intensive business like a vegan organic inn. . . . I call us a bed (dinner) and breakfast. Ron spends at least three hours creating his scrumptious meals that continually get rave reviews from the guests even if they are not vegan. It seems that they are finding us. This has been a banner year for us. Last year *Vegetarian Times* did a piece on us and that helped a lot. We have been written up in many glossy magazines including a publication in the UK . . . across the pond.

It's my passion but I love the inn and the wonderful folks who come and share a bit of their lives with us. Mealtime is my favorite because the good vibes coming from the lively chatter of new friends of like mind meeting is heavenly. Dinner is a big production and lasts for a couple of hours and sometimes longer depending on the guests. Sometimes they are still sitting at the dinner table talking after we have gone to bed.

Erica Jurgensen, a twenty-four-year-old Boston vegan who first learned of the inn at a Boston Vegetarian Food Festival, recounts her visit to the inn in 2005:

When we got there we were extremely excited because there was a blackboard with the words "Welcome Amy, Erica and Heather." The B&B was cozy and right in between the mountains. The two rooms we rented were more than enough for us. Each night we were there, Ron, the co-owner and chef, cooked our dinners and our breakfasts, all vegan style! He was there for our whole stay and was funny and full of many interesting stories, making us laugh and feeding us tasty and delicious meals. A wonderful surprise for me was the lack of television, computer, and radio. It was wonderful. My friends and I are not people who watch a lot of television, but no music or computer was a change for us. There was a stash of games at the bottom of the stairwell, which we got ourselves into; the first night we played Men Are from Mars, Women Are from Venus. Well the cherry on top was that the soaps were vegan, and the products for cleaning were all natural cruelty-free. We ate delicious food like potpie, sausages, biscuits, blueberry pancakes, and chocolate cake. The trip was too short, and I do plan on returning soon but for a much longer stay.

On the other side of New England, on Cape Cod, an area featuring charming villages, rolling sand dunes, and miles of beaches, Anne and Dave Dennis decided to open Shady Hollow Inn in the town of Dennis (no known relation to the town's founders) in 2001. The bed-and-breakfast has since become a popular destination for vegetarians.

Bed-and-breakfast inns like Shady Hollow serve up more than just food to people who eat no meat. Traveling vegetarians commonly share horror stories, and Anne Dennis has one of her own.

My example of a bad travel experience happened in Savannah at a B&B in the historic district. The breakfast I was brought had sausage on the plate (I hadn't told the staff I was vegetarian so that was no one's mistake)—but when I asked for a breakfast without the sausage because I was vegetarian they just removed the meat and brought me back the same plate with all of the juice and grease on it. Well, yuck! I got myself out to a coffee place where at least a bagel was safe. We hear over and over again how relieved people are because they don't have to worry about the food here. And returning guests usually tell me what particular dish or muffin they are looking forward to having again!

Anne and Dave say they became vegetarians for a variety of reasons: health concerns, environmental considerations, and philosophical attitudes toward other creatures.

Quite frankly, from a completely pragmatic point of view it's hard to believe that every thinking person wouldn't choose this lifestyle. We started a new life together at age fifty—a B&B seemed like a good way to live on Cape Cod and have an income-producing property without having a retail operation. (David was in the natural foods industry in Canada for many years before selling his company.) As vegetarian travelers ourselves, we know how difficult it is to find good food in a situation like this, especially if you are vegan. So, the veggie B&B is our niche and it has worked out beautifully.

The response has been overwhelmingly positive from all of our guests—we pay great attention to detail in every aspect of our accommodation and people do appreciate it, as evidenced by the frequency of repeat guests that we have and their compliments in our guest book. Who could not like fresh fruit, organic coffee and orange juice, freshly baked muffins and bread and a main dish tailored to your dietary requirements?

First, our tofu scramble is probably the most popular breakfast entree, although our muffins and sweet breads (all vegan) get rave reviews. We have definitely had guests who while not veg or vegan expressed great interest in trying our recipes at home and expanding their diet to include dishes made without eggs and dairy. There is always lots of recipe sharing going on here.

Dozens of other inns that cater to people who don't eat meat have opened in the past several years. At an inn tucked in the foothills of the

Blue Ridge Mountains in Virginia, visitors get to pet a pig rather than eat one. The White Pig Bed and Breakfast at Briar Creek Farm was established in a renovated Victorian farmhouse in late 2001 by Dina Brigish, who stopped eating meat in her early teens and later co-founded the group Syracuse University for Animal Rights while a student. Brigish worked in the fashion industry in New York for several years, attended the Natural Gourmet Cookery School in Manhattan, and served as an intern at Millennium Restaurant in San Francisco. She decided to cut out all animal products after her mother gave her Norman, a pot-bellied pig who has become the namesake of the inn.

Along with Norman, a dozen other pigs live on the property. The inn "looks to introduce non-vegans to delicious vegan cuisine and maybe shed a new light on the wonderful, sensitive and intelligent creature we call the pig," says Brigish, who has heard through secondhand information that at least one guest has quit eating meat and a vegetarian decided to become a vegan after their stay. "About 60 percent of the guests are not vegetarians, but their spouse or significant other is vegetarian or vegan."

Like Shady Hollow and Sweet Onion, the White Pig Bed and Breakfast offers a variety of vegan meals. Some of the favorites include chocolate pie and "cheesecake" and, for entrées, marinated baked tofu in lieu of meat substitutes. "But my guests claim that my blueberry pancakes are the best they have ever had," notes Brigish.

Over the centuries, vegetarians have gone beyond restaurants and opened health resorts. One of the most popular, Hippocrates Institute in West Palm Beach, Florida, offers a Life Change program that teaches people about diet and how to live a healthy life, and other holistic wellness and healing regimes like colon hydrotherapy and acupuncture. The institute traces its roots to the mid-1950s, when raw food and wheatgrass advocate Anne Wigmore first opened it in Boston. Once people leave Hippocrates, the vast majority remain on a vegan or vegetarian diet or "closely adhere" to one, says director Brian Clement, a vegan. On the average, about 80 percent of guests at the resort are return visitors, he says.

DIFFERING VEGAN DIETARY REGIMES

Not all vegans are alike when it comes to what they put on their plates. A small minority of them choose to eat only fruit (fruitarian), which, says Nellie Shriver, includes "whatever is given by the plant, tree, bush, or vine." Fruit has the highest per-acre yield of any food—450,000 pounds of fruit can be grown on an acre, says Shriver. "No food on this planet is nonviolent. Fruit is the only food not derived by

David Wolfe. Courtesy David Wolfe.

killing or stealing. Of all the categories of food, fruit is the broadest, including tens of thousands of varieties of seeds, nuts, berries, tree fruits. Cucumbers, squash, and tomatoes, for instance, are fruits. Fruit is the only food which can reforest the world."

A much larger percentage of vegans, although still a minority, opt to ignore the stove and eat a mainly raw food diet. Advocates of raw food diets say that cooking food above 115–118 degrees destroys or degrades the digestive enzymes in many foods, though many mainstream nutritionists state that the body already has such enzymes. Moreover, raw food aficionados claim that nothing can be healthier than eating fruits, nuts, berries, and other foods the way nature has prepared them.

David Wolfe, arguably the most popular promoter of raw foods in the Western world, states:

Living, raw plants create the possibility of all animal life on Earth. Living chlorophyll is the basis of the food chain. Out of all possible diet strategies, a diet that consists of a large amount of fresh, living plant matter (especially vegetables) makes the most sense to me. Where else could we derive the power and joy of living but from eating living foods? Raw organic plant foods are completely intact without having been corrupted by heat, fire, and chemicals or processing of any type. Living plant cells are hydrating juice bags of nutrients containing the building blocks of healthy skin, organs, tissues and, most importantly, of a sound Earth-friendly consciousness. Heat creates chemical changes. No creature on Earth naturally boils, broils, roasts, chemicalizes their food. The most popular diet on Earth, by far, is raw food. Due to millennia of living in cities and villages where fire processing was the only food preservative, the human body has been forced to adapt. But to continue to eat all this fire-processed food now when we can have the best raw organic food ever (if we choose) seems to be absurd.

Wolfe, who has eaten an all-raw foods diet since 1995, recommends that most people should eat 80 percent raw organic food "because that is easy to do for most people and is, in fact, good enough." The king of raw has made it his mission to "make raw-food nutrition an option for anyone on the planet." He has two Web sites—www.rawfood.com and www.davidwolfe.com—and several books (*Naked Chocolate*, *Eating for Beauty*, *The Sunfood Diet Success System*), and has made numerous television and radio appearances, and public lectures.

A May 2, 2005, appearance on Coast-to-Coast AM radio exposed Wolfe to about 15 million listeners, resulting in a flood of hits to his Web sites and widespread recognition.

> Phones rang off the hook for a month. I was even recognized on the streets of New York by numerous individuals a few days after the show. Now...this is a *radio* show...not television. That means that people went to the Web sites, saw pictures of what I looked like, and then were able to recognize me on the street! As if in answer to a prayer, one guy recognized me as I was getting out of a cab just when I really needed someone's help unloading an entire trunkfull of my books, goji berries, and cacao beans out of the cab. He helped me unload the cab, thanked me for the information on the radio, and we went different directions. I love New Yorkers.

The raw food trend, promoted by celebrities such as actor Woody Harrelson and model Carol Alt, has spawned a number of restaurants and cafés. According to Wolfe, the number of restaurants devoted to raw foods that he knows of jumped from two in 1995 to fifty in 2005. "This is not a trend but a wave that has been building for a decade. People are attracted to raw food because they like to feel good, awake and aware. I believe that the explosion of raw food in Hollywood has been in large part due to a concerted plan that we set into motion many years ago. We chose specifically to go after Hollywood, because once Hollywood is sold on something, then the world will soon be hearing about it."

Raw food enthusiasts look upon Juliano's Raw, a restaurant in Santa Monica, California, with the same reverence vegetarians have for Millennium. The restaurant, owned by Juliano, a tireless raw foods promoter who uses only his first name, draws celebrities such Alt, Harrelson, actress Alicia Silverstone, singer Cher, and designer Donna

Karan. Juliano, the author of *Raw: The UnCookbook*, told the *Denver Post* that he "flies around the world on his private jet to cook."

In Las Vegas, Rod Obradovic and Lu Vuckovich offer customers an all-raw menu at their two Go Raw Café restaurants. Entrées include Gimme the Beet, a veggie burger made with beets, carrots, sunflower seeds, and parsley served on living bread with tomato, lettuce sprouts, and avocado; Neat Loaf made with mushrooms and nuts, vegetables and tomato sauce, and served with "fries"; and traditional pizza with living crust topped with "cheese" and a choice of basil pesto or marinara sauce. "Nothing is cooked and no animal products are used, even though there are words such as 'cheese,' 'fries,' and 'salmon' on the menu. Those are made with nuts, vegetables, and herbs and spices," Obradovic, originally from Yugoslavia, told the press.

Whether it's raw, vegan, or vegetarian, those who want plant-based foods without meat are much more fortunate than their counterparts of the past. Don Potts, a real estate broker from Jackson, Mississippi, says it is easy to be a vegetarian today. Even fine restaurants feature a few such entrées. "In the past, salad and baked potato were all a vegetarian could find to eat at most restaurants," says Potts, whose wife and children are also vegetarians.

Potts told a reporter from a local paper that aspiring vegetarians should stay away from tofu until they're ready. "I know people that have tried to start with tofu, and they didn't know what to do with it. They didn't like it." Instead, he suggests "starting with the basics like switching from regular milk to soy milk or trying a veggie burger instead of beef."

VEGETARIAN ENTREPENEURS

In decades past, vegetarians relied on a handful of companies marketing products free from animal ingredients. Twenty years ago, it was easier to find a gold nugget on a sandy beach than to find a vegan marshmallow. There was no Internet to search for products that had no animal ingredients, nor were there many catalogs catering to vegetarians.

As the vegetarian culture becomes more accepted and entrenched in the United States, businesses are scrambling to meet the demand for products free from animal ingredients. Even nonleather shoes are readily available. Years ago, vegetarians seeking shoes not made from animal skins had to shop in discount outlets that offered inexpensive plastic footwear, which was often uncomfortable and unstylish.

Erica and Sara Kubersky are two vegans who took action to solve this dilemma in 2001 by founding MooShoes, a New York City retailer.

"We founded MooShoes because as non–leather wearers ourselves we found it difficult to find shoes. It seemed like our only options were places like Payless or ordering from overseas Web sites," said Erica. MooShoes, which now has an online catalog, also offers handbags, wallets, belts, jackets, jewelry, accessories, and many other items of interest to those seeking apparel not made from animal products. According to Kubersky, these goods "are equal to their leather counterparts in durability, quality, and breathability."

Footwear aside, vegans face countless hardships when it comes to living their ideals. Animal products are used in thousands of nonfood consumer products, which might contain honey, beeswax, bone-char processed sugar, dairy derivatives, carmine coloring, and silk products. Before making a purchase, vegans have to ask questions such as, "Does this plastic contain animal ingredients?" "Does this paint or stain contain milk protein?" And often, to the vegetarian's dismay, the seller has no clue what the ingredients are.

Vegans are forced to play detective—it's not uncommon to see one in the health food or grocery store meticulously checking out the ingredient labels on products. Very few people realize that animal products are often used to process sugar or wine, or lurk in the liquid of contact lens solutions. Stephen Bartell, founder of Clear Conscience, points out that contact lens solutions often contain animal by-products, such as enzymatic cleaners for removing protein deposits. Bartell, a vegetarian, founded Clear Conscience in 1998 after realizing that there were no animal product–free solutions on the market. Now over 1,000 health food stores, optometrists, and Web sites sell his product nationwide.

So many products are either made with animal products or are filtered or purified with animal products. Much to the surprise of not a few vegans, wine falls into this category. To purify and stabilize their product, winemakers add fining agents to barrels of wine, which are removed before bottling. Sometimes these agents include Aquacol (a liquid gelatin made from fish skins) or Isinglass powder (from selected fish bladders), as well as egg whites and milk products, according to Frey Wines, a California producer that makes organic and vegan wine. Similarly, Worcestershire sauce usually contains anchovies. But Edward and Sons, formed in 1978 by vegetarians, manufactures a vegan version, along with several other popular animal product–free foods.

After decades of widely publicized protests over animal testing, most vegans know that cosmetics pose a double-sided problem—not only might the products contain animal ingredients, but they might be tested on animals. Some cosmetic companies have caved in to the pressure and stopped the testing, but their products might still contain collagen or some other animal-derived ingredient.

Once again, vegans jumped into the market. Brian Duprey, along with his brother Jim, founded Duprey Cosmetics in 2004 after a quarter of a century of work in the fashion industry as makeup artists.

> The vegan community is my community. Because our products were given to our friends to try first, we can literally say that our products were tested on vegans! Vegans have high expectations. They are tired of the lack of good performing product and really want something good. They are picky and want to know what every ingredient does. They are the best test field. Unfortunately many vegans are not used to paying a lot for many things, like clothes and cosmetics. Our prices surprised some, but many were so ready for the quality and glamour that they didn't bat an eye.

In 2005, the Dupreys hired actress Traci Lords, a former porn star who left the industry and successfully became a mainstream Hollywood actress. Her saga fit in well with the company's modus operandi: "We are aware the vegetarians are not our only market. In fact it's the animal-tested product users' hands that I really hope our products falls into. She has an amazing inspirational 'you can change your life' story that I really wanted to incorporate with our own philosophy," says Duprey.

Vegans have long sought cosmetics and other products marketed by Ecco-Bella, a New Jersey skin care and cosmetics company founded by Sally Malanga, who started the company in her townhouse in North Caldwell, New Jersey. "My one-car garage was the warehouse. When I needed to make copies, I had to move my two sleeping Siamese cats off the copier," recalls Malanga, who notes that business has doubled in the past two years. One of the latest products introduced by the company includes the Women's Wonder Bar, a chocolate bar made in Switzerland that features rose essential oil, chaste tree berry, and cranberry seed oil.

Malanga finds no logic in using ingredients typically found in cosmetics, such as talc, mercury, synthetic colors, fragrance, formaldehyde-releasing preservatives, and a wide range of ingredients derived from petroleum. "Earth is a paradise . . . there are so many plant-based materials to use. It's up to us to protect paradise and reap the benefits."

In 2004, the company surveyed customers and found out that just about 5 percent of them eat no meat, fish, or fowl—an amount slightly higher than the number of such people in the general population. "Some are aware of the cruelty involved in animal testing but aren't making the leap to vegetarianism," said Malanga, who also volunteers for Friends of Animals.

With the advent of the Internet, people who want products free from animal products and testing can visit several Web sites for one-stop

vegan shopping. Some of the favorites include AlternativeOutfitters
.com, which specializes in footwear, cosmetics, hair care, and accessories, and won People for the Ethical Treatment of Animals' 2004
Proggy award for best cruelty-free online vendor. Vegetariansite.com,
founded by David Sudarsky, sells clothing, hemp products, videos,
juicers, footwear, and grocery items. Sudarsky donates 10 percent of
sales to nonprofit organizations such as the Vegetarian Resource
Group. The site also features stories and essays on a range of topics of
interest to people who don't eat meat, such as "Animal Farming and
the Environment," and Sudarsky also lists current news stories.

Some of these Web sites grew from catalogs. Veganessentials.com, a
Web site that sells hundreds of products, traces its roots back to 1997,
when Courtney Ernster and her sister Sue purchased inventory and a
year later formed Veg Essentials, a catalog that was sent out to 3,500
people. The response was robust, and a second catalog was offered a
year and a half later. Then in the summer of 2000, the Web site became
a reality, and it continues to expand.

Pangea Vegan Store (www.veganstore.com), an online merchandise
catalog founded in 1995 and arguably the most popular of all vegan
product sites, was voted favorite company by readers of *VegNews*
magazine for three consecutive years. Founder Shari Kalina states:

> We were the first company to use the one-stop approach for a wide
> range of vegan products. When we started in 1995, there was no single
> place a person could go to get all the kinds of products we offer—
> nonleather shoes and belts, vegan food, cruelty-free body care, etc. We
> received a huge response from veg shoppers who were excited to have a
> centralized source for products to help them maintain their ethical
> lifestyles without having to read labels or check ingredients. In addition
> to carrying products manufactured by a wide variety of other companies,
> we also manufacture products ourselves when a suitable alternative to an
> animal-based good doesn't already exist (for example, our VeganSweets
> line of confections, which includes vegan marshmallows, dairy-free
> white chocolate, etc., and our No Bull line of leather alternatives). We
> make it easier for veg customers to shop without having to worry about
> whether the products they're buying have hidden or obscure animal
> ingredients. We are also diligent about avoiding products made in
> countries where no labor laws exist to protect the workers (such as
> China). This helps show others that vegans are concerned with human
> rights as well, countering the myth that vegans are only interested in
> helping (nonhuman) animals.

Manufacturers of shoes, accessories, and other products that traditionally contain animal products are beginning to take note of the

increasing market for vegan products. Joy Zakarian, who opened her
store All Vegan in 2003, says,

> When we were planning the store, it was exciting to find out that many
> "regular" shoe companies already make vegan shoes that don't necessarily
> make it into the "regular" stores. At first these companies didn't know what
> we were talking about when we came up at a shoe show and asked to see
> their nonleather styles. Now just three years later it's fun that these
> companies start showing us their vegan shoes right away when they see us.
> I think they might be starting to acknowledge vegans as customers, so
> maybe that will translate into more vegan shoes in the future. (Although
> the pessimist in me must acknowledge that we are still a very tiny blip on
> their radar screen—one large company whose shoes we've been carrying
> recently decided to add a small piece of pig's skin to the inside heel of all of
> their shoes—I got the impression that disgruntled vegans weren't high on
> their list of considerations when making that decision!)

Similarly, jewelry manufacturers don't seem to be concerned with
putting out products specifically for vegans. Jeanine Taylor decided to
do something about it. In 1999, she founded what she believes was the
first company to make and market animal product–free jewelry,
Snooty Jewelry. "I had been feeling that something was missing from
my business, but as soon as it occurred to me to combine my values
with what I loved doing, everything fell into place," said Taylor.

The vegan jewelry entrepreneur said that the vegan and vegetarian
community has been "wonderfully supportive." Usually, mainstream
companies who happen to make products without animal products

Jeanine Taylor, founder of Snooty Jewelry.
Courtesy Jeanine Taylor.

have drawn vegetarian and vegan consumers. But Snooty draws customers that are not vegetarian. "Thankfully, Snooty Jewelry has a strong
following of 'mainstream' customers as well. Every so often I'll get an e-
mail from a Web site customer telling me that although they don't share
my values, they're buying Snooty Jewelry because I have values."

Other subcultures in the United States have established business
networks so members can trade with other members. When members
support other members financially, everyone benefits. Why not hire a
carpenter or a financial planner that shares your lifestyle or philosophy? The logic of networking wasn't lost on Jeanine Taylor, who
founded what she calls her labor of love, www.VeggieNetwork.com:

> In the fall of 1999 I was about to spend a good chunk of change to have
> some work done on my house, and preferred the money benefit someone
> who shared my (vegan) values. After fantasizing about how wonderful it
> would be to have "Vegan Yellow Pages," I decided to add a page to my
> Web site listing veg*n business owners and service providers. What
> started as nothing more than a list of veg friends, who owned businesses,
> grew quickly as word spread. Who knows when my fantasy of being able
> to find anything from a vegan auto mechanic to a vegan dentist in my
> area will come true, but in the meantime, I'd like the Veggie Network to
> serve as a representation of the wide range of professionals who embrace
> a compassionate, plant-based lifestyle.

A sizable percentage of people embracing a compassionate, plant-
based lifestyle like to extend it to their pets. Though most veterinarians
say that pets need meat to survive, vegetarians who feed their pets
meat-free food say that conventional pet food contains unhealthy by-
products from slaughterhouses. James Pedan, who introduced a line of
vegan pet food (Vegecat and Vegedog) in the 1980s, reveals some of the
ingredients found in pet food on the Web site Harbingers of a New Age:
"Carcasses of pets (some with flea collars and containing sodium
pentobarbital used for euthanasia); diseased livestock, some still
wearing plastic ID tags, and filled with unwanted insecticides and
pharmaceuticals; and rotting supermarket rejects including plastic
and styrofoam packaging."

Entrepreneurs, chefs, and other food service professionals have
greatly enhanced the vegetarian subculture. Next, we'll dig deeper and
discover how else vegetarians have staked out their own culture. One
example: cartoonist and vegetarian Scott Adams has created the Dil-
berito, a burrito sans meat available at grocery stores. Adams eschews
meat for health and to think more clearly.

3

CULTURE

Those who have never heard Mr. Graham's instructions from his own lips, can form no just idea of their importance; and from this cause, as well as from the unbounded misrepresentations that have been made of his doctrines, an almost total and universal error of opinion and prejudice of feelings have gathered around his course and exceedingly retarded the progress of his great enterprise of philanthropy.

David Cambell, editor of the *Graham Journal of Health and Longevity* (Boston, April 1837), a magazine dedicated to the work of Sylvester Graham, father of vegetarianism in the United States

No one has posted a "Welcome to the Vegetarian World" sign on Main Street. At a glance, vegetarianism appears not to be a subculture, as meat-free cuisine is a trend, cookbooks clog the bookstore shelves, and fast-food restaurants advertise meat-free burgers. But that belies the reality that not eating meat still sets people apart from the dominant culture, and as a result vegetarians have created culture: customs, products, media, arts, events, businesses, and social and activist groups.

VEGETARIANS AND THE MEDIA

Dominated by ads for meat and other items derived from animals, and the federal government's dietary guidelines promoting meat-eating and milk-drinking, the corporate "mainstream" media is the least likely source for accurate representation of the vegetarian community.

Lingering stereotypes and dubious "facts" plague the depiction of the lives and habits of vegetarians and vegans. One observer, Carol Bullock, a consultant in the medical field in Everett, Washington, who "went lacto-ovo at the age of eleven (after seeing a film on the inner workings of a slaughterhouse) and vegan at thirty-five," shares her insight into television shows:

> I don't know that I've ever seen a positive representation of a vegan in the media. The show *ER* had characters making derogatory comments about veganism regularly. Example: Jerry's sister made vegan muffins that he brought into the ER. Everyone turned their nose up at them. Susan is going on a blind date to a vegan restaurant with a vegan man who shows up at the hospital and asks how much longer she'll be (albeit in a snarky tone). She decides she doesn't want to go out with him after all, telling him, "I'd rather go out for a steak anyway." The other show that stands out is *Good Eats*, a cooking show. Oh, and the *Drew Carey Show*—of course— had the series of episodes that had Drew dating a vegan who (unrealistically) ditched her beliefs by eating a hamburger.

Leah Mickens, a college student who lives in Georgia, shares similar criticism: "Vegetarians are portrayed as being hippies and wackjobs. In any of these 'mom-switching' shows, crazy vegetarian moms are compared with 'common-sense' middle America types. They are portrayed as violent militant activists on shows like *Law and Order* or self-righteous and annoying on sitcoms (*Growing Pains* is the one that comes to mind)."

Like members of minority religions and ethnic groups, and third-party politicians, vegetarians create their own media to communicate with the like-minded and reach out to the majority.

New York City talk radio show host Shelton Walden covers a variety of social issues on his program, *Walden's Pond*, including vegetarianism. He quit eating meat for several reasons and says, "I still feel human health comes first." He is not sure if it is necessary for vegetarians to have their own media.

"One of the things that has bothered me is the tendency to make ourselves into a separate entity; therefore we tend to be labeled as a semi-cult and consequently not taken seriously and dismissed. In addition, I would be worried about the tendency towards political stridency and political correctness that has infested every aspect of American society. I wonder if the veggie media entity would shut out other political viewpoints and become a left or right knee-jerk entity," explains Walden.

Some shows devote their entire content to vegetarian topics. Several years ago, Bob Linden started his own show, GoVegan radio, on KRLA in Los Angeles for an hour a week. *Los Angeles Times* Pulitizer prize-winning media critic Howard Rosenberg in 2001 described Linden's show: "Go Vegan! with Bob Linden, a kickbutt new AM radio show on KRLA 870 in Los Angeles, a city where vegans and other animal activists are given access to the airwaves about as often as it snows in Disneyland. Linden's pro-health, pro-animal hour of interviews, humor, and preachy factoids ('Over a million will be murdered for food just during this show today') airs at 10 A.M. Sundays on a commercial station whose regular lineup of programs is about as progressive as Vlad the Impaler."

Internet talk show host Meria Heller keeps the Internet crackling with intelligent talk on controversies like mad cow disease and other vegetarian-related topics. Her shows are streamed live, and then archived for replay at any time. Heller calls her program "red pill journalism," in reference to the movie *The Matrix*. On the air these past six years, Heller, a vegetarian and supporter of animal rights, also advocates for American freedoms. "People who want freedom for themselves have to want freedom for all living things. It's all connected... just like in *Animal Farm*—we are living the animals' revenge, paying the price. Freedom and soul—how can a soul that carries murder and terror think clearly?"

A majority of Heller's listeners tune into her top-rated show via the stream link on her site, as they do for another very popular program. Syndicated talk radio host Jeff Rense's Web site, Rense.com, receives more than 10 million hits a month and contains more than 150,000 pages. Rense explains that many consider his Web site "the world's number one site for truth and honest journalism.... I am extremely grateful about this and humbled by the astonishing support and respect it receives. The biggest compliment of all came in September 2005 when the U.S. Department of State named 'Jeff Rense and Rense.com' as the world's number one source of 'misinformation and conspiracy news.' If anything, the Department of State described itself."

Fearless and controversial, Rense offers plenty of evidence to support his astonishing assertions about food. "I've carefully—and with as much deliberation as possible—been presenting the facts about eating meat and dairy products on the air for the past twelve years now," says Rense. "I consider the intentional poisoning and killing of Americans via the dairy, meat and processed 'food' they are fed to be mass murder and genocide. The cancer stats alone tell the story."

Rense believes that vegetarianism and animal rights have a place in the freedom movement. "They are inexorably linked. We seek the truth about our health and welfare and are supposed to have the freedom to talk about it. Without the truth, we really don't have the full freedom to make choices," he explains. "We will never evolve as a species as long as we continue to kill and eat our animal neighbors. It won't happen. In fact, we are devolving now. The spiritual issues of killing and eating over 12 billion living things in the U.S. every *year* are huge. It has to stop."

Like most every vegetarian, Rense encounters staunch meat eaters who challenge him. "It's always sad to encounter people who are addicted—and that's what it is—to fast 'food' and the 'great' American diet. When I say I am a vegan, the first question out of their mouths is almost invariably (and rather incredulously): 'Well...what do you *eat?*'" The renegade radio talk show host credits others, including John Robbins, whose book *Diet for a New America* led Rense to vegetarianism. He calls Robert Cohen's NotMilk.com, Howard Lyman's MadCowboy.com, and Dr. Lorraine Day's DrDay.com three of the most important sites for life and health on the Internet. Well-known Web sites within the vegetarian community, like VegSource.com and Vegetarian Resource Group's vrg.org, feature video, podcasts, or just pages of information and blogs.

Those who prefer television to radio may tune in to *VegTv.com*, which offers cooking and health shows and celebrity interviews. Acclaimed cook and reporter Marie Oser hosts the show. On the Public Broadcasting System (PBS), Christine Pirello, host of *Christine Cooks*, offers a hopeful message that good cooking goes with good health. After developing leukemia when in her twenties, Pirello changed her diet. Now an example of robust health, she cooks foods of the plant kingdom and uses no animal products on her syndicated television program. Pirello is one of a long list of famous vegetarians. Entire Web sites are devoted to lists of these individuals.

Celebrity watchers report that some celebrities are meat free, such as Alicia Silverstone, James Cromwell, Ed Asner, Woody Harrelson, Bob Barker, Moby, Pam Anderson, Bea Arthur, Rue McClanahan, and Joaquin Phoenix, who, like his late activist-actor brother River Phoenix, is a vegan and strong supporter of animal liberation. Some stars are honored at the Genesis Awards for kindness to animals.

Books remain an integral part of the culture, and New York City-based Lantern books publishes numerous vegetarian authors, including Ruth Heidrich, PhD, Kerrie Saunders, PhD, Michael Greger, MD, Judy Carman, Keith Akers, Pamela Rice, Richard Schwartz, PhD, and Carol Adams.

"It's my belief that veganism lies at the heart of the change that must take place if the ecosystems—natural, cultural, ideological—are to survive and thrive. Because I believe that ideas matter, it's my hope that publishing books on these subjects can make people reevaluate their lives and make lasting changes within themselves and do the same to others," says Martin Rowe, Lantern founder and publisher.

Rowe cofounded *Satya*, a monthly magazine based in New York City devoted to in-depth stories and interviews about vegetarianism, animal rights, and other social causes. Past articles and commentaries include "Carbophobia!" by Michael Greger, MD, "The Real Vegan Police," and "Rights and Wrongs: Civil Liberties in Peril." Before Lantern Books was founded about 2000, the Book Publishing Company, the publishing arm of The Farm commune, had been the leading publisher of books on vegetarianism and related topics.

Several other magazines are dedicated to the practice and philosophy of plant-based eating, among them *Vegetarian Voice*, published by North American Vegetarian Society, and *American Vegan*, from the American Vegan Society. Like Satya, other vegetarian magazines are available on newsstands:

- *Veggie Life* specializes in diet and nutrition and color photos that show readers how to cook vegetarian style.
- *Vibrant Life* is a health and vegetarian magazine with a Web site and radio show—all with a Christian slant.
- *Vegetarian Journal*, the magazine of the Vegetarian Resource Group, reports on health news, new products, and controversies, and provides vegan recipes.

Vegetarian Times leads the pack with a circulation of 220,000 and has a long history with the vegetarian movement. Paul Obis founded the magazine in 1974 and merged it with *Vegetarian World* a few years later. *Vegetarian Times* has since transformed from an independent, primarily covering the philosophy and politics of vegetarianism, to a commercial periodical oriented toward cuisine and health. Yet in some ways the magazine has remained the same. Editor Val Weaver says,

> Thirty years ago, when *VT* was launched (it was a garage magazine), it really created a sense of community among vegetarians. There was pretty much nothing knitting them together then—no place to share either convictions or even recipes. *VT* filled that gap with a passion; it became a virtual meeting place for the veg community decades before anyone used "virtual" in this sense. That role has remained a prime one for the magazine, and the current version of *VT* gives an entire spread every issue to letters sharing opinions about a particular topic. (We ask a provocative question every month—and we get a *lot* of mail back.)
>
> The magazine's other main impact has been to help bring vegetarianism into the mainstream—making it accessible and understandable to a much larger share of the population than vegetarians themselves account for. While the number of vegetarians and vegans has stayed rel-

atively constant, the number of people who now understand the whys and hows of vegetarian eating has grown enormously. Vegetarians are often looked at admiringly today, especially on college campuses and in the under-thirty and over-sixty age groups—whereas once, they were just considered weird.

Weaver reports that a little over half of her readers are vegetarians; another 3 percent are vegans. The rest are flexitarians, "people looking for a healthy way to eat meatless a few times a week; people dealing with weight, heart or other health problems; people who are parents of vegetarian kids looking for family-friendly dishes; and people who are experimenting with vegetarian eating," she says.

Unlike *Vegetarian Times*, readers of *VegNews* are overwhelmingly vegetarian or vegan—95 percent to be exact, says publisher Joe Connelly. Female readers outnumber males four to one, and all tend to be professionals with upper-middle-class lifestyles, he adds. The bimonthly magazine, which debuted on the newsstands in March 2004, features celebrity interviews, veg-friendly travel destinations, profiles of people who are making their living in vegetarian-related businesses, and reviews of the latest foods, products, books, and other media of interest to vegetarians. A culture column spotlights vegans involved in the arts, from painters to musicians to dancers to restaurateurs.

Connelly discusses the publication's past and its ongoing appeal:

> *VegNews* began as a community-based publication with the simple mission of unifying the vegetarian movement. The roots of *VegNews* stem from a little publication called *The SAVES Paper* that was published by the Syracuse (N.Y.) Area Vegetarian Education Society from 1996–2000. Through that experience grew the idea for *VegNews*, which started as a clearinghouse, so to speak, of veg information from around the country, much of which originated from what local, community-based veg societies were doing. *VegNews* has since morphed into a lifestyle magazine, of course, but only because that is what the veg community asked for. Based on our rapid growth and the way the magazine has been embraced by vegetarians everywhere, I think it's fair to say that the community appreciates our efforts.

Vegetarian Times and *VegNews* have new company on the newsstands. *Herbivore* attracts a readership with countercultural leanings. Early on, founder Josh Hooten assumed his goal was to make veganism and animal rights appear mainstream. "It seems like the unwritten goal of vegetarian publications, to make us appear like normal people," he says.

But Hooten soon changed direction, and began shifting *Herbivore*'s content to appeal to a countercultural demographic. "You can never be all things to all people, so you shouldn't try. I decided I should do what I'm best at and leave the mainstream up to other publications and groups." Hooten and and his co-publisher, Michelle Schwegmann, now include people and organizations deemed controversial even by animal rights and vegetarian advocates.

One story covered VegPorn.com, a Web site he describes as "woman positive, sex positive, pro-animal rights," which sells products like vegan condoms and "Goddess Vibes." The woman who founded the site has difficulty finding mainstream animal rights groups that will accept donations from her, says Hooten. "She's definitely a challenge to what people think of as 'normal' in both mainstream society *and* the animal rights movement. She gets rejected by both on some levels." Also, *Herbivore* has featured Erik Marcus, an author Hooten says has the "courage to challenge some of its biggest groups and campaigns. He's been criticized from within the movement for this, but we think the dialogue he's starting can do nothing but help the movement become more effective."

Vegetarians might have *Herbivore* and the other magazines, but they decry the mainstream media's coverage of issues of concern to them. Vegetarian Howard Rosenberg, formerly media columnist with the *Los Angeles Times*, says the situation has improved. "A few years ago it was total misunderstanding, but overall, it has improved from outright ridicule to moderate understanding. You can extend that to any social cause out of the mainstream." Heather Chase, model and founder of Models with Conscience, located in Sedona, Arizona, also believes that the media's depiction of vegetarians has improved. "The depictions are moving away from stereotypes (hippies, etc.) to regular people. For example, in the children's program *Braceface*, the lead character is a bright vegetarian girl. Similarly, in the film *My Big Fat Greek Wedding*, the lead male character is a very 'normal' man who is also a vegetarian."

Motion pictures made for children have given vegetarianism the most positive portrayal. Highly popular films such as *Dr. Doolittle*, *Charlotte's Web*, and more recently *Babe*, *Chicken Run*, *A Shark's Tale*, and *Finding Nemo* seem to have tugged at the heartstrings of little ones (and their parents) rooting for animals people eat.

ARTS

Subcultures craft their own films, free from the censor's scissors. Tribe of Heart, an organization founded by James LaVeck and Jenny Stein to promote compassion for people and animals, released *The Witness* and *Peaceable Kingdom*, documentaries about animal rights activists and vegetarians that won awards and acclaim.

In 2005, filmmaker Shaun Monson released *Earthlings*, a feature-length documentary about the treatment of animals in puppy mills, animal shelters, pet stores, and factory farms, which reveals the hidden underbelly of the leather and fur trade, and the sports and entertainment industries. *Earthlings*, narrated by actor and vegan Joaquin Phoenix, won the 2005 Boston International Film Festival Indie Spec Best Content Award. Monson calls his film a "powerful tool in educating others on the importance of a vegan lifestyle. A picture is worth a thousand words, as they say. *Earthlings* is ninety minutes long. Ninety minutes of pictures. And I don't say this from a boastful standpoint, because the issue is quite staggering and life-changing once you become aware of it, but I think *Earthlings* is one of the most persuasive documentary films ever made."

California filmmaker and actor Monson says the film even changed him: "I've been a vegetarian since my mid-twenties, but became a vegan during the process of making *Earthlings*. Seeing is believing, and I sat at an editing table pouring through hours and hours of some of the most horrific atrocities ever done to the animal kingdom and recorded with a camera." And it has changed others as well: "Every screening we've ever held for *Earthlings* has turned some viewers into vegans. People aren't insensitive, just uninformed. Making the switch to vegetarianism or veganism after watching *Earthlings*, or the like, isn't the challenge. It's getting people to take a look at these issues that's the real challenge...just getting them through the door, and persuading them to sit down and watch the film."

Documentaries exposing cruelty to animals may be expected from vegetarians, but a sense of humor is not usually associated with vegetarians, unless the joke is on the vegetarians. Vance Lehmkuhl of Philadelphia turns that around. The author and artist of *The Joy of Soy* vegetarian cartoon collection explains:

> Humor and art share the quality of being able to carry new opinions in around the filters and barriers people have against direct assaults to their worldview, and they also generally make the individual momentarily feel good, loosening them up—so that's one point in favor of humor. Another is that the overall situation is so absurd—a majority with a juvenile, stubborn attachment to an unhealthy, unnecessary food calling "oddballs" those who have enough will and vision to live like we mean it—that speaking honestly about it requires a sense of the ridiculous. But there's a completely different way too, because it's easy for us to get caught up in the literally life-and-death details, and importance of what we're doing and turn into grim moral foot soldiers; humor has the capacity both to lift our spirits and to offer us the chance to laugh at ourselves, to get over ourselves. We make missteps, some of us take things to extremes, we

don't all agree on exact rights and wrongs—all of these are important to be conscious of, as well as a good source of jokes. So ultimately, if it works, vegetarian humor is *fun*, and proves we can have more fun doing the right thing than otherwise: i.e., fresh, healthy, ethical eating can be fun; slaughter never can.

Dan Piraro, the creator of the popular *Bizarro* syndicated newspaper comic, pokes fun at daily life, including meat eating. "With *Bizarro*, I've been able to draw in a large number of daily readers with my humor. Once I have their interest, I can introduce ideas about our food and lifestyle choices that they might not otherwise be exposed to. In this way, I've been able to get lots of people thinking about cruelty and compassion, health and environment issues, and eventually veganism," he explains. His humor doesn't end with the newspaper column inch; Piraro tours the United States with his live, one-man comedy show called the Bizarro Baloney Show. The show includes puppets, songs, videos, animation, cartoons, audience participation, props, and costumes to depict various aspects of his twenty-year career as a syndicated cartoonist. Piraro, a vegan since 2002, received the Humane Society's Genesis Award for Outstanding Cartoonist in 2002 and 2003, and the National Cartoonists Society's awards for Best Newspaper Panel in 1999, 2000, and 2001, and Cartoonist of the Year in 2005.

These days, people who attend veggie events might catch Lehmkuhl drawing cartoons for the crowd, or hear folksinger Dana Lyons revving them up with his song "Cows with Guns." The tune tells of armed cows turning against a burger chain and is the subject of an animated film featured on Internet sites. Another singer-songwriter, Bob Pyle of Maryland, entertains at vegetarian events with songs of social relevance, including songs about food. About forty radio stations worldwide have aired Pyle's CD release *Apples and Oranges*, featuring rhymes like, "Now I've improved my alkaloids and my glucocordacoids and fit into my corduroys without so much wriggling."

Saiom Shriver of Ohio crafts rhymes in her poetry about animal rights and vegetarianism, causes she has promulgated since the 1970s. From the pages of *Vegetarian Times* during its early years to lectures at the World Vegetarian Congress and an appearance on the *Mike Douglas* syndicated television program, to the Web pages of the Internet, Shriver's words urge readers to think about vegetarianism. Here is a sample of her poetry:

How to Serve a Suffocated Fish

First cut off his fin
It's his steering wheel

Then chop off his lungs
He can't breathe without
his gills.
Then gouge out his eyes
for he no longer needs to
see
And scrape off those
inedible diamonds
...his diving suit scales.
Tattletell
of the size of his tail...
and how you left
in the water
a wake of bloody trail.

De-gut him, deluded
into thinking...his
guts are more putrefied
than the rest of his flesh.
Then grill his gills
and fry his eyes
and bake his mad fish muscles
and maybe wish on his bones.

How to serve a fish:
cast your bread upon
the waters in which he
freely swims.

Unturkey Day

What was her name...this turkey...
before she was defeathered?
What was her soul?
Was she shy or bold?
Did she struggle or cry
when she
was killed?
Do ecoli and salmonella
and leukosis grow
now in her rotting flesh...
as she in Spirit
hovers above the table?

Will evidence of the crime
remain ... in wishbones
... or will all the evidence
be consumed

Turkeys give thanks
to vegetarians.

Poetry does not always soothe the soul, just as paintings produced by celebrated artist Sue Coe bring the viewer into the darker realms of life. Scenes of slaughterhouses painted by Coe, including her "Porkopolis" series and "Dead Meat" with coauthor Alexander Cockburn, cause people to see the hidden underbelly of everyday life.

Poet-writer and artist Constantina "Connie" Salamone portrays a vegetarian point of view in her work that includes woodcuts and other art of women who comfort animals other people consider dinner. Salamone writes:

Chicken, Female Friend,
I cannot wonder what,
Men would have thought to do,
If egg of mine, like yours,
Came out big, pristine and shelled.

Musicians, too, contribute to social change, a fact not lost on brother and sister Rob Beloved and Eleni Binge of Beloved Binge. "Musical expression has always been a huge part of my life. When I became vegan, it was a natural transition to include animal rights–inspired themes into my music," writes Rob Beloved.

"Music can be effective to promote positive change on several levels," explains Eleni. "The first and most basic are the songs. For example, with our song 'Why Vegan,' many of those who have heard it tell us it has made them think of their diet and consider reducing or eliminating meat. A student created a video for the song recently and submitted it to several film festivals, which further promotes the message through the less confrontational technique of cut-out animation." The band places animal rights and vegetarian literature on their merchandise table, performs at benefits, and donates a portion of their income to select organizations.

Vegetarians also tune into "hardcore," a type of punk music associated with straight edge, a social movement of abstinence from alcohol, drugs, tobacco, and promiscuous sex. Some straight edgers include a reverence for life or nonviolence ethic that includes vegetarianism, and some also oppose abortion. Kurt Schroeder, founder of Catalyst Records of Indianapolis, Indiana, says that straight edge includes a significant number of vegans.

> I would say that it is currently on the increase, after hitting a major decline in the late nineties. At that time, veganism (along with any kind of idealism) became out of vogue in the hardcore scene, partially as a backlash against a strong political, straight edge, vegan growth in the early and mid-nineties and the popularity of vegan straight edge bands such as Earth Crisis. But like anything else, those who really took the message to heart remained dedicated, and now many of them are starting their own bands and trying to make a mark and spread the word. I also think there is a growing backlash in many areas against the commoditization of hardcore, and a nostalgia for "the old days" of a few years ago for many people—when bands were about something, had important things to say, and newcomers were pretty sure to be exposed to new ideas when going to a show.

Hardcore music is loud, fast, and angry, but beneath lies a humane philosophy, explains vegetarian Schroeder:

> Part of what makes hardcore (as a music style) is that aggressive sound. I would say a lot of the music is about anger, and plays to people who are angry about a number of things in the state of the world today— oppression and injustice for instance. Still there is a definite "edge" to it, the tattooing, the style of dancing, the aggressive music. I won't deny that the aspect is there. I would also say that there is some sense of "hatred" towards many oppressive and unjust institutions of this culture, whether vivisection, institutionalized racism and sexism, 6 billion animals tortured and killed a day, our nation killing 200,000+ civilians in a third world nation, poverty, etc., the list could go on indefinitely. But this should not necessarily be confused with an attitude of hatred towards people. Vegans or people in the hardcore scene aren't just walking time bombs, or akin to Nazi skinheads.

In these days of corporate-controlled music and style usurped from the younger generation and fed back to them as a trend, young adults struggle to set themselves apart and maintain their own identity. Catalyst's Schroeder says that hardcore has roots in the "do it yourself ethic...making something, a place or a culture of our own with our own rules, and without the interference of mainstream culture. This is an ideal of course, and recently 'hardcore,' like most other subcultures eventually are, has been influenced and co-opted by mainstream culture."

ANOTHER MEANING FOR SOUL FOOD

Like hardcore, some hip-hop musicians have vegetarian values. Rhode Island resident Sage Francis is deemed a "rare beast in hip-hop: he's a vegetarian emcee/spoken word artist and he's not timid about saying so." Most well-known hip-hop artists, however, are African American. Some urge their young audiences to consider a new way of eating. A vegetarian-themed documentary by Supa Nova Slom, *Holistic Wellness for the Hip-Hop Generation*, features top artists like Erykah Badu.

Since the seventies, civil rights activist and pioneering comedian Dick Gregory (dickgregory.com) has promoted the meat-free diet in the African American community. Like his comedy, Gregory's vegetarian message reached people of all colors. He was a featured speaker at the World Vegetarian Congress held in Orono, Maine, in 1974, where he talked about world hunger. In the 1980s, Gregory promoted a meat-free diet on television to help obese people. He recently told *Ebony* magazine regarding diet, "I'm the one who changed the whole thing in the Black community." Dexter Scott King, son of slain civil rights leader Dr. Martin Luther King Jr., became a vegan after meeting Gregory. The late Coretta Scott King was a vegan. She believed in justice for people, and for animals used for food, vivisection, the fur trade, and entertainment. Black Vegetarians cofounder Tracye L. McQuirter went veg after listening to a lecture by Dick Gregory.

Does forsaking traditional meat-laden "soul food" present special challenges for African American vegetarians? Shakela Richardson of the Campus Vegetarian Society told the authors,

> Well, generally, no. Everyone has the power to change their lives. However, we do stereotype ourselves. . . . I am African American, and I grew up not eating any fruits or vegetables. There wasn't even a decent grocery store in my neighborhood. I think it is more of a class issue than race. Growing up, it was normal to eat fried chicken and pork chops. Often, and before the encounter with Soul Vegetarian I didn't think there were any black vegetarians. I was shocked that I found not only that tens of thousands were, but that Soul Vegetarian Restaurant was owned by Black people.

Shelton Walden believes that living meat free might be more challenging among African Americans. "Possibly," writes Walden, "because many African Americans trace their roots in the South, which has a long tradition of meat eating. It is very difficult to break away from that tradition."

Accusations of racism were raised in 2005 when PETA produced a vegan campaign comparing the treatment of farmed animals with the treatment of African slaves from America's past. Kris Candour and Tashee Meadows, founders of Justice for All Species, an organization of people of color advocating vegetarianism, animal rights, and human rights, in an interview with Washington, DC-based Black Vegetarians, said they were not offended by the comparison.

BIRDS OF A FEATHER

Those who do not eat pig or chicken might choose to surround themselves exclusively with the like-minded and visit or join a vegetarian community, or a person might grow up in such an environment. For example, Salem Children's Village in New Hampshire is a residential care facility where formerly abused or neglected children eat and grow vegetarian food, and are taught respect for all creation and the need for compassion.

Down South, in 1971, Stephen Gaskin, a Korean War veteran, English professor, philosopher, and LSD guru, led dozens of young hippies from the Haight-Ashbury area of San Francisco to establish a community in Summertown, Tennessee. The press reported, "Members at the time had to take a vow of poverty and turn over all possessions and money to the Farm, be completely vegan (no leather goods either), and make a commitment to be as compassionate as possible toward each other, to the animals, and to the land. Abortion and premarital sex were frowned upon."

No longer strictly classified as a commune, The Farm invites visitors and consists of a group of people who are self-sufficient. The original residents learned to use alternative energy, produce soy foods, and establish businesses like the Book Publishing Company. In 1974, Gaskin and The Farm founded Plenty International, a humanitarian organization; when the waters of Hurricane Katrina flooded New Orleans and surrounding areas in 2005, Plenty assisted survivors.

The Farm's Plenty has plenty of company in the humanitarian cause. Food for Life volunteers were also serving vegetarian food to the victims of Katrina. The Hare Krishna movement, also known as ISKCON, formed Food for Life in 1974 and serves food to people in sixty countries, including places on the front lines of war-torn areas. Within hours after the hurricane took its toll on New Orleans, Food for Life volunteers served nourishing "karma-free" meals cooked in the kitchen of their nearby Mississippi farm.

Another vegetarian community, Gentle World, formed in Florida during the 1970s, helps feed the poor and disadvantaged. Gentle World has since moved to Maui, Hawaii, where they established the Vegan Restaurant. Gentle World gained attention during the 1980s for fancy vegan buffet meals created for Hollywood celebrities, and for *The Cookbook for People Who Love Animals*. Gentle World has published books, a musical album, greeting cards, and other art depicting Eden-like peaceful scenes.

Other communities, while not advocating vegetarianism, nevertheless support it. "At Sirius the rights of vegetarians are deeply honored and respected—strong spiritual convictions are fully supported," writes Jill Kelly, who is part of the Sirius Community, located in Shutesbury, Massachusetts. "The community meals are all vegetarian...vegetavegetables, too, here are grown without harmful chemicals and with great love." Respect and love for life are at the heart of the vegetarian philosophy that is as old as human existence: helping animals, the Earth, and one's own human species.

COMPASSION IS IN FASHION: MODELS AND MOVIE STARS

Back in the 1970s, Marcia Pearson, a model and advocate of vegetarianism from Washington state, lived her ideals on the job at great cost. The founder of Fashion with Compassion, Pearson's vegetarian values prevented her from pursuing lucrative opportunities in modeling promoting particular products like fur.

Today others also work to change the fashion industry by persuading cosmetics companies to stop animal testing and remove animal ingredients from their products. Duprey Cosmetics, established by vegetarians, does not use ingredients derived from or tested on animals. Model Heather Chase believes that change has been occurring at other companies mainly due to activism and increased coverage by the media and the entertainment industry.

"In the film *Legally Blonde 2*, the lead character works to ban the testing of cosmetics on animals. I think that it is fair to assume that seeing films like this increases viewers' interest in, and possibly their demand for, cruelty-free products," explains Chase, who is author of *Beauty without the Beasts*. She explains that it is nearly impossible to avoid absolutely all harm to animals, "but we can do our best to significantly minimize the harm. I get much more joy by cuddling a live animal in my arms than hanging the remains of a dead one on my shoulders. I find that implementing these suggestions brings increased meaning and satisfaction to my life, as they help me to thrive while allowing my fellow beings to thrive as well."

In the world of high fashion, top designer Stella McCartney, like her dad Sir Paul McCartney, does not eat meat and supports animal rights. She uses no animal-derived materials in her work; for example, instead of silk produced from boiling worms, she uses parachute silk.

The culture of vegetarianism continues to expand. At Veganica.com, Derek Goodwin gives artists, poets, photographers, musicians, and others a forum to "present their case more artistically and professionally." Goodwin established a vegan radio program on a low-power FM station with cohost Megan Shackleford, who owns a vegan bakery called Oh Sweet Mamas. Their Web site, www.veganradio.com, features podcasts of their shows. A photographer, Goodwin has earned recognition for his photographs of farm animals. "I think that a lot of the photographs and paintings of farm animals in the world are made to be cute but not to confront people with the fact that these are all individual beings with souls and feelings and unique personalities. I am trying to create photographs that will convey this to the viewer and make them feel uncomfortable about eating these noble beings," explains Goodwin, who resides in Northampton, Massachusetts.

The culture of vegetarianism includes far more than can be featured in one chapter or book; for example, events like the annual North American Vegetarian Society Summerfest and the Compassion and Animals Festival. In 2005 the latter event, headed by Kim Stallwood and Tom Regan, PhD, carried the theme "Power of One" and drew hundreds of vegetarians. The event showcased the latest ideas in helping animals, including where that idea intersects with the vegetarian world.

"In general, the most powerful forces in Western culture, both religious and cultural, have combined to direct food choices towards animals and animal products. The cultural paradigm is: Animals exist for us. Why else would they be here? Every time an individual overcomes these forces and chooses instead to eat with knowledge and compassion, the power of one is demonstrated. It is as if that person has managed to swim up Niagara Falls. Everytime this happens, it is an inspiration," explains Professor Regan.

Culturally, vegetarians are carving their own niches rather than passively accepting whatever the meat-eating majority metes out. "It is important for vegetarians to have our own culture within the dominant meat-eating culture," claims Pamela Rice, author of *101 Reasons Why I'm a Vegetarian*. "Darn. Those meat eaters make the lives of vegetarians downright miserable. Just a little bit, we vegetarians need to shed our 'live and let live' attitude. We need to advocate for ourselves for a change. We need to make some noise and bitch a little. We need to turn the tables on meat eaters, because it is they who are hurting animals, fouling the environment, and causing so many people around us—them, in fact—to limp and gasp and cower in pain and cough and be constipated. And who needs that?"

4

BODY AND SOUL: MOTIVATIONS FOR ABSTAINING FROM ANIMAL FLESH, FROM PHYSICAL TO PROFOUND

I have now no remaining doubts of the vast importance that would result to mankind, from an universal training from childhood, to the exclusive use of vegetable food. I believe such a course of training, along with a due attention to air, exercise, cleanliness, etc., would be the means of improving our race, physically, intellectually and morally, beyond anything of which the world has yet conceived.

William Andrus Alcott, MD, *Vegetable Diet: As Sanctioned by Medical Men by Experience in All Ages* (Boston, 1838)

Modern medical authorities may deem people like Dr. Alcott a quack, yet, a significant percentage of people who do not eat meat agree about the positive transformative power of a pure plant-based diet for the human race, regardless of whether they have ever heard of Alcott. As in 1838, physical, intellectual, and moral concerns motivate Americans to reject animal flesh for food. When asked, "Why are you a vegetarian?" respondents' answers might be brief, such as "ethics" or "health"—or lengthy reports on preventing dietary diseases, eradicating world hunger, respecting pigs and chickens, or eating only foods God intended for human beings.

Psychologist Rachel M. MacNair, PhD, a vegetarian, has conducted research that shows a person initially motivated by one reason to reject meat usually adds others. "Compassion for animals is one of many motivations for becoming vegetarian or vegan. Health is another major one. Also common are environmental, world hunger, spiritual, aesthetic, and even anti-big-business concerns. This multiple reasoning is important. My focus groups, along with an informal e-mail survey of fifty-four vegans, confirm that adding reasons for being vegetarian or vegan is a common practice. Having more reasons bolsters the case for vegetarianism."

HEALTH

Several surveys indicate that a slight majority of people become vegetarians for health reasons. A 1992 *Vegetarian Times* reader survey revealed that nearly half of them switched to a plant-based diet for health reasons, followed by ethical, religious, environmental, and other reasons. Vegetarian sources report on the flood of studies accumulated over the years presenting proof that a plant-based diet reigns supreme over its omnivorous counterpart. Studies showing that a plant-based diet is integral in the prevention or reversal of arthritis, diabetes, heart disease, and cancer are rarely disseminated in the mass media.

"Vegetarian diets are outside our culture, so there's little to support that style of eating. Intellectually, a person can understand that a vegetarian diet may be health-supporting. But in the day-to-day, practical world, sticking to a vegetarian diet can be challenging. That's especially true, I think, if your motivation for going vegetarian is health," writes Suzanne Havala Hobbs, DrPH, RD, clinical assistant professor at the School of Public Health, University of North Carolina at Chapel Hill.

"Health benefits aren't readily apparent every day, so it's easy to lose the motivation to eat that way. People who are ethically motivated to eat a vegetarian diet are, I believe, more likely to be motivated to eat that way consistently," explains Dr. Havala Hobbs. What is the current attitude toward vegetarianism among the medical establishment? Havala Hobbs, author of *Being Vegetarian for Dummies* and nutrition advisor to the Vegetarian Resource Group, perceives an attitude of "intellectual acceptance, generally," among the medical establishment of "the concept that vegetarian diets—and even vegan diets—confer health benefits. The medical establishment is not, generally, educated about veganism, but there is certainly growing curiosity and awareness of the option. I think most nonvegetarian health professionals are still wary of a vegan diet, but they are gradually coming around to appreciating the health benefits that vegetarian diets confer."

Author Michael Klaper, MD, president of the Institute of Nutrition Education and Research, explains, "There is no money to be made by physicians and other health professionals dispensing this kind of advice, and such [a] vegetarian approach is far too threatening economically, culturally, and politically to the status quo to be widely promoted at this time."

Money has been made, by proponents of high-protein, low-carbohydrate meat-based diets who told the nation not to deprive themselves of steak and dairy products, but to eat them and lose unwanted pounds. During the torrent of publicity for those trendy diets, veteran advocates of vegetarian and vegan diets were hardly heard. One former bestselling author who espouses the vegan diet was even told he was "too eighties" and needed to write a high-protein diet book, according to a press account. The tide of research and opinion regarding the benefits of plant-based nutrition that had been building for more than a century was nearly drowned by the rushing river of human beings to the meat case. Nevertheless, John McDougall, MD, stayed the course.

"The fat you eat is the fat you wear. Regardless of how much some people would wish otherwise, high-fat diets promote heart disease, cancer and diabetes," wrote McDougall in a letter to the *San Francisco Chronicle* during the height of the high-protein mania. Dr. McDougall and his wife, Mary McDougall, RN, are authors of several books on the vegan diet, including *The McDougall Plan*. A popular author since the 1980s, McDougall conducted a study that revealed that about 70 percent of people with moderate to severe arthritis will benefit from a low-fat vegan diet. He has also had success in helping patients reverse other health conditions through diet. Like McDougall, Neal Barnard, MD, and his Physicians Committee for Responsible Medicine have conducted studies showing a vegan diet can lead to reversal of disease.

A vast forest of studies show the power of a plant-based diet, but just about every vegetarian has been warned by a concerned friend or relative, even a physician, dietitian, or teacher, to be careful—meaning that a diet without meat, and particularly without meat and cow's milk, might lead to dietary deficiency and illness. However, writes Dr. Barnard, author of *Breaking the Food Seduction*, "Vegetarian diets, which contain no meat (beef, pork, poultry, or fish and shellfish), are naturally low in saturated fat, high in fiber, and full of vitamins, minerals, and cancer-fighting compounds. A multitude of scientific studies have shown that vegetarian diets have remarkable health benefits and can help prevent certain diseases, such as cancer, diabetes, and heart disease. We encourage vegetarian diets as a way of improving general health and preventing diet-related illnesses."

William Harris, MD, director of the Kaiser Permanente Vegetarian Lifestyle Clinic in Hawaii, explains in his book, *The Scientific Basis of Vegetarianism*: "Documented benefits of a pure vegetarian [vegan] lifestyle include permanent reduction in weight, blood pressure, serum cholesterol, and blood sugar, as well as risk reduction for cardiovascular disease and half a dozen common forms of cancer. Allergies, arthritis, and asthma also respond to vegan nutrition, which means no meat, fish, chicken, dairy, eggs, or even honey."

Unlike Klaper, McDougall, and Barnard, other advocates of meat-free eating are rarely speakers at events put on by vegetarian or animal rights organizations, but nevertheless have influence:

- Gary Null, PhD, in his many books and magazine articles, and on his popular syndicated radio program has informed a multitude of Americans about vegetarian diets, and has won awards for exposing corruption within the medical industry.
- Jay Kordich, known as the Juiceman, promotes a raw food vegan diet in his books and television infomercials.
- Lorraine Day, MD, a trauma surgeon, promotes a natural hygiene–type regimen that includes a raw food vegan diet, prayer and positive thinking, abstaining from alcohol and tobacco, and getting plenty of exercise, pure air, and water. Dr. Day, famous for television infomercials, who developed a large breast tumor and was told she would die, regained her health. She rejected chemotherapy, surgery, and radiation, which she says are dangerous and even deadly.
- Husband-and-wife team Ollie C. Fisher, DMD, and Perdita J. Fisher, DMD, of the Fisher Wellness Center in St. Louis, Missouri, also take a holistic approach to health. Through the wellness center that bears their name, the couple encourage their patients to consider a plant-based diet. "People are more receptive to change today than at any time in the past. They are tired of the fad diets that were proven harmful or the cures that never worked." The Fishers have assembled a team of massage therapists, nurses, acupuncturists, colon hydrotherapists, dentists, and prevention educators at the center, and own Eternity Vegetarian Deli and Juice Bar, where they offer free wellness seminars and serve foods such as lasagna, collard greens, and sunflower seed paté.

People who promulgate meatless meals for health reasons have plenty of evidence to prove their case. A few of the main studies referred to by advocates follow.

When trying to persuade the meat-eating masses, mention of a study in a newspaper like the *New York Times* adds credibility. In 1990, the *Times* quoted Cornell University scientist T. Colin Campbell, PhD: "We're basically a vegetarian species"—words that still roll off the presses of vegetarian publications. The *Times* reported on Campbell's findings from the China Study, which it termed the "Grand Prix of epidemiology." Campbell had helped develop dietary guidelines to protect against cancer for the U.S. government. Then, with a team of researchers from China and Oxford University, he studied 6,500 Chinese from sixty-five counties who ate very little or no meat, assessing hundreds of variables on their health, eating habits, and food sources. China served as a perfect setting for the study, with a homogenous population who lived in the same area and ate the same food for most of their lives. The findings indicted a meat- and dairy-centered diet; diseases such as diabetes, osteoporosis, heart disease, and some cancers were rare or nonexistent among the Chinese, who ate little or no meat and milk. Campbell's book is *The China Study*.

Heart disease has surpassed cancer as America's leading killer. In the 1980s, Dean Ornish, MD, assembled forty-eight volunteers suffering from heart disease. At his Preventive Medicine Research Institute, these patients were split into two groups: a control group who received conventional care and an experimental group that was put on a vegetarian diet including no more than 10 percent of its calories from fat, along with a regimen of meditation, yoga, and exercise. Eighteen of the twenty-two patients in the experimental group ended up with unclogged arteries and no chest pain, while the patients in the control group experienced increased blockage and more pain.

Ornish wasn't the only physician demonstrating that a meat-free diet can reverse the effects of heart disease. Cleveland Clinic surgeon Dr. C. B. Esselstyn, who grew up on a cattle farm, conducted a twelve-year study of a diet and drug combination that saved patients from life-threatening heart disease without the use of surgery. Eighteen patients followed the Esselstyn program at the clinic. The patients were put on a vegetarian diet allowing only 10 percent of its calories to come from fat, but with no meditation, yoga, or heavy exercise. In all but one case, after five years, all patients were alive and well, and tests showed reversal of heart disease.

Dr. Michael Klaper, author of *Vegan Nutrition: Pure and Simple*, says, "The human body has absolutely no requirement for animal flesh. Nobody has ever been found facedown twenty yards from the Burger King because they couldn't get their Whopper in time." The doctor's own Vegan Health Study, with 900 participants, showed that a number of chronic diseases and medical conditions, including osteoporosis, cardiovascular disease, type 2 diabetes, and certain cancers, as well as some kidney disorders, immune-inflammatory diseases, toxin exposure, gastrointestinal diseases, and eye disorders can be prevented or even reversed with a low-fat diet free of animal products.

Kerrie Saunders, PhD, in her book *The Vegan Diet*, covers what might be lurking in animal products: hormones, antibiotics, pesticides, and genetically modified organisms used on animals or in their food, or even salmonella.

Some vegetarians are motivated by the belief that humans are not meant to eat meat, because if they were, people would react like grizzly bears and happily rip prey apart and eat it raw. People would be attracted, not repulsed, by slaughterhouses. Nineteenth-century vegetarians promulgated the idea that human beings are not herbivores like the bison, but instead are frugivores like the gorillas, whose great strength and size are developed on a Genesis-type diet. Reuben Dimond Mussey, MD, Dartmouth medical professor and president of the American Medical Association during the Victorian era, championed this point of view, and was one of many who cited the work of Curvier, the renowned naturalist who pronounced humankind naturally frugivorous.

Two centuries later, vegetarians still rely upon experts to prove their point about anatomy. For example, a report called *The Comparative Anatomy of Eating* by Milton R. Mills, MD, associate director of preventive medicine at the Washington-based Physicians Committee for Responsible Medicine, provided evidence for this diet: "While most humans are clearly 'behavioral' omnivores, the question still remains as to whether humans are anatomically suited for a diet that includes animal as well as plant foods." The evidence supports a plant-based diet, claims Mills. "Humankind does not show the mixed structural features one expects and finds in anatomical omnivores such as bears and raccoons. Thus, from comparing the gastrointestinal tract of humans to that of carnivores, herbivores and omnivores we must conclude that humankind's GI tract is designed for a purely plant-food diet," writes Mills. Rex Bowlby, author of *Plant Roots: 101 Reasons Why the Human Diet Is Rooted Exclusively in Plants*, points to concrete science, studies, and experiments indicating that humans are meant to eat plants and not animals. "The argument is a holistic one, encompassing biology, chemistry, evolution, anatomy, psychology, sociology, philosophy, religion, ecology, and ethics. We should look at the argument as if it were a jigsaw puzzle with each piece as supportive evidence, but not conclusive proof. Then when you have enough pieces that fit together—and there are more than enough pieces to satisfy even the most skeptical—the picture of humans as natural vegetarians is clear and in focus."

AESTHETICS

Generally, Americans use euphemisms when speaking of meat, which popular culture refers to as hamburger, roast beef, and filet mignon, not cow flesh, cow remains, or cow carcass. The dominant meat-eating culture does not directly acknowledge that meat is the muscle or other part of a dead animal.

Most people don't want to know the facts on the origins of meat, nor would they want to personally slaughter animals for their dinner. Vegetarians say this serves as further evidence that people are meant to eat fruits and vegetables and not venison and veal. One non–meat eater posted on an Internet board: "I really just think it is gross to eat dead animals. To me, everyone else can eat whatever they want. I don't try to 'convert' anyone. It's a little difficult eating other places because I want to make sure there isn't 'meat juice' in anything."

Americans are deeply conditioned to avoid thinking about subjects that may be painful to ponder. Polite society considers war, world hunger, torture, and the bloody actuality of animals turned into meat as taboo subjects. The unsuspecting vegetarian who casually remarks that he or she does not eat meat or prefers tofu to the turkey entrée may be met with an anxiety-filled monologue beginning with "Don't try to convert me!" or "I love meat!" or even "Cows are so stupid!" Such responses usually originate from the fear of learning the frightening details of slaughter. Among other possibilities, the person might assume the vegetarian is preachy, or the meat eater may fear that, deep down, he or she might prefer being vegetarian but loathes the idea of becoming "different" from other people.

A sensation was created in the late 1990s when light flooded into the darkness of the slaughterhouse. Muckraking author Gail Eisnitz, like a modern-day Upton Sinclair, made headlines on the front page of the *Washington Post* for her whistle-blowing exposé *Slaughterhouse: The Shocking Story of Greed, Neglect, and Inhumane Treatment Inside the US Meat Industry*. Eisnitz, an undercover investigator for the Humane Farming Association, revealed the workings of an abattoir and reported on what most people, meat abstainers or not, might label atrocities, including the skinning of live cows. People shaken awake to the blood-drenched reality of slaughter by viewing film footage shot in slaughterhouses and shown at vegetarian food festivals or animal rights demonstrations may suddenly decide the resulting meat is also repulsive, rationale enough for avoiding steak, turkey, lamb, and pork.

David Wolfe, author of *Eating for Beauty*, adds fish: "Who wants to bite into a smelly fish when you could be drinking a coconut on the beach in Hawaii! What is more fun than eating chocolate with your lover? How about squeezing mango juice on your wife, girlfriend, husband, significant other? Everybody knows somewhere deep inside that the picture of paradise is on a beach sipping a coconut, not swinging an ax at an innocent animal's head."

ATHLETICS

Vegetarians point out that the belief that protein from animal flesh, or at least milk or eggs, aids athletic performance was scientifically disproved long ago, yet it still lingers. However, it has lost much of its strength as athletes prove that a plant-based diet provides all the power they need.

Americans often elevate athletes from football, baseball, and sports to demigod status—a phenomenon not lost on the vegetarian-vegan sub-culture, which lists meat-abstaining athletes, past and present, in its publications and Web sites. Over a century ago, vegetarian publications reported on the adventures of Karl Mann, a champion vegetarian athlete. In 1898, Mann, one of eight vegetarians in a twenty-five-man walking race held in Berlin, Germany, won the seventy-mile journey in four hours and eleven minutes, according to *Food, Home, and Garden* magazine. The top six finishers were all vegetarians, a fact that prompted Cornell University professor Goldwin Smith to state to the press, "the vegetarians have shown a remarkable superiority in endurance over the eaters of meat."

Today, some popular names appearing in vegetarian literature, even from past decades, include tennis stars Martina Navratilova and Peter Burwash, basketball stars Bill Walton and Pete Maravich, football players Joe Namath and Fred Dwyer, baseball pitcher Bill Lee, triathlon champion Dave Scott, football coach Marv Levy, running back Ricky Williams, baseball coach Tony LaRussa, wrestler Killer Kowalski, and runner Carl Lewis.

Athletes who eat foods exclusively from the plant kingdom rather than beef, fish, or fowl say that their diet enhances their endurance and performance. Ruth Heidrich serves as a sterling example. She suffered from breast cancer and had a mastectomy, then switched to a life-saving vegan diet at the urging of John McDougall, MD, in 1982 at the age of forty-seven. Fueled by her recovery and diet, the Hawaii resident has earned enough trophies and medals to fill dozens of shelves: 900 gold medals and trophies for every distance from 100 meter dashes and 5K road races to ultra marathons and triathlons. She has also completed more than sixty marathons all over the world, set three world fitness records in her age group at the Cooper Clinic in Dallas, Texas, and won eight gold medals in the Senior Olympics in Hawaii, Arizona, and Nevada.

"In my own case, my advanced breast cancer was stopped in its tracks by a change to a vegan diet without chemotherapy and radiation. Next, I noticed that my running got faster, that I could run longer, and that on this diet, I had completed the Ironman Triathlon (a 2.4 mile swim, 112-mile bike, and a 26.2 mile marathon) and won gold medals in my age group. Not only that, I found that I could recover so much faster and be ready to race again the next weekend."

Heidrich, who has a PhD in health management and works as a fitness trainer, cofounded the Vegetarian Society of Hawaii and serves on the council of the Vegetarian Union of North America. She cohosts a weekly talk show, *Nutrition and You* on KWAI, Honolulu, Hawaii, and has written several books, including *Race for Life* and *Senior Fitness: The Diet and Exercise Program for Maximum Health and Longevity*, and produced videos. She also was named one of the Top Ten Fittest Women in North America in 1999, and was nominated by People for the Ethical Treatment of Animals in 2003 as one of the Sexiest Vegetarians Alive.

Athletes like Heidrich work hard to smash the protein myth, which still lingers in the athletic community and mainstream society. A century of scientific evidence has debunked the idea that one has to eat meat to get adequate protein. In the early twentieth century, a series of experiments at Yale University conducted by professor Russell H. Chittenden and economist Irving Fisher revealed that the requirement of 118 to 145 grams of protein was inflated. The scientists discovered that vegetarian athletes significantly outperformed their nonvegetarian counterparts, and that a daily intake of 35 to 40 grams was adequate.

"The myth of getting as much protein as possible to build muscle is still very prevalent. They seem to think that muscles are built in the kitchen—by downing protein powders and/or pills—as opposed to in the gym. People are usually not taught that fruits and vegetables have just the right amount of protein, and certainly are not taught that meat, with its excessively high protein content, can cause many diseases," says Heidrich.

Scott Jurek, a thirty-one-year-old champion runner, who dumped meat from his diet eight years ago and then became a vegan after reading Howard Lyman's *Mad Cowboy*, hears the question "Where do you get your protein?" from fellow athletes. But Jurek lets his accomplishments answer this and other skeptics' questions. In 2005, the Seattle resident won his seventh consecutive Western States 100-miler, and, trekking 135 miles from Death Valley in 115-degree heat to Mount Whitney, captured the Badwater Ultra Marathon by shattering the course record and finishing two hours ahead of the nearest competitor.

A Seattle-based physical therapist, Jurek credits his vegan diet with allowing him to recover more quickly from workouts and injuries, and getting him through a demanding training regimen. He believes that a meat- and dairy-free diet can help athletes prevent debilitating diseases and injuries that often occur later in life.

To support vegetarian athletes and to educate people who participate in sports on the benefits of a plant-based diet, Bradley Saul, a
twenty-seven-year-old South Carolina native, formed Organic Athlete,
an organization that forms sports clubs made up of vegans. To date,
Organic Athlete has formed chapters in Atlanta, Arizona, California,
Colorado, Florida, Wisconsin, Canada and the United Kingdom.

"The successes of vegan athletes like Carl Lewis have been known for
a long time, but there has not been a cohesive effort to demonstrate the
power of vegan living by athletes. Organic Athlete was founded to
educate people about the benefits of plant-based nutrition and environmental stewardship," said Saul.

Several athletes are showcased on the website (www.organicathletes
.org), along with the reasons why they chose to eschew animal products. Professional surfer Katie Coryell states that switching to a vegan
diet has improved her performance and has dramatically cut her recovery time from injuries.

Dr. Douglas N. Graham, advisor to Organic Athlete and president of
Healthful Living International, recommends a mostly raw vegan diet
to improve athletic performance. Graham, who has trained professional and Olympic athletes including tennis legend Martina Navratilova, states that athletes generally fail to recognize the benefits of diet.

> Surprisingly, most athletes aren't that interested in utilizing lifestyle
> modification as a method of tweaking their performance. As adults, we
> sometimes forget that the athletes we watch on television are mostly kids
> in their twenties. The up-and-coming athletes of the future are just
> teenagers and younger. These young people have yet to learn the lesson
> of the importance of healthful living. They tend to think that they know it
> all and that they have it, or can buy it all. It is a rare athlete indeed who is
> willing to commit to a raw vegan program. I truly believe this will change
> in the foreseeable future, as the competition gets stiffer and the facts
> about diet and performance become more readily available.

SPIRITUALITY

Judy M. Carman cofounded Worldwide Prayer Circle for Animals
"to create a circle of compassion around the world by asking people
to pray a simple prayer each day for the animals suffering under
the domination of human beings.... The Prayer Circle for Animals is
a nondenominational circle of people devoted to using action and
the power of prayer, meditation, and/or focused thought to liberate
all animals from human oppression and exploitation." Cofounder
Will Tuttle, author of *The World Peace Diet*, was raised in Concord,

Massachusetts, an area renowned for its New England transcendentalist history. He recalls his and his brother's experiences with vegetarianism when they were young adults in the 1970s: "We had been born and raised ... in a traditional New England family with deep roots to the first Pilgrims and Puritans. I learned to swim in Walden Pond, went to Thoreau and Alcott schools, and at the insistence of my father, a writer, pianist, and owner of the local newspaper, memorized some of Emerson's poetry. By the time I got to Colby, I had perhaps unconsciously imbibed the lingering spirit of the Concord transcendentalists, but I had barely heard of Buddhism or vegetarianism." Tuttle's travels eventually led him to a monastery in Korea, where veganism has been practiced for over 800 years, and where the monks will not even kill mosquitoes.

Author Richard Schwartz, PhD, president of the Society of Ethical and Religious Vegetarians, is "working with people of other religions to promote vegetarianism in religious communities. ... I learned that the first Biblical dietary law (Genesis 1:29) was strictly vegetarian, and I became convinced that important Jewish mandates to preserve our health, be kind to animals, protect the environment, conserve resources, share with hungry people, and seek and pursue peace all pointed to vegetarianism as the best diet for Jews (and everyone else) today."

Across the Internet street from Schwartz's Web site—JewishVeg .com—and around the corner from Carman and Tuttle's Web site, people seeking a Christian ministry specifically welcoming vegetarians can connect with the AllCreatures.org community and publishers Frank and Mary Hoffman. The Internet ministry began in 1988 when the foundation that bears their name was formed. At the request of Bostonian Maynard Clark, a long-time vegetarian movement organizer, the Hoffmans hosted a veg-Christian e-mail discussion group. "We found ourselves doing a lot of church-type ministry on the Internet ... and began our 'Internet Church' ... we post a sermon every week and do a lot of corresponding with people in need," write the Hoffmans. On AllCreatures.org, which receives about 3 million hits a week, visitors will also find the Hoffmans' and others' inspirational art and photography of nature and animals, as well as poetry, essays, Bible teachings, and more.

AllCreatures.org hosts Catholic Concern for Animals, an organization that reaches out to church members. Roman Catholic Jan Fredericks explains,

> Catholic tradition and theology has been concerned about abstaining from eating animals. It has been practiced in the past and probably has increased because of the exposure of factory farms, however it is not taught in our churches for the most part. Catholics are taught to have

well-informed consciences and I believe the Holy Spirit is moving amongst us to live more in tune with God's intended diet (vegetarian). While the Holy Spirit teaches us all things (see 1 John 2:27), vegetarianism should be part of Catholic social teaching, relief services and environmentalism. Since gluttony is a sin in the Catholic Church, perhaps the large consumption of meat should be included in the examination of our consciences. Sometimes part of the liturgy has "The Lord is good to all and compassionate toward all his works" Ps. 145:9, NAB—as His children made in His image, we too should have compassion on His creatures. . . . Someday we will give an account to God who cares about all of His animals including each victim in the agri-business's animal factories. ("No creature is concealed from him, but everything is naked and exposed to the eyes of him to whom we must render an account." Hebrews 4:13 NAB.)

Over at DietfortheNewAge.com, Internet travelers find the writings of Jody Patton, including her book *Diet for the New Age to Come*. Patton, a Christian from Minneapolis, Minnesota, explains why her young family hasn't consumed animal products for more than five years:

We changed our diet primarily for health reasons at first, but within a short time we learned about the ethical and environmental impact of our food choices, too, which are equally important reasons for us now. Our decision to live a vegetarian lifestyle also has huge spiritual significance to us. We took our first inspiration to live this lifestyle from the story in Daniel, chapter 1, in the Bible, and took that step of faith. It is more than just a story to us, though. It is an example of how to eat in Babylon, or at a time that we believe is the end of the age. It is one way for us to follow the teachings, or to apply the teachings of the Bible, in anticipation of the complete fulfillment of God's promises."

The topic of vegetarianism and Christianity generates great storms of controversy; some of the gales from this storm originated in the Virginia headquarters of PETA, which claims that Jesus was a vegetarian. Named one of the "50 Most Influential People Under 38" by *Details* magazine in 2003, Bruce Friedrich serves on the advisory board of the Christian Vegetarian Society and serves as the vegan campaign coordinator for PETA. In an interview with the *San Francisco Chronicle*, Friedrich stated, "Jesus mandates kindness and mercy for all God's creatures. He'd be appalled by the suffering that we inflict on animals today to indulge our acquired taste for their flesh. Catholics, and all Christians, have a choice. When we sit down to eat, we can add to the violence, misery and death in the world, or we can respect God's creatures with a vegetarian diet."

Peace activist Father John Dear writes, "I don't think you can conclude conclusively that Jesus was a vegetarian, that the early apostles were, or what St. Paul actually said. But for me, as a public Christian, that is not a problem!" The Christian Vegetarian Association (CVA) believes that what Jesus ate or wore 2000 years ago should not be a mandate for 2005. "We are blessed with a wide range of healthful, tasty, convenient plant foods, much like in Eden," states CVA's Web site. Stephen R. Kaufman, MD, CVA cochair, writes, "Most people seem to find our argument compelling. However, it is definitely a minority who are inspired to change their diets. Some people object to our biblical interpretations."

Volatile debate continues to erupt over whether Jesus was a vegetarian. Does evidence support the claim that Jesus did not eat animal flesh? Author Rev. J. R. Hyland, IMF, states,

> Only if there is another discovery of the caliber of the Dead Sea Scrolls, and it deals with the dietary choices of Jesus, can we find some measure of "proof" re the vegetarianism of Jesus. But whether or not it can be proved that Jesus was a vegetarian is not the issue for me. His revelation of God's love and compassion for all creatures—a continuation of the teachings of the Latter Prophets of Israel—is a leavening agent in Western civilization. Just as the abolition of slavery and the enfranchisement of women developed from the foundation of a Judeo-Christian culture, so, also, the humane treatment of other creatures is evolving in our culture to include farm animals as well as "pets." And with this understanding, it becomes increasingly obvious that you cannot "Be Kind to Animals" as long as you continue to kill them, and eat them. . . . The Bible was misused to bolster the barbarism of slavery and the subjugation of women, but those attempts failed. And today, the scriptures are being misused to try and hold on to the barbarism of human carnivorism. But, ultimately this, too, will fail.

Could it be that evidence for the vegetarianism of Jesus Christ exists but remains suppressed or just ignored by officials of Christianity, including the original church, Roman Catholicism? Keith Akers, author of *The Lost Religion of Jesus*, writes,

> They are being ignored, not suppressed. The whole idea [that] "secret manuscripts in the Vatican reveal shattering new truths about Christianity long suppressed by the church" is nonsense. *The Da Vinci Code* promotes this idea—it was a great novel, but lousy history. Nicholas Notovitch and Edmund Szekeley, two widely quoted authors who promote this idea, have produced documents which are fairly easily exposed as frauds.

Actually, there *are* manuscripts in the Vatican which reveal shattering new truths about Christianity. They are called "The New Testament" and the "Early Church Fathers." Romans 14, I Corinthians 8–10, and Galatians 1–2 show Paul in conflict with Jewish Christians in the early church who are not only vegetarian, but think that vegetarianism should be required of all Christians. The "Recognitions of Clement" and the "Homilies of Clement" are later documents which continue this Jewish Christian tradition. The Ebionites, who followed those in the early church (including the leadership!) who were vegetarian, believed that vegetarianism should be required of all followers of Jesus, and when questioned as to why they didn't eat meat, said, "Christ revealed it to me."

This tradition of vegetarianism can be traced back to Jesus himself, says Akers.

What was Jesus doing in the temple in the last week of his life, in the incident which in Sunday School was referred to as "Jesus chases the dishonest money-changers out of the temple"? It wasn't about the money-changers, he was disrupting the animal sacrifice business! In the gospel accounts, the money-changers are nowhere at the top of his list (in Luke they are not even mentioned); it is the dealers in pigeons, sheep, and cattle whom he attacks. He drives the buyers and sellers, and their animals, too, out of the temple. This was an act of animal liberation.

Abstinence from animal flesh is the practice of about half of Seventh-Day Adventists, a church whose members believe the body is the temple of the Holy Spirit. The church also disseminates vegetarian information through more than 600 health centers, publishing houses, TV and radio programs, and Country Life vegan restaurants. Dick Nunez, a church member, manages the Black Hills Health Education Center in Hermosa, South Dakota, where, he explains, "We are a wellness center that houses people for three weeks. We reverse many of the conditions plaguing society such as heart disease, cancer, diabetes, depression, autoimmune disorders and obesity. We have three MDs, three RNs, one physical therapist, one exercise physiologist, and numerous therapists."

Christopher Foster, PhD, of Provo, Utah, who founded Mormons for Animals in 2001, explains why members of the Church of Jesus Christ of Latter-Day Saints (LDS) should be vegetarian: "Eating meat causes extensive animal suffering for a comparatively [small] amount of human 'enjoyment.' Prophets have taught that we should be very concerned about animal welfare and refrain from activities that harm them. The scriptures repeatedly advise us to eat meat only when necessary (and for the animals' sakes).... The raising of animals for food practices unrighteous dominion over the earth and its animals—all of God's creation over which we have stewardship."

Pagans

The number of Wiccans or pagans in the United States doubles about every couple of years. Peoples' perception of pagan practitioners has largely been molded by Hollywood stereotypes, but some pagans claim vegetarianism fits their philosophy. Crescent Lynn, president of the Vegetarian Network of Austin, says many pagans today choose a plant-based diet. "The Wiccan creed says, 'As it harm none, do as you will,' meaning that we can do whatever we like as long as it doesn't cause harm. Since eating meat and dairy products are not required for survival or even health, if we take the creed seriously, we should avoid animal products."

Tricia Perry, a police officer and Massachusetts resident, agrees: "My Pagan beliefs had a great deal to do with going vegetarian. I follow the creed of 'Harm none' and I believe that includes animals, birds and fish. As fellow Earthlings, they should be respected." Laura Mason, a twenty-seven-year-old mailing list coordinator who lives in Maryland, says awareness seems to be higher in the pagan community, but believes the actual number of them who never eat meat might not be higher than in the general population. "The members of my particular sect of paganism are all vegetarians (I'm the only vegan) but when I go to more public events I am definitely the minority."

Despite the fact that some pagans sacrifice animals on altars instead of stoves, others prefer to pet animals rather than slay them. Lynn, a former social worker and teacher who now homeschools her children, says, "Ancients believed that the gods and goddesses required blood sacrifices to ease their anger or to get on their good sides. We no longer believe this. Yes, it is true that violence and bloodletting raises energy, but most of us acknowledge that the energy raised in that manner is negative. There are some heathens (Norse practitioners) who do practice this as well as Santerians and voodoo practitioners, but it is quite rare! Most pagans today—even those not vegetarian or vegan—acknowledge that there are much better ways of raising power and accomplishing our goals."

Other Practices

Advocate of vegetarianism Marcia Pearson describes the Order of the Cross, which is based upon the writings of J. Todd Ferrier (1855–1943), a minister and ardent antivivisectionist. "The members of the Order of the Cross *live* the phrase 'Peace begins with me.' It is probably the only

Susan Smith Jones. Courtesy
Susan Smith Jones.

membership group which requires vegetarianism because they believe
that purity of the body and the purity of living and purity of the soul are
dependent on each other," explains Pearson.

Some beliefs seem out of science fiction. "[T]he conversion to vegetarianism (or any other life change) can be interpreted as an expression of ongoing personal evolution and the continual challenge to
improve one's moral, intellectual, and physical condition," wrote
George Dvorsky in *Humanist* magazine. He labels himself a "trans-
humanist," that is, a humanist who believes in enhancing human beings through science and technology.

Susan Smith Jones, PhD, of California, has taught thousands the
vegetarian way. An athlete and expert in nutrition, antiaging, and
exercise, Jones was told she might never walk again after a terrible
accident. But using natural methods and positive thinking, she fully
recovered. The author of the book series *Unleash the Power of Nature-
Foods*, Jones states, "being committed to a vegetarian lifestyle reaps
priceless rewards. For example, I'm blessed to live disease-free without
ever taking any medication; I am told I look years younger than my age;
and I have the energy and vitality of someone thirty years my junior."

Jones, a motivational speaker, holistic lifestyle coach, and author of
twenty books, including the Pulitzer prize-nominated *Choose to Live
Peacefully*, connects the physical aspects of food with a higher reason
for abstaining from animal flesh.

It is said that a picture speaks a thousand words. Our society seems to be "youth oriented"—most people desire ways to turn back the clock and live without disease. When we see a person radiating a youthful vitality—through natural ways—simply by choosing a vegetarian diet and living a healthy, balanced lifestyle, we're inspired to give it a try. Positive actions (diet and exercise) and thoughts combined with discipline and a deep commitment towards ourselves and our planet Earth equals priceless rewards and peaceful lives.

Victoria Moran, a certified life coach who has made a pair of appearances on the *Oprah Winfrey Show*, believes that vegetarianism based on endures while vegetarianism based solely on health lies on a shaky foundation. "The prevailing thought on health changes all the time," says Moran, author of a *Creating a Charmed Life* and *Lit from Within: A Simple Guide to the Art of Inner Beauty*. "During the high protein diet craze, a lot of vegetarians turned to meat eating. But the people who cared about living in a way that reduces suffering were unmoved."

PEACE AND PRO-LIFE

Food Not Bombs (FNB) feeds vegan meals to the poor and to people at rallies. Volunteers with the twenty-five-year-old group will likely start microbanks, community gardens, info shops, bike repair collectives, wind generation centers, and community health centers, says cofounder Keith McHenry. With chapters across the nation and around the world, FNB promotes peace and social justice, but McHenry and volunteers were once deemed "prisoners of conscience" by Amnesty International. FNB volunteers have been beaten and tortured by police in the United States, and have come under surveillance by the government, an oil company, and even the Anti-Defamation League, according to information on the group's Web site.

Assisted by a student vegetarian group at Louisiana State University in Baton Rouge, McHenry's FNB was one of the first organizations to feed the hungry people whose lives were disrupted by Hurricane Katrina in 2005. His paternal great-great-grandfather was Dr. James McHenry, who signed the U.S. Constitution and served as a general in the Revolutionary War and as secretary of war under George Washington. He writes about vegetarianism:

If America's mainstream embraced a nonviolent diet and economy it would be the most fundamental change in U.S. history. Millions of Americans would have greatly improved health. Thousands of people who would have died prematurely from heart disease, strokes and diabetes will live longer more fulfilling lives. Americans would think more clearly and their self-esteem would increase making it more difficult for politicians and corporate leaders to find popular support for policies that are against their own interest. Americans fill [their] empty feeling by consumerism and patriotism. If you believe in nonviolence it's difficult to support violence against animals and it makes sense to be vegan or vegetarian. Food Not Bombs shares free vegan meals at our literature tables to show by example the connection between our personal lives and the effort to build a world at peace.

Vegetarianism and the peace movement in the United States have a long association, dating back to at least 1817, when the Bible-Christians of Philadelphia, recently arrived from England, advocated vegetarianism, abolition, and pacifism. Father John Dear, SJ, a leader in today's peace movement and author of several books on the subject, including the booklet *Christianity and Vegetarianism: Pursuing the Nonviolence of Jesus*, shares his perspective:

> Nonviolence is completely inclusive, embracing creation and all existence. In a world where life is cheap, where millions are starving and thousands killed by war every year, we are all learning the meaning of nonviolence and peace. I have hope that we will all continue to make the connections of peace and nonviolence, between our own inner selves, all humanity, all animals and the earth itself. This is a great spiritual journey, and we have to keep encouraging everyone and inviting everyone into the depths of nonviolence.

During the last quarter century, author Colman McCarthy has worked for peace and vegetarianism. A former columnist for the *Washington Post*, McCarthy has taught thousands of students through the Center for Teaching Peace, which he founded with his wife.

> In my high school and college classes, in which I've taught nonviolence and pacifism to more than 7,000 students in the past twenty-five years, I'm aware that most students feel helpless to act meaningfully against the world's wars or conflicts. The violence is too distant, too entrenched. Students repeat this refrain every semester, and every semester I suggest that there is a war they can take action to end: the war on animals. People eat them, wear them, ride them, chain them, hunt them, exploit them, imprison them—and pay billions of dollars to corporations to keep doing it for our pleasure or benefit. We do everything to animals but let them live in God's peace and freedom.

McCarthy, who writes for the *National Catholic Reporter*, recalls the reaction of one student the day he brought a turkey into class, the week before Thanksgiving. "The presence of this living, gentle and intelligent bird in the classroom—she curious about us and we curious about her—was enough to bring about an instant conversion to an herbivore diet."

Vegetarianism is part of the peace and pro-life ethic, believes McCarthy, as does Vasu Murti, author of *They Shall Not Hurt or Destroy*, who was raised in a family of Hindu Brahmans:

> I believe there is a karmic connection between the killing of animal beings and the killing of human beings. Abortion, like war, is the karmic reaction for killing animals. Pro-lifers look in horror as an entire class of humans are systematically stripped of their rights, executed, and even used as tools for medical research—but this is what we humans have been doing to animals for millennia. Pro-lifers speak of the "slippery slope," the belief that acceptance of abortion leads to a devaluation of life and paves the way towards acceptance of infanticide and euthanasia. I merely assert that the "slippery slope" begins with what we humans do to animals. Pythagoras warned that "those who kill animals for food will be more prone than vegetarians to torture and kill their fellow men."

Ironically, the animal rights movement, largely made up of vegetarians, seems to lean toward support for legal abortion, while the

Vasu Murti, pro-life vegan. Courtesy Vasu Murti.

pro-life movement seems uninterested in supporting animal rights. But both movements have more similarities than differences, says Murti, author of *The Liberal Case Against Abortion*:

> In both cases, we're talking about extending our moral sphere of concern to embrace a disenfranchised class of beings; beings that are on the fringes of society and only accorded marginal personhood. Both groups compare the mass killing of animals and the mass killing of unborn children to the Nazi Holocaust. Both compare themselves to the abolitionists who sought to end [human] slavery. Recognizing the rights of another class of beings limits our freedoms and our choices and requires a change in our personal lifestyle—the abolition of [human] slavery is a good example of this. Both movements have picketed the homes of physicians who either perform abortions or experiment on animals. The controversial use of human fetal tissue and embryonic stem cells for medical research brings these two causes even closer together. Both movements show the public graphic photos of tortured animals or aborted fetuses, in order to awaken the conscience of the nation. These two causes (animal rights and prenatal rights) are moving along parallel lines, much like the movements in the nineteenth century for the rights of African Americans and the rights of women.

Like Murti, Rachel M. MacNair, director of the Institute for Integrated Social Analysis, believes in "noncruelty to helpless beings— whether unborn beings or animals." This has a historic basis, as early feminists tended to support vegetarianism and oppose abortion.

MacNair maintains that health connects the two causes. "Abortions, and eating animals, are both unhealthy," she explains. A psychologist and past president of Feminists for Life, MacNair says vegetarians who are pro-life—that is, support both human and animal rights—find themselves challenged by meat eaters among the antiabortion movement. "A lot of pro-lifers get worked up: [They ask] why are you saving baby eagles and not baby humans? On the other hand, vegetarian pro-lifers are displeased with vegetarian pro-choice people, whom they perceive as all believing it's okay to kill baby humans and not animals," says MacNair, author of *The Psychology of Peace*.

Vegetarian feminists may be divided on the subject of abortion, but they are united in their belief that female human beings, like animals of other species, are exploited, abused, and murdered by patriarchal society. "As ecofeminists we recognize that the abuse of women and nature is intimately connected in patriarchal society. As ecofeminist animal advocates we view the exploitation of women and animals as an expression of a common patriarchal worldview, which manifests itself in both sexism and speciesism," Feminists for Animal Rights: An

EcoFeminist Alliance states on their Web site. Women are treated like meat and animals are turned into meat. Thus, a feminist should not partake of the food of exploitation and violence, claims Feminists for Animal Rights, along with writers such as Carol J. Adams, author of *The Sexual Politics of Meat.*

ANIMAL LIBERATION

People may avoid meat because of feminism or health reasons, but motivation such as sympathy, pity, empathy, love, or respect for animals will more likely meld this way of eating into a person's daily life. A survey of thousands of visitors to Vegweb.com reports that 44 percent of female respondents (10,920) list animal rights as their primary motivation, while 35 percent (6,353) list health. Male respondents listed animal rights (37 percent, 2,345) and health (30 percent, 1,935).

Nathan Runkle, the executive director of Mercy for Animals, states:

> Life on "Old MacDonald's Farm" isn't what it used to be. The green pastures and idyllic barnyard scenes portrayed in children's books have been replaced by windowless sheds, wire cages, and other confinement systems integral to what is now known as "factory farming." Today the majority of farmed animals are confined to the point that they can barely move, denied veterinary care, mutilated without painkillers, and finally mercilessly slaughtered. The competition to produce inexpensive meat, eggs, and dairy products has led to animals being treated as nothing more than commodities, resulting in an enormous amount of suffering in the pursuit of profit. Every year approximately 26 billion cows, pigs, chickens, turkeys and fish, each a unique individual capable of experiencing happiness, joy, loneliness, and frustration, are killed to satisfy America's appetite for animal flesh, milk, and eggs. Every time we eat, we are making a powerful choice that has profound consequences on the lives of animals.

Mercy for Animals has made television commercials exposing how animals are treated on factory farms and slaughterhouses. Another young organization, Compassion Over Killing (COK) also airs television commercials. Executive director Erica Meier says:

> COK's MTV Commercial Campaign (2004) stands out as one of the most successful and cost-effective ways to expose millions of viewers to the horrors forced upon farmed animals every day by the meat, egg, and dairy industries. What's more, by targeting MTV's teen and young adult viewing audience, COK is able to get the animals' message directly to

those shown by research to be the most receptive to vegetarian eating. All of COK's thirty-second spots offer hard-hitting messages about how our dietary choices have far-reaching effects on the lives and deaths of billions of animals, and they further direct viewers to their TryVeg.com Web site to learn more about compassionate eating.

ENVIRONMENT

Vegetarians may have been inspired to quit eating meat because of humanism, religion, or animal rights, or because of concern for planet Earth. Vegetarians and others claim that big corporate animal-based agriculture results in damage to the land, trees, water, and air, as well as to animal and plant species displaced or made extinct. Statistics on the amount of water needed to raise animals or the loss of topsoil because of ranching show up on anything from grocery bags to leaflets distributed by vegetarians.

Author Pamela Rice states, "[V]egetarians cannot beat the feeling of knowing that they are saving the planet a world-full of environmental havoc. Meat production is a significant contributor to water pollution (manure, fertilizer, pesticides), air pollution (manure odor, hydrogen sulfide, ammonia, dust), global warming (methane from cow burps, rain forest deforestation), water depletion, oil extraction (meat production is a significant user of fossil fuels), topsoil erosion, and fish-stock extinction and ecological disruption. And I probably forgot a few."

David Kidd, founder of American Free Tree Program and Vegetarian Club of Canton, committed himself to nonviolent principles while serving in the Vietnam War, agrees: "Clearly the livestock industry is the biggest cause of deforestation and loss of topsoil in the U.S." Kidd, who wanted to help remedy some of the damage, organized tree-planting projects that have planted over 12 million trees in Ohio and several other states.

Animal-derived foods that people consume affect the environment, even when that animal is a bee, says Noah Lewis, publisher of Vegetus .org. "Eschewing bees' honey is no more about strictness or purity than is eschewing cow's milk—both are the products of sentient beings and are to be avoided to the same extent. Just as there are no morally relevant differences that justify exploiting mammals, birds, and fishes, an honest look at insects reveals that they, too, should not be subject to systematic exploitation. The effects of such exploitation have been dramatic—the profit motive of industrial beekeepers led to the importation and spread of the *Varroa* mite, which decimated free

Pattrice Jones of Global Hunger Alliance expresses a concern shared by many vegetarians:

> A person eating the average American meat-based diet consumes enough resources to feed twenty people a healthy vegetarian diet. When you eat an animal, you're gobbling up all of the food that animal ate over the course of his or her lifetime as well as all of the water used to grow that food, all of the water drunk by the animal, all of the fuel used to transport food to the animal and then transport the animal to the slaughterhouse, and all of the energy used to kill, cut up, and package the animal's body. Animal agriculture pollutes and depletes a host of natural resources, the increasing scarcity of which menaces all of us but which is particularly hazardous in regions where people are already struggling with hunger and malnutrition.

POLITICS

Generally, the dominant culture believes that vegetarians are politically liberal, especially those who are animal rights advocates. But an increasing number of vegetarians are coming from the ranks of conservatism, libertarianism, and even the Christian conservative camp. A few years ago, Matthew Scully, a vegetarian speech writer for the George W. Bush administration, made the best-seller's list with *Dominion*, a book that raised eyebrows and awareness of the suffering of animals. Conservative writer and commentator Patrick Buchanan's *American Conservative* magazine advocated against factory farming.

Political philosophy can indeed influence food choices, as in the following case of a young New Yorker: "My outlook changed from socialist to libertarian about a month after I became a vegetarian," says Rhys Southan, who once interned for *Reason* magazine and ABC News's John Stossel. "At first I thought both changes were coming from completely different realizations. But in fact, they were related in a very basic way—an aversion for the use of force. Yet that's not a connection that a lot of people make, and vegetarianism is still often considered an emotional, idealistic, and irrational decision—unless it's completely apolitical and health related."

Southan further explains how libertarianism fits with his dietary choices:

> The prototypical vegetarians are sandal-wearing hippies who ride their bikes to the co-op grocery store and protest for fun in the rare moments they aren't studying Marxist economics or the sociology of gender. There's some truth to this stereotype, but it's important to realize

honeybee colonies and made human intervention virtually re
the survival of all honeybee colonies."

Not all vegetarians agree that the environmental proble:
ated with meat production pose grave risks to humanity. Er
author of *Meat Market* and a popular lecturer, writes: "[T]h
mental impact of meat production is far less costly than 1
tarians suggest." For example, Marcus claims that the o
claim that it takes about 5,200 gallons of water to produ
pound of beef "has no real evidence to back it up" and th:
likely number could be as low as 441 gallons.

"Several leaders in the movement have reacted unha:
setting the record straight," says Marcus. But advocates
bious figures could find themselves in a difficult predicam
"I think it backfires every time somebody hears it, rais:
brows, and decides that it's probably not a credible cla
further pro-veggie claims on different subjects should
missed." However, Marcus believes there is compelling
cattle ranching has ruined more square miles of land i
States than any other activity, and that the "consequ
world's appetite for fish have become ruinous to the oce

A growing number of people who don't eat meat pr:
gardening, or gardening without using animal product fe
Duggan and Olga Schifani of Center for Vegan Organic
that this method reduces "food safety risks such as F
human form of mad cow disease (Creutzfeldt-Jakot
creases dependence upon slaughterhouse and fisheries
eliminating the use of bone, blood, feather, and fish me:
improves long-term soil productivity; and preserves
quality, reduces waste, feeds more people."

HUNGER

During the 1970s, a sizable but unknown number
ing meat out of concern for world hunger. The rec
Adventist–sponsored Fourth International Congres
Nutrition at Loma Linda University featured hu:
"Approximately 10 billion livestock animals are F
animal-product diet system in the United States ea
livestock population out-weighs the U.S. human po
5 times. Approximately 250 million metric tons of gr
livestock each year. This is sufficient grain to feed :
million people as vegetarians."

that vegetarianism has nothing to do with fiscal irresponsibility and the expansion of government power. Eschewing meat simply means applying the libertarian concept of negative rights (basically, the right to be left alone, and the responsibility to take care of yourself) to animals. For instance, animals should have the right to free speech—unless your girlfriend's dog's barking infringes on your ability to sleep. If liberals were to apply their concept of human rights to animals, it would mean giving animals health care, higher education, and retirement benefits. Lady bugs would become welfare queens.

Then there are those left-wing "fronts" saving animals at the expense of humans, like the Animal Liberation Front. It's this disastrous mingling of violent left-wing tactics with the libertarian principle of animal rights that gives vegetarianism a bad name. The left likes to consider compassion amongst its primary values (thus the resentment over the term "compassionate conservative"), the main reason why vegetarianism is considered a hippie thing: "Ahh, look at the cuddly animals, we don't want to hurt them!" But in fact, a lot of the literature on animal rights is rational and brilliantly argued. By being a vegan who is also a libertarian—a political paradigm that detests emotional policy decisions that do more harm than good—I might help people see that animal rights isn't just for save-the-everything idealists. And, in the other direction, animal rights activists might realize they don't have to be socialists just because they love animals. Or that those who disagree with a lot of government spending must obviously be horrible bunny-hating bastards. A lot of vegetarians have a holier-than-thou attitude, so it's good for them to see holiness in people who aren't necessarily fellow travelers.

Southan puts it succinctly: "I'm vegetarian because I want to cause as little harm as possible. That's the same reason I'm a libertarian."

On the other side of the spectrum, Richard Kahn, ecopedagogy chair at University of California at Los Angeles's Paulo Freire Institute, states:

Today, capitalism is the primary cause of animal suffering and ecological crisis the world over. Corporations, which exist only to return profits, are the irrational engines that are driving a terrible and perilously rapid mass extinction of species that is unprecedented over the last 65 million years, and people who function as blind consumers of corporate products are only fueling a murderous problem by aiding and abetting it. Rather than become furious with the current situation, I tell people, "Don't get mad, get vegan!" I think of veganism as an attempt to produce a revolutionary alternative to the status quo and as a process of ongoing self-reflection about how one relates to the world that dovetails into political action.

Popular culture, even vegetarian culture, doesn't usually recognize differences among vegetarians, particularly on controversies such as global warming, animal agriculture pollution, and restrictions of endangered species law, yet these differences are strong. Contrary to popular misconception, arguments for vegetarianism are based on logic and practicality, as well as morality, spirituality, and philosophy. Giving up meat does not normally deprive a human being of the pleasure of eating or cause him or her to develop dietary deficiencies. In fact, people who cease to eat meat report that this is a source of satisfaction and joy in their lives, even when the meat-eating culture they live in disapproves.

5

SPREADING THE GOOD NEWS

Most conscientiously have I desired, and sought to find out the
truth, for the truth's sake, and to promulgate it for the good of man.
Sylvester Graham, Father of Vegetarianism in America, 1849,
Lectures on the Science of Human Life

Scantily-clad women who call themselves the Vegan Vixens are
flaunting themselves on television to bring vegetarianism and animal
rights to the public's attention. The Vixens might not be everyone's
idea of the proper promulgation of the ancient practice and philosophy
of vegetarianism, but they are gaining attention for themselves and
their way of life. PETA, too, employs sexy women.

The question of using sex to sell vegetarianism draws mixed responses from advocates. Truly Ankerberg-Nobis, MS, of Physicians
Committee for Responsible Medicine, sees nothing wrong with using
beauty and feminity to sell vegetarianism. "When people say that PETA
'uses' women, they are relegating women to the very role we have
fought to be rid of, namely, 'things' that need to be ordered around and
kept in their place.... When you see women dressed 'sexily' for activism, do you see a victimized woman with nothing to offer the world
other than her body? Or do you see a woman who intelligently and
freely chooses to use her body to make a point? Your answer may lead
you to your own hidden sexism."

On the other hand, Dan Stuntebeck, member of the Campus Vegetarian Society at the University of Wisconsin at Madison, believes that

Connie Salamone spreads the vegetarian
word through her art, writing, and slide-
show. Courtesy Connie Salamone.

idea fails to work. "You either get guys who just ogle over some scantily
clad girl or maybe get a blurb on the news (which likely furthers the
'wacko' stereotype of animal activists). Secondly, it itself is a form of
exploitation, which is what we are fighting against."

Standing out from the ordinary is part of being a vegetarian. Not
surprisingly, people accustomed to being normal Americans, never
stepping out of the conformity line—and new to not eating fish,
chicken, pork, and beef—might become concerned when they are no
longer part of the majority, at least not in eating habits, and likely not
in philosophy. But this sense of alienation or even fear may evaporate
when they reach out to others who share the same eating habits or
values. For all the talk of individualism in the United States, when one
is suddenly "different" due to beliefs or values, or to the food one does
not eat, one may be astonished to find that the dominant meat-eating
culture often fails to readily accept differences and may respond with
ridicule or even hostility.

Jenna Torres, PhD, coauthor of *Vegan Freak*, suggests that people
who find themselves in the predicament of being different stop trying
to fit in.

We say that if you're worried about not being seen as normal when
you're a vegan, then we encourage you to rethink the value of actually
being normal. Granted, this isn't easy for most people who live in places

where they don't know any other vegans. Thankfully, you can find a lot of support on the Internet.... It's helped keep us sane. One specific recommendation we have for a large range of situations is that you show the benefits of veganism through example—that you eat well, live well, and live by your conscience; people are sometimes genuinely curious about veganism because they just can't fathom it, so it helps to patiently respond to their inquiries. Being confrontational usually turns friends and family off, but avoiding arguments doesn't necessarily mean that you have to keep your opinions to yourself.

Vegetarians, particularly fledgling ones, often turn to the Internet for information. Of the hundreds of thousands of Web sites dedicated to vegetarianism, likely only a few generate annual visits in the millions. Vegsource.com, arguably the leader of the pack, features the advice and writings of leading physicians, chefs, activists, and authors, as well as message boards, news, and video clips. Jeff Nelson, who founded the site in October 1996, tells of its rapid growth: "The site is so vast that even its publisher is unsure of its actual size. Including our hundreds of active discussion boards, it's impossible for me to say how many pages we have on the site—it's in the tens of thousands. We're one of the oldest vegetarian Web sites on the Web and we get around 1.4 million visitors per month. We can put out an article or bulletin and reach a very significant segment of the veg world in a short time."

Internet surfers can find paradise online, or at least the seemingly endless Web pages of *Vegetarians in Paradise* (VIP), an online magazine published in Los Angeles, California since 1999 by Reuben and Zel Allen. The latter, a professional belly dancer turned caterer and dessert inventor, wrote the book *The Nutty Vegan*. Restaurant listings of vegan, vegetarian, and vegetarian-friendly restaurants in Los Angeles County, and a database of vegetarian food companies that briefly describes the offerings of each company are popular with some 80,000 readers, say the Allens.

Another popular Web site presents serious vegetarian topics, but coated with sarcasm and humor. The Funhouse section of Veganstreet .com, for example, features "Tabloid News" with stories like, "Teen Vegan Makes Entire Family Uncomfortable" and a spoof of the popular television game show *Who Wants to Be a Millionaire*—"Who Wants to Be a Vegetarian." Veganstreet presents annual awards for the "five biggest blunders, stupid acts, and points of embarrassment for bad people, corporations, and government agencies disguised as corporations." In 2005, the U.S. Department of Agriculture was one of the chosen five: "The USDA. Technically not a corporation, but, really, who are they kidding? With the rotating door between the USDA, Monsanto and the FDA, it's really one big happy family anyway. Imagine their summer picnics! Anyway, after all their years of bowing to corporate interests and treating consumer protection as though it's a poker card they desperately want to get rid of, we hereby decree that the USDA is an honorary corporation (perhaps USDA, Inc.?)."

Some vegetarians promote plant-based dining by using e-mail to send news and views. Susan Roghair, a.k.a. Englandgal, of Tampa, Florida, regularly e-mails her popular Animal Rights Online newsletter to subscribers. Roghair formed Animal Rights Online in 1997 with a coterie of activists to speedily keep people informed. For Roghair, the Internet has become indispensable as an advocacy tool:

> I could see that the Internet as a resource for information has exploded. Millions of people every day turn to online services for information, conversation and entertainment. The Internet is truly a free form of expression. It isn't biased—or controlled by editors. It's not dependent on ratings to determine what you learn about or see. It's not watered down, cropped, edited, or made "to fit the available time slot." There are no "sound bites," no photo ops. It is, to date, a pure media form.
>
> A housewife in a small town in southern Iowa can learn things that she might never hear in the commercial media, may never obtain at her local library, or ever know without the contacts the Internet provides. A vegan can find support online and obtain new recipes! People all over the world can be apprised of events and news releases that would never be covered by the ratings-powered commercial media. Because of the sheer number of animals that suffer in factory farmed conditions, we focus heavily on this issue. Each year in the United States alone, ten billion animals are slaughtered for food. The slaughter itself, while horrible, is only the last chapter in a life of misery. This is why most of our staff are vegans and the rest vegetarians. This is why we work so hard to promote the plant-based diet.

Others promulgate plant-based eating in person, as well as on the Internet. Professional dancer Dixie Mahy, a vegetarian since 1957, has worked to spread vegetarianism in San Francisco for decades. She serves as president of the San Francisco Vegetarian Society, which was formed a year prior to her joining. The organization spreads the word by holding potlucks, lectures, dinners, and by publishing *Vegetarian News*, a bimonthly newsletter, and according to Mahy, has spun off several groups over the years. Mahy and the society's efforts have yielded quite a harvest: When she arrived in San Francisco in 1956, there were no vegetarian restaurants or groups, and only one health food store that sold meatless products. However, readers of *VegNews* recently voted San Francisco as the most vegetarian friendly city in the nation.

A still older group, and likely the oldest vegetarian group, Vegetarian Society of the District of Columbia, established by Madge Darnielle in 1927, attracts the public by holding dinners, talks, and providing exhibits at a variety of social events.

In the Pacific Northwest, Vegetarians of Washington includes "people from every income and ethnic group in our region, and from all political persuasions," says vice president Stewart Rose. "There seems to be a stereotype of vegetarians being almost all liberal in their politics. This is patently false. Our organization has a very substantial representation of conservatives, numbering approximately the same as their liberal counterparts. However, we emphasize that, unlike some other vegetarian organizations that have political subagendas, Vegetarians of Washington does not engage in any political activity whatsoever, but instead remains highly focused on its vegetarian mission."

Rose outlines additional reasons for the success of the group:

We have no particular spiritual platform or activity, but we welcome people from many religions and consider the spiritual motivation for following a vegetarian diet as equivalent to any other. When Vegetarians of Washington was formed, a very careful analysis was made of both what was going right and wrong with the vegetarian movement. We did not consider the vegetarian movement to be as successful as it should be given the compelling case it makes. We endeavored to incorporate those aspects that were going well and reject aspects of the movement that led to disastrous results or that violated our sense of ethics.

Vegetarians of Washington has published a cookbook and a guidebook called *Veg-Feasting in the Pacific Northwest*. A third book is on the way. "We do not consider ourselves activists. We make our mission and identity very clear to the public. We hold events where people can learn, feel supported and have some fun." One of these events, the Vegfest, occurs annually each spring. The 2005 event featured 500 different kinds of food from over 125 companies. Over 207,000 food samples—from Italian baked tofu and garbanzo bean curry to American cuisine such as veggie burgers, veggie hot dogs, flavored soy milks, and soy yogurts were served.

Thousands of miles away, Jill Howard Church, president of the Vegetarian Society of Georgia, which was founded by Louise Stewart in 1990, says the organization provides a social support network for people choosing a meat-free lifestyle.

In the early years it focused on hosting potluck dinners and helping vegetarians and vegans network with each other. As vegetarianism has become more mainstream, and veg products more easily available, the focus has shifted to be more comprehensive. Today we focus on educating people about the many benefits of reducing and eliminating meat, egg and dairy consumption. We recognize that people become vegetarian and vegan for a variety of reasons (animal welfare, health, environment) and we try to address all of those concerns. We are trying to make better use of the Internet as an educational and outreach tool. Our most popular event is our annual vegan Thanksgiving dinner, where we celebrate and give thanks for all life.

Emily (Sammy) Samfield, an aerospace medicine technician from Douglasville, Georgia, focuses on a specific form of advocacy: "I started Atlanta Veggie Kids. I think having our kids healthy and active is the number one reason to go vegan and has the biggest impact on others. My son and I both promote veganism by the healthy life we lead."

Shakira Croce, a seventeen-year-old high school graduate from Gainesville, Georgia, has already built a résumé of vegetarian advocacy:

> I founded Gainesville High School's first ever animal rights club in Gainesville, GA, the city that prides itself as being the "poultry capital of the world," so I have met my share of opposition to my veg activism. Other than winning the battle of founding my animal rights club and advising other students across the country to found their own veg clubs, I have also successfully petitioned for vegetarian options in my middle school cafeteria and successfully implemented a permanent alternative to dissection—a computer program—at the high school. I have written countless letters to the editor in support of animal rights and veg issues, and I have held World Farm Animals Day and National MeatOut Day events at my high school.

Another Southern state, Texas, features several vegetarian organizations, most of them under the umbrella of the Lone Star Vegetarian Network, including the Fort Worth Vegetarian Society, San Antonio Vegetarian Society, Vegetarian Dallas, Vegetarian Network of Austin, Vegetarian Society of Houston, Voice for Animals, and the Vegetarian Society of El Paso. The El Paso society was founded by Sukie Sargent, a seventy-two-year-old retired civil servant who became a vegetarian sixteen years ago and a vegan a year later after reading about the egg industry in a PETA newsletter. "I made a covenant with the animals after I retired," she says.

Sargent discusses her society's efforts:

> El Paso is not a vegetarian-friendly city—we don't even have a vegetarian restaurant, let alone a vegan restaurant. But there are lots of

vegetarians here and our events are well attended. All our events are vegan even though not all attendees are vegan. We are encouraging El Paso restaurants to include vegetarian/vegan options by publishing a restaurant guide for El Paso. The volunteer in charge of this project personally visits the restaurants and encourages them to include veg options, so we can give them a free advertisement by including them in our guide. We also have potlucks, dinner and a movie, workshops, restaurant hoppers, [and] cooking classes and we publish a twenty-four-page quarterly newsletter. I am also the founder of Voice for All Animals, the first-ever animal rights group in El Paso. However, the vegetarian society is more active at this time.

Similarly, the San Antonio Vegetarian Society (SAVS) hosts a variety of activities, including regular meetings that alternate between potluck dinners and catered restaurant meals. SAVS, founded in 1989, celebrates annual events such as Earthwise Living Day in February, Great American Meat Out Day in March, Earth Day in April, World Vegetarian Day and the statewide Vegetarian Chili Cook-Off in October, Thanksgiving, "Winter" and the Fourth of July with vegetarian parties, celebratory feasts, and barbecues. SAVS member Gloria Weers says her group does direct outreach by handing out food samples at health food stores and holding cooking classes at the local whole foods grocery store.

Kaz Sephton, SAVS president, discusses life as a vegetarian in Texas: "Texas is about 1 percent vegetarian and I know them all....people look at you up and down as if you lost a body part. On the other hand, it's not underground anymore and it's grown on a small scale."

Alexanda Svoboda, a Nebraska native, reports on a small but somewhat viable vegetarian scene in her home state:

My connection to a vegetarian scene in NE was always homebound vegetarian/vegan potlucks, breakfasts, etc. There was no organization that promoted vegetarianism, but unofficially and strangely enough a large majority of my roommates from several different houses were vegetarian, some vegan. This all took place in Lincoln, where the only vegetarian restaurant to date is Maggie's Vegetarian Wraps—small, but delicious, only open for breakfast and lunch. All other dining options weren't advertised as vegetarian, but it was easy to find really good food at one of the many small, family-run ethnic restaurants, or the local co-op (Open Harvest), or at a local bakery that serves awesome vegetarian soups (Grateful Bread). Omaha is larger than Lincoln and as far as I know has only one all-vegetarian restaurant. Outside of these two cities, I can't imagine there being another restaurant in Nebraska that advertises itself as vegetarian. Nebraska is the beef state (or cornhusker state, depending [on] who you ask) and vegetarian issues aren't pushed as such because there's no need to be militant about one's diet in a state that wouldn't be very receptive. Of bigger concern are issues that don't come down to individual lifestyle choices like sustainable agriculture. I think vegetarian/veganism is a privileged diet because the conscious decision to restrict what you eat (on whatever moral grounds) comes from having enough to eat not being a problem in the first place.

Alissa Finley of Vegetarians of Oklahoma promotes vegetarianism through education, interaction, and mutual support:

We believe that the reduced consumption of animal products promotes healthier lives, environmental conservation, and compassion for all life on the planet. Vegetarians of Oklahoma (VegOK) was formed in 1989, initially under the name Vegetarians of Oklahoma City (VOKC). Over the years, the group came to encompass members not from just OKC, but many of the surrounding city-outgrowths and small towns. We eventually became the only vegetarian group in Oklahoma. These two factors together led us in 2004 to vote to change our name to the more inclusive and expansive Vegetarians of Oklahoma.

Also, in 2004 we formed two other subgroups under the umbrella of VegOK: Veg PAK and Animal Allies. I formed Vegetarian Parents and Kids (Veg PAK) to help create a sense of vegetarian community for families, especially the children. Veg PAK has monthly gatherings separate from VegOK meetings complete with kid-friendly vegan snacks, free information, a lending library, and a safe place to just hang out and play. The kids don't have to ask their parents, "Can I eat this? Is this vegan?" and amongst themselves they can share any experiences or concerns they may have surrounding being vegetarian. It is also just as important for the parents to have a support community to discuss raising vegetarian children, e.g., dealing [with] nonvegetarian grandparents, going to eat at friends' houses, school issues, nutritional information, recipe exchanges and such. I have two vegan-since-conception children myself, and I didn't want them to grow up feeling like "the only ones." They are proud of their veganism, and have a circle of vegan friends that are being raised with similar values.

PART
II

VEGETARIANS IN A
MEAT-EATING COUNTRY

6

PARADOX

Men get angry, and rave against Vegetarians as if they have committed some mortal offense. A man cannot make a simple natural meal, without suffering a sort of martyrdom, from all the flesh eaters around him. Men do not like to be reproved, even by the example of those who live better than themselves. To the impure, purity is a reproach. One would think, to hear some flesh eaters talk, that devouring the bodies of slaughtered beasts was the height of human virtue.

Thomas Low Nichols, American Vegetarian Society, 1851

Vegetarian foods, fashions, and festivals attract America's attention. Slowly, vegetarianism has seeped into the mainstream of society and the dominant meat-eating American culture seems to accept non-meat-eating people. People who choose a plant-based diet believe that the mainstream accepts vegetarianism far more than it did some twenty or even five years ago. After all, who doesn't know a vegetarian, or a few, or have one in their family, workplace, or classroom?

Jeff Nelson, founder of VegSource.com, doesn't consider vegetarianism a subgroup or fringe. "We're just normal people who've discovered a really great way to live. Part of the VegSource mission is to demystify and demythify what a vegetarian or vegan is—we're people with families and jobs and kids and lives. The fact that we don't eat animals doesn't mean we're 'strange.' That's a message that VegSource stands behind."

But in everyday American life, outside the vegetarian community, does the meat-eating majority truly accept people who will not touch fish, chicken wings, or other meat? At first glance, this appears to be the case.

Dilip Barman, president of the Triangle Vegetarian Society in North Carolina, believes so: "Most of the time, I get synergy—'Oh, I'm trying to cut back my meat consumption,' or 'I'm also a vegetarian!'" Likewise, Erin Pavlina, editor of *VegFamily* magazine and author of *Raising Vegan Children in a Non-Vegan World*, says life for vegans continues to improve since more products for vegans are available and a growing number of restaurants offer meals without any animal products.

Pavlina would like Americans who eat meat to know: "Vegans are not fanatics, we are not weird. We are concerned about our health and the environment so we eat a plant-based diet. We care very deeply for animals and do not want to see them suffer. We know we can easily survive, and in fact thrive, on a vegan diet and are happy to be doing our part to protect the animals of Earth. The food we eat is varied and diverse, and delicious. Contrary to popular thought, it does not taste like cardboard."

However, acceptance of vegetarians hinges on an unspoken "don't ask, don't tell" policy whereby meat eaters show tolerance unless vegans start talking of the slaughter of animals, or insisting that human health problems are derived from devouring meat, drinking milk, and eating eggs. Vegetarians, and especially vegans, whether or not they are outspoken or activists, experience discord of varying degrees from the dominant culture.

Most vegetarians and vegans have felt the sting of prejudice from family members, doctors, employers, and other meat eaters. Gail Davis, author of *Vegetarian Food for Thought: Quotations and Inspirations*, explains her perspective: "Here in Indiana, one doesn't have a lot of vegan company.... This is a state where parents have had their adopted child taken away from them for nothing more than practicing their vegan lifestyle. I have learned not to discuss my personal dietary preferences with certain people. My family doctor thought I was nuts for not eating *anything* that comes from an animal, but then was astounded by my cholesterol levels. My Midwestern in-laws find me even loonier, and I think they worry that their son will one day die from that dreaded diseaselackomeatomia." Davis's experience is not uncommon.

This is a paradox: Several million Americans do not eat meat, and sales of vegetarian food and products are soaring. Vegetarians report that they experience acceptance, even admiration, but also misunderstanding as well as alienation, suspicion, and rejection. Their forebears did as well. At the advent of the vegetarian movement in the

1830s, the culture characterized those who did not eat meat as emasculated, heretics, feeble, even insane.

Another paradox: If recent polls are correct, the per capita percentage of vegetarians has increased only modestly in the past few years, lagging significantly behind the explosive growth of foods and products that don't contain animal products. Yet the number of young vegetarians, and especially vegans, seems on the upswing.

Sociologist Donna Maurer, PhD, author of *Vegetarianism: Movement or Moment* and a vegetarian, studies the progress of vegetarianism in the United States:

> It's difficult to define what constitutes "success" for a social movement. If a movement that maintains a body of adherents, an organizational structure, and a fairly cohesive philosophy can be regarded as successful, then yes. If success means helping to create a culture that is more conducive to enacting that philosophy—then, to some degree, yes. If success means effecting large-scale, broad changes in society on a political level, then no. If it means attracting an increasing percentage of the population that consistently practices a vegetarian diet, then studies would suggest the movement has not been very successful.... While people are generally more accepting of vegetarian diets and vegetarian food, and there seems to be a larger proportion of partial vegetarians, there does not seem to have been a dramatic rise in the percentage of the population that consumes no meat/poultry/seafood.

THE JOYS AND FRUSTRATIONS

Paradox notwithstanding, people report that they enjoy being vegetarian and vegan. Anne Weaver, an octogenarian from North Carolina who stopped eating meat in 1989, says, "The joy of being a vegan is that food actually tastes better and that I feel that I am healthier. But the frustration is that places to eat out are scarce." Pavlina explains,

> The greatest joy of being vegan is having a clear conscience. Knowing that I am doing the best I can to prevent animals from suffering makes me feel great. Raising vegan children is also extremely rewarding because my children get to start out their lives with a clean conscience. I feel good knowing I am not polluting their bodies with animal protein, fats, and artery-clogging cholesterol.
>
> I think the greatest joy comes from exposing someone to this way of life and watching their internal lightbulb go on. When someone really "gets it" there is no greater satisfaction for me. This happened just

yesterday when I saw my hairdresser. She told me that since our last meeting and conversation a month earlier, she had given up eating dairy. She reported that she felt a lot healthier, and was happy to not be contributing in that way to the misery of animals. The frustration comes from so many more people not "getting it."

Despite the march of time, fallacies, including the belief that vegetarians eat fish, persist. For example, best-selling science fiction and fantasy author and vegetarian Piers Anthony recalls an experience he had in the military years ago: "In the Army another soldier asked me whether I was a vegetarian, and I said yes. He asked whether I ate fish, I said no. Then he said that his cousin was a vegetarian, and he ate fish, so I wasn't a vegetarian. A few months later I was told that this person committed suicide. I remain slightly bemused."

Millions of Americans, however, are understanding and moving toward vegetarianism, which offers hope to those who work for this change. "I have personally influenced change in the lifestyle of many people who have become vegetarian or vegan after following my example—this has been very personally rewarding and encouraging," writes Dash Dennis, a member of the Vegetarian Society of Stillwater in Oklahoma. On the other hand, Dennis has been harassed: "I had a heckler last year wearing an 'EAT MEAT' T-shirt."

Rachel Mertz, a young adult from Fargo, North Dakota, who enjoys being a vegetarian and educating others, says stereotypes are a problem. "I think that vegetarians are mainly still seen as radicals. The media still depicts most of us as being gay, weak and annoying. I do think it will change when more and more people become educated, which is where most of the work of activists lies right now." Mertz maintains her sense of humor. "In a city in nearby Perham, Minnesota, there is a billboard-size sign on a farmer's lawn which reads 'PETA: People Eating Tasty Animals,' which I find ridiculous. My stepfather distributes People Eating Tasty Animals bumper stickers, which adorn every old rusty pickup, to redneck country folk, as I mail his hunting friends vegetarian starter kits as a joke!"

Other problems plague vegetarians. Diane Payne, a paralegal in Rehoboth Beach, Delaware, says she encounters difficulty finding restaurants that are "veg friendly" when traveling or just dining with family or friends.

> When going out with family/friends who are nonvegetarians at times it is difficult, for certain restaurants do not accommodate and I must be prepared to eat a salad and side dishes. Then, there are the restaurants who always try to prepare a pasta dish as a solution. There is a lack of creativity at times with food preparation.... The worst experience I

have had is dealing with staff at restaurants who are not versed with their restaurants' food preparation. The restaurants do not educate their staff as to what products offer no animal products. Soup is always the issue. I always have to ask if their soup is made with a chicken/beef broth.

Despite these annoyances, Payne loves being a vegetarian and sharing with others:

There are many joys. My conscience is not weighed down by guilt of how the animals are treated who are used for human consumption. I live a healthy lifestyle due to being a vegetarian, which provides me with more energy. . . . I would have to say the times that bring a smile to my face and my heart is when my telephone rings and it's my twelve-year-old nephew (nonvegetarian) who lives in another state, calling to tell me about something he has read or seen, such as a group protesting fur or a restaurant in the area that has veg friendly dishes for when I come to visit, etc. My being a vegetarian has brought awareness to him that he may not have considered before. That makes my heart sing.

Rod Colletti, too, enjoys the fruits of a plant-based diet. The founder of the New Orleans Vegetarian Association, which was a viable organization before Hurricane Katrina struck the city, experiences joy knowing that his diet helps to reduce animal suffering. But Colletti says vegetarians who do little to promote the veggie lifestyle or the animal rights movement frustrate him, as well as "Sicilian/ Italian Catholics, who tell me, while eating meat, 'If you only knew how 'good' this tastes.'" He says, "My best friend (for forty-eight years) tried to justify eating animals by saying, 'That's why they were *put here*.'" Colletti told his friend, "Animals were not 'put here'— they grew here, just the same as everything else on this planet 'grew here'!"

Jennifer Rubenstein, executive director of EarthSave Louisville in Kentucky, says, "The joy is the great feeling you get three times a day when you eat and know you are having a powerful impact on the world. The frustration is the 'unevenness' of veg awareness (people/restaurants with awareness and options—some are very aware, others are clueless) and the lack of connection to some folks who choose to remain meat eaters because of custom/taste, even after they are aware of the facts."

The joy of being a vegetarian, says Rob Pierson of New Mexico, "is eating well and encouraging positive change" while the frustration stems from the "lack of cultural acceptance of personal/ethical integrity as a real motivation for choosing a vegetarian lifestyle." Pierson explains: "The most persistent annoyance is some variation on the cheerfully delivered 'I know you're a vegetarian, but you do eat chicken/fish, right?' The most troubling comments are from individuals who accept the health benefits of vegetarianism but are incredulous that either (a) animals suffer or (b) we might care."

Alyssa Aftosmes, a twenty-two-year-old student at Providence College, enjoys being a vegetarian, but knows problems accompany the choice not to eat meat.

Being a strict vegetarian in America definitely presents challenges on some front. On the one hand, there are usually options for me at restaurants (although you can only go out to a nice dinner and order salad so many times), and usually people find my decision interesting and want to know more about it. I like striking up discussions about what I believe is right for me, but I refuse to get on a soapbox on the issue; people are much more receptive if you make the point that you respect how others feel, but vegetarianism was a very personal decision. On the other hand, organic and vegan products tend to be on the pricey side. As a college student, I'd like to see the food I love to eat be as affordable as other products available to nonvegetarians. I do love the aspect of feeling like I belong to a special community of people; people who are practicing nonviolence and who are willing to make huge life changes to take a stand for what they believe in.

The women's studies major says people have asked her some rather strange questions.

"If you were stranded on a desert island, and the only thing left to eat anywhere was an animal . . ." You get the idea. I find that most people are just interested in learning more about why I decided to live this way. At the same time, people approach the subject with hesitation, as though scared that they'll offend me. Patience and respect for others' decisions are certainly important. I find that I am able to express myself and give heartfelt explanations when I don't get all riled up and offended. From family, most brushed my decision off as a phase, others told me I was being ridiculous. There were concerns about me getting enough nutrients and vitamins out of my diet, so I bought some great books that really helped me to balance everything.

Vegetarian leaders also report similar joys and frustrations. Erik Marcus, author of *Meat Market: Animals, Ethics, and Money*, says, "Every time I can get a young person to become vegan, I've saved at least 2,000 animals from a lifetime of misery and a brutal death."

Alyson Powers, grassroots activist. Courtesy Alyson Powers.

Naturally, not everyone will go along with Marcus. "The unfavorable comments are too numerous and explicit to mention."

Bruce Friedrich, known to millions as the vegan campaign coordinator for PETA, says, "It's a joy knowing that what I'm doing is decreasing the amount of suffering in the world. I wake up every morning excited about going to work!" Unkind or ignorant comments directed at Friedrich do not deter him—"Like water off a duck's back. The provocative comments are an indication that people are listening."

Ingrid Newkirk, cofounder and president of PETA, tells of what delights her in promoting veganism: "Seeing people no longer have acne, cramps, bronchitis, and no longer be at such high risk for heart disease, stroke and cancer, the diseases that killed my father." As the leader of the world's premiere animal rights group, Newkirk receives plenty of praise, but draws criticism and evil acts of revenge. She writes, "Oh, I don't take anything personally so I see any nasty words are just an indication of the guilt I may arouse. PETA's advocacy scares the pants off the meat industry and dairy people, so they can get pretty vindictive in trying to kill the messenger, something that reflects on them, I'd say. The worst is knowing animals suffered to 'get back' at me or PETA, when someone hurts one deliberately and sends the body or limbs or organs through the mail."

Cruelty toward vegetarians who feel empathy for farmed animals is not uncommon, yet it's usually from ignorance.

Alyson Powers, founder of the Farm Animal Welfare Network, a resource and activity group for the University of Iowa, explains how it feels to care:

> The joys of promoting veganism are many. On a personal level, it makes me feel good to know that I am out there doing something for the animals instead of just doing nothing but feeling despair over the suffering animals endure. It is easy to get discouraged and overwhelmed thinking there is nothing one person can do to spare lives and lessen the immense suffering of farm animals. I can sit at home and feel sad and angry about the situation or I can turn that energy into positive action that educates the public about what happens at factory farms. It is also a fun way to meet people and engage in interesting conversations about important issues. It is also nice to see people's defenses lower and to see their stereotypes break down about vegans and animal rights activists. People often reveal their stereotypes when they tell me things like, "Oh, you're a vegan? You look really healthy!" or are surprised to talk with animal activists who are friendly and discuss their views calmly and rationally.
>
> And of course, the *ultimate* joy is when people tell me that they have become vegetarian or vegan because of some literature I gave them when I was leafleting or a discussion we had at an info table or a film that they saw on TV that we submitted. Even people telling me that they've cut back on meat or are only buying eggs from free-range farmers makes me happy. I know the materials I help distribute have planted a seed and they will continue to think about the reality that animals' lives are involved in the production of their food.
>
> The frustrations of promoting veganism are that many people do not want to think about the source of their food because it makes them very uncomfortable—for obvious reasons. They don't want to change their habits that rely so much on meat, eggs and dairy. So although not everyone I encounter will be receptive to the message, I still feel that on some level I am making a difference. Even if they go home that evening and gripe about someone handing them a brochure about factory farming or veganism, at least they are talking about it. Also, the next time they hear about these issues, it will not be such a foreign topic to them and they may be more receptive than they were the first time they heard it and reacted defensively.

Chris Heinrich. Courtesy Chris Heinrich.

University of Idaho senior Chris Heinrich's decision not to eat
animal products really hit home:

> My family has always been in the food industry. My brother is a chef in
> Las Vegas, my dad was in the meat brokerage business for over twenty
> years, my other brother distributed meat products throughout the
> Northwest, and my family owned a deli/grocery/catering business in
> north Idaho for a year. My dad especially didn't understand why I had
> these feelings to stop eating animal products. We would go out to
> restaurants, and he would get extremely upset. I tried to explain to him
> why I was vegan. Now he goes out of his way to find foods that I can eat
> and restaurants we can go to. The main thing I learned is to not get
> defensive. If I explain myself without making myself seem superior or
> better than meat eaters, things work out a lot better.

Heinrich can't recall a bad experience. "Most people just don't understand the reasoning behind what it means to be vegan. It's interesting how people can make fun of other people for doing something
that represents compassion and being cruelty free."

People who eat meat rarely confront Steven Baer, a Massachusetts
vegan and animal rights activist.

> Maybe because I'm a tall, level-headed, muscular male that most rude
> comments either never get said to me or they just don't stick with me.
> People tend to speak to me in endearing terms like calling me the "vegan

man" as if I were some idyllic late nineteenth century, rough-tough, plainsman that cigarette commercials embellished. At my job I have been called "Primate Protector" and my phone "The Monkey Phone," a take-off on Batman and the bat phone. Neighbors, passersby, and many others have complimented me for caring more about animals than I do about people—some have said, "People have rights too!" Usually, no matter where I go when I am educating people about human abusiveness towards animals, someone invariably will say, "Get a life, get a job," or "Why don't you protest xyz issue?"

Baer experiences a somewhat different frustration:

One of the frustrations of being a vegan in a meat-eating culture is seeing a physically attractive woman morph into a repulsively vulgar flesh-ripping cannibal at the drop of a dining plate. It is equally difficult to see the charred remains of an animal neighbor laid out disemboweled on a kitchen or restaurant table. Being in the company of carnists for long is difficult also because the conversation invariably touches upon restaurants or food that were tried, and then it begins to sound to me like a rehash of a stone age conquest of an unsuspecting gentle individual that was cornered, attacked, and chopped to bits in some more uniquely deviant way than the last. The joy I feel as a vegan comes from looking into the eyes of a cow, a sheep, a pig, a dog, a cat, a chicken, a squirrel, a snake, or any manner of creature and think-speaking—we are safe in each other's company; no one here wants to cause harm to the other; and then feeling agreement from the creature upon that thought.

Meat eaters might poke fun at vegetarians, or they might express admiration and say that they aspire to one day "kicking the meat habit." Others make rude, strange, or hostile comments. Author Brenda Davis, RD, offers her theory on these comments:

When you hold a mirror up to someone (which is what you are doing when you behave in an appropriate, yet unpopular way), you force them to see themselves and their behavior in an unflattering way. Many people will react to this by lashing out at the mirror (you). In other words, I think that on a very deep, intuitive level, all people know that killing is wrong. By eating in a way that does not involve killing, while in the company of others who are dining on flesh, the violence on their plates becomes all the more obvious. It then feels uncomfortable to the person consuming the flesh, who may become defensive and strike out at you, instead of really looking at themselves or questioning their own dietary choices.

Mark Braunstein, author of *Radical Vegetarianism*, gives his perspective on sharing food with people who eat meat: "Sometimes I cannot sit at the same table with acquaintances and friends while they dine on the dead bodies of my animal buddies. The offensive odor has much to do with it, but so does my defensive posture. The disappointment I feel about them is my burden, not theirs, and the loss of companionship is solely mine. Yet I easily tolerate strangers who eat meat at the table next to mine. Go disfigure."

The decision to not eat meat can come between relatives, spouses, and friends like a wedge. While the parties involved might remain intimate, the fact that one eats meat and the other does not could cause problems—not uncommon whenever two people do not share the same values.

Professor and author Tom Regan, PhD, philosopher of animal rights, has written an essay on this subject in booklet form titled *Vegetarianism and Friendship*. When asked about the possibility that a vegetarian and a meat eater can be truly close friends or romantic partners, or if differences regarding diet and attitudes toward farm animals will always be beneath the surface, Regan replied, "Friendships come in degrees. They are deepest when friends share the same vision and care most about the same things. This includes what we eat, and what we don't. In this sense, and for this reason, while vegetarians can have nonvegetarian friends, friendships of this sort never will be of the deepest variety."

Vegetarians who aren't in the limelight share similar joys and frustrations. Brian Duprey, founder of Duprey Cosmetics, says, "The joy is simply knowing that vegan is simply the human truth and way we should live. I find extreme joy that I have been able to find my way to it in a world that teaches us otherwise. Many other people may not agree with my frustration but I am frustrated at the boom of vegan junk food products. It is now possible for vegans to have many of the same weight-related issues due to diet as meat eaters do."

Jinjee Talifero of California tells us, "The joy is in inspiring others with the hope that they can be healthy. They don't have to be sick. They can take responsibility for and thereby power over their own health. The frustration is that most people don't really want this responsibility. They do like to complain about the abusive power of the medical industry though. We need to wake up to the connection here. When you give away responsibility you also give away power. It is up to the individual to become more responsible."

She finds it odd that people still believe that vegans need to get vitamin B_{12} from supplements. "They ask, 'Where do you get your B_{12} if not from cows?' Well where do cows get it from? Grass! What is B_{12}?

Is it a protein? Fruits and vegetables all have every one of the eighteen amino acids needed for bodily function. Or else how could vegetarians still be alive? You'd think this myth would have died already."

Law student Jill Ballard explained the best and worst aspects of her vegetarianism: "The best is the empowerment of making one's own choices, eschewing conformity, saving money, and of course, the *food*. The worst is being so aware of the horror, being surrounded by ignorant murderers, and getting stuck in situations where the stench of death is all around." Ballard says someone even tried to trick her. "In class last semester, a veggie classmate gave me a bag of vegan marshmallows. The woman who sat next to me asked in an insecure tone, 'You guys are *vegetarians*? What do you do for protein?' Ironically, the same student tried to trick me into eating cheese pizza when the contracts professor brought in a pizza where the cheese looked like the crust with oil on it and green pesto."

Generally, vegetarians are pleasantly surprised when a meat eater understands vegetarianism. On the other hand, they are fustrated when meat eaters are unconcerned about the plight of animals raised for food. Jill Cirivello, of the Citizens for Animal Rights of Eastern Iowa, says, "The joy is when someone gets it. The frustration is that it feels like there is a holocaust going on with the animals and no one wants to listen." Some of the comments she has received include these: "Guilt about eating meat themselves and apologizing for the freezer full of meat they have in their basement. . . . statements like, 'You won't convert me; I *love* my meat!' or 'Why don't you worry about more important issues that involve human beings?' "

Some say that people in urban areas tend to be more favorable toward vegetarianism. Heather Wise, twenty-four, of Brooklyn, perceives a "split attitude" toward vegetarianism and veganism. "I think in urban areas there is an acceptance and welcoming. New vegetarian restaurants are opening here every day. I basically never have to worry about going to a restaurant and not having options. But in more conservative, traditional areas outside the city I think the attitude is mainly negative. In those areas the vibe I get is that it's silly and a nuisance and what the hell *do* you eat anyway."

Lingering stereotypes, no matter what locale, frustrate people who do not eat meat. Dick Nunez, a vegetarian and Seventh-Day Adventist who lives in South Dakota, says, "People think you can still eat fish and chicken and be vegetarian. That is frustrating, especially being a total vegetarian. Remember, a vegan does not use leather either. I am not vegan since I still wear leather shoes. I am a total vegetarian. Also, people think you will get weak on this diet. I have weighed as much as 292 lbs. with a 500 lb. bench press." Unlike others, Nunez rarely gets pelted with rude comments regarding what he eats. "I guess at 292 lbs.,

Dick Nunez enjoys vegetarianism. Courtesy Dick
Nunez.

no one 'pops off' to me about being vegetarian. However, I in turn do
not make people feel bad if they still eat meat."

Leah Mickens, a college student studying library science at the
University of South Carolina, finds stereotypes problematic. "Aside
from finding food in smaller, less diverse towns, the biggest hassle is
stereotypes. Everyone thinks that if you're vegetarian, then you're a
hippy or socialist or just plain crazy. But I do feel that as a vegetarian
that I am able to enjoy a much greater variety of foods than the average
meat-eating American."

Like others listed here, Mickens hears the occasional odd comment.
"Aside from the peculiar notion that fish is a vegetable, someone
wanted to know, 'What the (expletive) is a vegan?' So I guess it really
hasn't permeated regular culture that much. . . . The worst is when
people leave nasty notes on my car accusing me of not caring about
children just because I care about animals."

New York City resident Pamela Rice, author of *101 Reasons Why I
Am a Vegetarian*, turned fifty on April 15, 2005, "in fact the exact same
day that McDonald's also turned fifty. Yes, I was born the exact day
that Ray Kroc opened his first restaurant, and as luck would have it just
a matter of a few miles from that ominous event." Rice thinks the best
part about being a vegan "is the personal satisfaction that comes with
it, both mental and physical. The worst part is the world around me.
The ignorance and utter meanness of meat eaters is a constant source
of strife and anguish. I try to segregate myself from the meat-eating
world as much as possible. At the moment, I don't have to interact with

meat eaters too much. I know that most vegetarians do not have this luxury and often have to endure a lot of boorish and tasteless abuse."

Rice shares an experience: "Once, when I was passing out my pamphlet [later the basis of her book] at a street fair, a woman asked me why I'm a vegetarian. I was, of course, wearing a signboard at the time that read, 'Ask me why I'm a vegetarian.' I make a point of being very polite when people probe my reasons on this subject. However, in this case, the woman asked the question, 'Why are you a vegetarian?' while she gnawed on a dead turkey leg stump (commonly known as a 'drumstick'). I remained polite in spite of the display, although to this day I kind of regret that."

Mary Margison, a communications major at the University of Rhode Island, wrote, produced, and directed a film about the pet bird trade. She explains her joy in abstaining from all animal products: "The best thing about being vegetarian for me, besides not eating animals, is when people ask me why I'm vegan. I thrive on finding opportunities to tell people that milk and cheese are not benign by-products of keeping cows, and that eating eggs is ethically equivalent to eating chickens. Then I offer a cup of soy milk and a vegan cookie." She is also pleased to set an example for children. "Ethical children will grow from watching ethical adults in action." Among people of her own age group, Margison finds, "Most people give me a look and ask me what I eat. I give them a long list of food (grilled veggies, portabella mushrooms, pasta with garlic and olive oil, veggie burgers and tofu dogs, all sorts of amazing faux meats, rice with veggies, peanut butter and jelly sandwiches, etc.). Their next question is usually to ask why I am vegetarian. Over time my answer has been shortened to, 'If you knew where your meat came from and what was in it, you'd be vegetarian too.'"

Some meat eaters perceive veganism as a challenge. Margison recalls when older relatives at a party "cornered my sister (who is also vegetarian) and I and told us that we're going to hell for not eating meat because Jesus said in the Bible that you have to eat meat to be a good Christian, or something. . . . Of course, when asked to show where exactly it says that, they get huffy and walk away." Overall, Margison has met "very few people who were actually against the idea of vegetarianism. I hear more of 'I could never do that' than anything else, which says to me that far more people than we think have really thought about it for themselves. I think this is a huge change from the past, and it indicates to me that vegetarians and vegans are far more accepted now than we have been in generations."

Shaun Monson, documentary filmmaker and actor from Burbank, California, states that for him veganism results in "only peace of mind and joy." But the Hollywood and documentary filmmaking community has not exactly welcomed Monson and his *Earthlings*, a documentary on the commercial use of animals, with open arms.

> Not yet. At least not enough for me as a documentarian. *Earthlings* has been turned down by more than one documentary film festival, which I always find the most disheartening. Distributors have told me *"Earthlings* will never see the light of day." Cable companies have told me to "sweep it under the rug." Even a close friend of mine at the Humane Society said, *"Earthlings* is the definitive film of all time that Americans don't want to see." I'm often asked to cut the film down, or edit around the most disturbing aspects of the film. But the documentary is the nonfiction film, so for me to cut any of that footage out would be to cut truth out, as far as I'm concerned, and I won't do it.

However, the documentary film industry, like the commercial film industry, needs to make money, "which means they need to be a crowd pleaser and be entertaining," says Monson, "so audiences don't like to experience discomfort when watching a film, including documentaries, as well as the six o'clock news."

Far from Hollywood, in Vermont, Judy Miner shares the ups and downs of going against the meat-eating current of society:

> The joy of being vegan is knowing that in some small way I am helping to prevent a miserable life and early death for animals. In that way I am also reducing the suffering in a world that has far too much of it. Being vegan has led me to try many foods I may have otherwise ignored. My diet is far more interesting (and delicious) than the typical meat-heavy American diet. My biggest frustration is my inability to persuade more people to become aware of the issues and change their diet choices. Another frustration is the difficulty of avoiding all animal products in things I use. We don't live in a vegan-friendly world and compromise is inevitable.

Miner was for several years an officer of the Vermont Vegetarian Society.

Like Miner, vegetarians in other parts of the United States face difficulties when it comes to acceptance. Being a vegetarian can be very difficult in Texas, explains Gloria Weers, who resides in the town of Converse, and who has two grown children who are also meat free. How do fellow Texans react to Weers's abstinence from meat?

"Our doctor sort of ignores us. Good friends either understand or think we are 'daft.'" People rarely make rude comments to Weers. "I am too old to get any of these out loud. The worst we hear are dead animal jokes, etc."

Some people who eat no meat are frustrated with people who have abandoned veganism. For the last six years, Krissy Vandenberg, executive director of Vegan Action of Richmond, Virginia, has given presentations across America on living the vegan lifestyle, the vegan product certification campaign, and how to veganize college cafeterias. Vandenberg, also the mother of a vegan baby, finds joy "meeting new vegans everywhere I go. I am regularly surprised when I meet vegans in the places I would least expect. The biggest frustration is meeting ex-vegans. For a lot of younger folks, vegetarianism and veganism have sometimes been fads in the last ten years and many of them have given it up for whatever becomes the new fad. Our greatest challenge and most important goal are educating people to be veg for life."

Lewis Regenstein of Atlanta, Georgia, founder and president of the Interfaith Council for the Protection of Animals and Nature, feels joy when "going to a great restaurant or dinner party and having tons of happy, healthy, humane dishes to eat." Regenstein, author of several books, and active with the Vegetarian Society of Georgia, also shares his frustrations:

> People are always asking, "You're a vegetarian? What can you eat?" I invite them to our Thanksgiving dinner. Roberta Kalechofsky of Micah Publications in Marblehead, Mass., has even published a vegetarian Haggadah for Passover. It is also frustrating that, having a Jewish mother, I am often presented dishes like lobster, and am told, "It's not meat, you can have it." Oy. And of course vegetarians are always being asked where we get our protein—usually by someone who eats so much meat that he or she must constantly be expelling calcium and developing osteoporosis.

California author Vasu Murti told us his perspective:

> The joy is in practicing a consistent ethic of reverence for life; finding new ways to live cruelty free, and sharing this knowledge with others, in the hopes of making a better world for the animals and for other human beings. The frustration comes from meat-eating America, which is often uninterested or unwilling to take this necessary step towards making it a better world. Perhaps it's because of the stereotype of vegetarianism being associated with "cults" that people react with fear towards vegetarianism. There was an episode from the original *Twilight Zone* series in which an alien from another planet comes to Earth and is gunned down, out of fear, in a rural village. It turns out the alien was coming to Earth with good news: a cure for cancer. With vegetarianism, we have a cure for cancer, heart disease, osteoporosis, overpopulation, etc. And yet, people react with fear.

Contrary to stereotype, not all Alaskans eat meat or hunt wolves from helicopters. Alaskan Delisa Renideo finds joy in knowing that she doesn't support cruelty:

> I have a measure of inner peace knowing that I am making a difference with my lifestyle. I also feel very healthy and energetic and know I will not get cancer, heart disease, diabetes, or any of the other diseases of affluence, so that brings me peace of mind. I love being out in nature and sharing my love with the wild animals, reassuring them that I am their friend and they have nothing to fear from me. As far as frustrations, the biggest is just not being able to bring about the change I so desperately want to see quickly enough.

Thousands of miles to the east, Diane Carr, of Lexington, Massachusetts, encounters lack of interest more than anything else. "Regarding joys, and frustrations, it is mostly frustration. The most frustration I feel is that relatives are not remotely interested to know more. They think it is 'my issue' and I tell them I don't own it. A joy would be when my husband orders tofu. The only other joy I can think of was when I spoke on a local TV show about foie gras, and everyone told me I did a great job—and I think they were influenced to oppose foie gras (but they didn't personally eat it anyway)."

Brenda Davis, RD, past chair of the Vegetarian Nutrition Dietetic Practice Group of the American Dietetic Association, explains her experience as a vegan:

> The greatest joy is in knowing that not a single animal has to suffer and die for me to eat. To me it is simple—eating an animal-centered diet results in environmental destruction, untold pain and suffering, and disease in people. Why would I choose such a diet when not only is it unnecessary to my survival, it impairs my survival? The biggest frustration is knowing that millions of kind, generous and loving people have not yet expanded their circles of compassion to include the animals they eat. They adore their pets, treat their dogs like the cherished members of their families that they are, yet eat equally intelligent and wonderful creatures at almost every meal. It is like living a nightmare.

Judy Carman, a Kansas author, offers her perspective:

> We enjoy our license plates for the front of our cars that read "Eat Tofu." We use these so that we can "talk back" to the many trucks around here that sport a front plate that says "Eat Beef." It's no secret that Kansas is an ultraconservative state. . . . When we show *Meet Your Meat*, narrated by Alec Baldwin, on the sidewalk downtown on Saturday

nights, we get many interesting comments. One night a man who had worked at the Emporia slaughterhouse stopped to look at the video. Some Kansas University students were standing there making fun of the footage, claiming it was faked. The ex-slaughterhouse worker set them straight. He said, "I worked there for four years, cutting the throats of cows, and believe me, it's a lot worse than that." He later told us he had quit his job when it suddenly hit him that these cows were animals with feelings who didn't want to die. He became vegan overnight.

Of course, we also get the occasional hamburger thrown at us, and young guys driving by yelling, "We love animals. They taste good." Some farmers will stop and debate with us, displaying their certainty that God put animals here on earth for humans to use however we want. Of course, many people stop to watch and talk who are either already vegetarian or vegan or considering making the commitment.

The greatest frustration is knowing that no matter what we are doing at the moment, in that moment billions of animals are dying horrible deaths or living in torturous confinement and needing liberation. The greatest joy, though, is that sense of connection—that wondrous feeling of kinship with all life. Knowing you are doing what you can to alleviate their suffering opens a spiritual pathway between you and them. In some mysterious way, I think we can feel their gratitude and their knowing that we will not give up until they are all truly liberated from human domination.

Being "too few," those who abstain from animal flesh are up against a culture that does not hold animals in high regard and does not easily honor the wishes of vegetarians. Despite all the excitement over vegetarian food, fashions, and festivals, are vegetarians and vegans truly accepted? Or as a minority, are they sometimes disrespected?

7

VEGUDICE

No man living can show an instance in which we have attempted to force on the people our peculiar views, or compel others by moral despotism or any other means, to conform to our dietetic regulations. Had we the power to effect all our purposes we should have no desire to compel the people of this country to submit to our dictum, or unwillingly to change any of their habits.

Reverend Sylvester Graham, father of vegetarianism
in the United States, July 20, 1839

During the 1830s, a prominent physician writing in the prestigious *Boston Medical and Surgical Journal* (later the *New England Journal of Medicine*) proclaimed that vegetarians were physical and emotional weaklings. The doctor claimed that a young adult male patient had become weak and emasculated, wet the bed, became insane, and then died—due to lack of meat in his diet. At the time, the press was characterizing the members of Boston, Massachusetts-based American Physiological Society, an early vegetarian organization, as feeble. Some APS members, weakened by long-term illnesses, came to meetings in search of health. On occasion an ailing member of the group died, thus wedding the image of weakness, sickliness, and death to vegetarianism.

Today's media present conflicting depictions of vegetarianism—from sexy and fit celebrity to "child abuser" and animal rights "terrorist."

Deliberate or ignorant misunderstanding of the diet without meat poses a problem, especially when the media perpetuates myths, untruths, and half-truths about vegetarianism and veganism. For example, author John McDougall, MD, uses the word *sensationalism* to describe the response of the mass media, which immediately implies condemnation of vegetarianism or veganism when a rare case arises of a child raised exclusively on foods of the plant kingdom who fails to thrive. Concerning one case in particular, McDougall writes:

> Whenever a story surfaces condemning eating vegetables, especially when the focus is on those eccentric vegetarians, it makes front-page news and is welcome reading for people longing to hear their meat- and dairy-centered diet is better than all that "health food nonsense." Let me begin by acknowledging there is a little truth in most stories that make the headlines. The truth here is that a vegan diet (a diet with no animal products of any kind), unless supplemented with B_{12}, is deficient in this vitamin, and has been found in very rare cases to result in problems of vitamin B_{12} deficiency. B_{12} is made by bacteria and is stored in the body parts of animals that eat these bacteria. If you search the medical literature carefully, you will find about a dozen cases ascribed to a vegetarian diet (search www.nlm.nih.gov)—and almost every one of these has made front-page news. Compare this risk to 1.25 million heart attacks (half fatal) annually in the USA that get almost no media attention and are accepted as part of our modern way of life.

Vegetarians may be typical Americans, but their practice and philosophy of not eating meat, and especially not consuming milk or dairy products, for whatever reason, sets them apart. Jenna Torres, PhD, coauthor of *Vegan Freak*, believes that some who eat meat see those who don't as threats. She tells of a sign on the border of a northwestern state painted with words like "Vegetarians not welcome." "Because we challenge the status quo just by choosing not to eat the Standard American Diet, people think that vegans are self-righteous, crazy ideologues who are out to threaten everyone's way of life. Even though we'd love it if more people became vegan, most vegans I know just wish their own dietary choices to be respected (by having something vegan to eat and not being harassed for it) and won't push their diet on anyone who isn't willing to learn about it," she writes.

Probably every person who always passes on the meat entrée knows the experience of being "the vegetarian" or, if also passing on the egg- and dairy-laden cake, "the vegan"—at a party, at work or school, even at the doctor's office. Vegetarians may be unduly scrutinized for signs of vitamin or protein deficiency, or put in a position of supposedly representing all vegetarians. One person might relish this opportunity to share knowledge of diet and health, world hunger, factory farming, nonviolence, or the emotional life of chickens. "I think anytime we meet someone living a different lifestyle than we are used to, we tend to see that person as a representative of the whole. It's a natural tendency for humans to make generalizations; although often incorrect, generalizations allow for efficient cognition," writes Danielle Marino of Mercy for Animals. Other people do not want or enjoy the role of "the vegetarian." This person does not want what he or she says, does, or eats to represent the vast vegetarian world. The role inevitably seems to invite nonstop questions, which might show genuine interest or might be a game of one-upmanship: meat eater versus vegetarian.

Stanley M. Sapon, PhD, philosopher and professor emeritus of psycholinguistics at the University of Rochester in New York, is well aware of the traps that befall unwitting vegetarians. Sapon recalls being approached, after a presentation he gave at a conference, by a young man who said:

> "I really find myself in trouble when people press me with questions about my values and my lifestyle. What answer can I give to somebody who knows of my concern with animal suffering in research laboratories, and asks me 'Do you really think the life of an animal is worth more than the life of a human being?' What can I say to somebody who learns that I'm a Vegan, and challenges me by asking, 'What would happen to the millions of animals who would *not* be consumed if the world became Vegan?' How do I reply to someone who asks, 'Don't you care about the thousands of hardworking, God-fearing cattle ranchers, dairy farmers and poultry producers who would lose their livelihood if everybody gave up eating meat, cheese and eggs? And what about their poor, innocent families?'"

His struggles to answer such questions set me to reflect on how my own professional experience might cast some light on a problem that Vegans so often encounter. The first thing to become clear was that he had been deceived by a grammatical form. *He had been attempting to answer...as questions...fragments of rhetoric that were not simple questions.*

What disarmed him, and made him so vulnerable, was his inability to determine *when a question is a genuine inquiry...and when it is not.* First of all, he failed to recognize that everything that has the grammatical *form* of a question is not always a request for information. The "questions" about animals in research and agricultural economics were certainly not requests for factual information that might be found in an encyclopedia. At best, they are challenges to the validity of Vegan ethical values, and at worst, thinly disguised attacks on Vegan lifestyle or perspectives. Second, he failed to realize that the person who phrases the "question" also frames the "rules of engagement" that oblige the respondent to accept the legitimacy of the proposition to be explored. Just because someone asks you a "question" does not mean that you are obliged to reply in accordance with the premises of the "question." Perhaps the most grievous tactical error of all derives from honest attempts to address the issues within the framework of a "question and answer." Categorically, it is impossible to answer a question that is nothing more than a challenge to a verbal, philosophical, or moral *duel*. The person who asks if you value an animal's life above a human's is not really interested in *your* views. What your interrogator is seeking is an opportunity to push you into defending an indefensible position, and solidly confirm the correctness of *his* views and the wrongness of *yours*. To attempt to answer the question—as phrased—is to acknowledge the validity of an "either-or" choice, as well as the fallacious assumption that killing animals saves human lives. If you fall into the trap, you will find yourself defending positions that have no basis in reality. You will be standing in quicksand, flailing at phantom issues, sinking deeper by the minute. *Defending* is the key word here.

Sociologist Bob Torres, PhD, coauthor of *Vegan Freak*, explains his take on this problem:

I always tell my students that there's always a price to pay for going against social norms. This is true regardless of the level of infraction; breaking social rules or running against expectations means that you could end up anywhere along a continuum that includes prison, ridicule, or even puzzlement. Though vegans and vegetarians aren't really breaking any rules, we do things that are contrary to what's expected in meat-eating America, and we pay for that by being ridiculed and/or mis-portrayed in the media, by being laughed at as crazies, or by being shunned during social occasions. These are the things that we live with as vegetarians, and for vegans, it is even worse, because we're seen as marginal extremists. We're either hippies or terrorists (or, if the particular source is nasty enough, both). So, with that said, there are challenges, and most of the challenges in being vegan or vegetarian come from learning how to live contrary to expectations. The joys of vegetarianism and veganism seem to stem from the same place, at least for me. We're pleasant reminders that there's something wrong with meat-centric America, and we remind people of that. When you connect with someone and your own choices get them to think twice about theirs, that's powerful. In terms of joys, America also offers a great variety of vegan foods, and overall tolerance for vegans and vegetarians isn't as bad as in some places, so on balance, it isn't all that bad.

More than 170 years have passed since American Physiological Society members gathered in Boston, which was the hub of vegetarian activity in those days. Yet stereotypes of vegetarians still abound. For example, the term *strict vegetarian* carries a negative connotation in pleasure-seeking America. The dominant culture perceives meat eating as pleasurable, so it perceives someone who rejects meat or all animal-derived foods as a pleasure anorexic—a pathological denier of the enjoyment of meat.

However, vegetarians are joyful about what they do—and do not—eat for dinner, and the problems they encounter as minorities do not diminish that joy or sway them to eat meat. But there are exceptions who run back to the meat counter when the heat of being different becomes unbearable. Sometimes the problem of being vegetarian is just an annoyance, such as when they are asked by meat eaters, "Where do you get your protein?" This question has over the decades become a joke among vegetarians. When a vegetarian tells another, "I was asked the *protein* question," a bond of understanding is forged. "Oh, you get that ridiculous question, too!" might be the reply. The vegetarian world knows that foods from the plant kingdom contain abundant protein, but the dominant culture and the meat industry seem to perpetuate the long-ago-dispelled idea that one must eat meat and even drink milk for protein, meaning for strength and health.

Another common annoyance occurs when waiters or waitresses, or perhaps well-meaning parents or grandparents, assume a meal containing chicken or fish is "vegetarian." Certainly, many meat-eating people realize the vegetarian diet provides plenty of protein, and all know that chickens and fish are not plucked from plants. However, the protein myth and chicken-fish dilemma continue, even among the younger generation, but to a lesser extent. People who eat no meat find it difficult eliminating misinformation and feel uncomfortable being the recipient of stereotyping.

Sometimes the stereotypes or prejudice lurk below the surface. Once Pamela Rice decided to stop eating meat, she took to the streets of New York City wearing a signboard, "Ask me why I am a vegetarian," and handing passersby her pamphlet, *101 Reasons Why I'm a Vegetarian*, which was published as a book in 2005. Like any author, Rice hoped to share her book with people she knows and brought it to a social gathering.

> Just a month or so since my book has come out, I was at a family gathering. Now I believe that if my book had had any other title under the sun, everyone there would have been cooing and fussing over it. They would have wanted to touch it, leaf through it, even read a page or two. But there was something about this title—*101 Reasons Why I'm a*

Vegetarian—which, I guess, upset them. You'd think my book was chametz on Passover....In other words, they treated it as if it were something to be swept up and disposed of. At the same time, it seems, I became invisible. I could tell that the people around me were demonstrably more uncomfortable than usual around me. They knew, I think, that the embodiment of my persona was wrapped up with that terrible little book, something that now seems to separate me from the people I love.

No one insulted or ridiculed Rice, but her experience was, in our opinion, just as real as any other form of prejudice. Call it "vegudice." Undoubtedly there are people who will think vegudice a stupid or trivial idea, or an insult to people who experience racism, sexism, and other acknowledged prejudices. Yet vegudice exists.

Vegetarians are not supposed to violate basic unwritten rules of society regulating what they can say and do and still be considered polite and appropriate. "Just as in any cohort, one bad apple can spoil the whole bunch. Specifically, I mean that a rude, 'holier-than-thou,' or disrespectful vegetarian can leave a nonvegetarian with the generalization that all vegetarians are that way," says Danielle Marino.

However, while Marino makes an interesting and important point, the parameters of what constitutes "holier-than-thou" or "disrespectful" behavior by vegetarians have been determined by the dominant meat-eating culture that tends to like to muzzle the vegetarian point of view, trivialize it, or call it preachy.

Unwritten rules of polite society preclude vegetarians from being vocal and judgmental, arguably a prejudice against vegetarians. Factory farming would not be a controversy today, and Americans would be totally in the dark on how animals are transformed into meat if not for "preachy" vegetarians.

Society's rules demand that a person never acknowledge that meat on the table was once an animal, except to joke ("Guess Thanksgiving isn't Tom Turkey's favorite holiday!") or to comment on the properties or characteristics of the former animal. ("That sure was a plump bird." "Did you hear that lobster when we threw it into the pot of boiling water? It was a real squealer!")

People who object to meat are well aware that polite, well-adjusted Americans are supposed to maintain silence and not dissent at the dinner table, bemoaning that a turkey drumstick was once part of a living turkey, that a filet was once a living fish, and that spareribs were not donated by a pig.

Author Carol J. Adams says the animal has become what she calls the "absent referent." Her journey to vegetarianism began when she was at Yale Divinity School and mourning for the pony she had loved when suddenly she understood the hamburger she was eating had been an animal. Adams began to consider the ethics of eating meat and a year later became a vegetarian.

Adams writes, "Behind every meal of meat is an absence: the death of the animal whose place the meat takes. The 'absent referent' is that which separates the meat eater from the animal and the animal from the end product. The function of the absent referent is to keep our 'meat' separated from any idea that she or he was once an animal, to keep some*thing* from being seen as having been some*one*."

Like the absent referent, most forms of vegudice are invisible or nearly so. Discussion of vegudice could result in accusations of whinyness, a colloquial term used in the mass media to describe those who speak up for their rights or promote unpopular causes or lawsuits. People who have not experienced vegudice don't notice it.

As time passes, the absent referent becomes more visible. What society now labels as rude or holier-than-thou might not be thought of that way tomorrow. For example, women who spoke out for the vote, and men and women who labeled slavery in vivid language befitting its horror were vilified. Today early feminists and the abolitionists are heroes to millions of people worldwide.

Generally, vegetarians, perhaps to maintain etiquette, out of fear of rejection, or due to a belief that society will not soon, if ever, transform to vegetarianism, do not discuss the fact that meat was an animal. Yet, when the topic does arise among meat eaters, the meat eaters might change their meal choices, even if temporarily. Harvard psychologist Ellen J. Langer, PhD, an expert on mindfulness and author of a book by that title, recalled in her book not wanting to eat roast duck she had ordered in a restaurant. Without thinking deeply, Langer ordered duck directly after she and some children had fed ducks at a pond outside the restaurant. The children were aghast at her order. Roused to the irony of the situation, Dr. Langer became mindful and changed her order. Suddenly the absent referent became visible—figuratively and literally. Although the ducks on the menu were not those who lived by the pond, having seen the ducks and interacted with them made her mindful of the irony of ordering duck flesh for dinner.

Psychology has a name for the process that enables human beings to disregard the fact that animals are slaughtered for meat when this information contradicts their perception of themselves as kind to animals and causes stress: cognitive dissonance.

Vegetarians who attempt to explain to a meat eater that animals raised for food suffer and are met with either a hostile reaction or utterly ignored, likely experience the effects of that person's cognitive dissonance. In other words, meat eaters generally do not want to consider the details of animal slaughter because they do not want to perceive themselves as acting in a way that leads to this suffering; that would not be acceptable to people who consider themselves good people, since, at least in American culture, part of being a good person is to be kind to animals and not cause them fear and death.

Elizabeth Aloisio, MEd, a psychotherapist and cofounder of Quality Behavioral Health of Cranston, Rhode Island, told us that the theory of cognitive dissonace helps explain how the mind's defense mechanisms enable people to consider themselves kind to animals, and yet not think of the reality that the meat on their plate was once an animal who did not want to die. For a person to claim to be an "animal lover" and even an advocate for a particular species of animals, while at the same time remaining a consumer of animal flesh, requires a distortion in thinking for the person to be more at peace with this dichotomy, says Aloisio.

> The individual's mind creates a defense mechanism that allows that person to accept what the inner self might know to be true, or what the inner self might find to be unacceptable. Therefore, the individual may need to deny that animals are cruelly slaughtered, or may need to rationalize or intellectualize the necessity of slaughtering them. To purport that one loves animals, and even defend their rights, while justifying consumption of their flesh requires a gross distortion in thinking to avoid the visceral image that animals were slaughtered to satisfy the individual's desire to eat meat.

Becoming a vegetarian takes more than just changing menu options; one must confront the cognitive dissonance American society encourages. Psychologist Paul Amato, PhD, and Sonia Partridge, in their 1990 book *The New Vegetarians: Promoting Health and Protecting Life*, say it is not uncommon for former meat eaters to report that they became vegetarians after having a sudden revelation that the meat on their plate, or in the grocery store meat case, which they found appetizing smothered in onions, covered in sauce, or served in a sandwich, were body parts of dead animals. Meat eaters even admit to experiencing disgust for meat when they are "reminded that they regularly eat the bodies of dead animals." However, "most of the time, people do a good job of 'forgetting' where meat comes from," the authors say.

Amato first started studying vegetarianism a few years after he stopped eating meat. "It occurred to me that this was an interesting phenomenon, yet no one had studied it from a social scientific perspective. As an area of academic study, it's still unusual. But I see an increasing number of academics writing about vegetarianism and related issues these days . . . one can study and write about vegetarianism without being considered a wacko these days."

Meat eaters who study aspects of meat eating are not considered biased, but vegetarians studying aspects of vegetarianism are still labeled as biased. How can vegetarians minimize or perhaps avoid vegudice? Amato suggests,

> Don't be a missionary and try to convert other people to being vegetarian. If you act that way, people will get defensive. It's better just to set a good example and let people make up their own minds. If you are an ethical vegetarian, don't ruminate or dwell on the issue of animal suffering. You'll only get depressed. Social change occurs slowly, and we have to get used to that. Vegetarianism is a healthy alternative to the mainstream American diet, and it's good for animals and for the environment. But it's not a religion, so don't become a fanatic or an obsessive compulsive about it. Try to have some fun with it.

Naturally, not all vegetarians agree with Amato, who predicts that vegetarianism will become more common and accepted.

Like their meat-eating counterparts, vegetarians are often guilty of stereotyping—that is, stereotyping other vegetarians. New Yorker Rhys Southan explains:

> When I worked for the University of Texas student newspaper, the *Daily Texan*, I had a bit of a rivalry with the token socialist columnist. Then one night at a staff party, he saw me refuse meat because I was a vegan. He was shocked. He was the "compassionate socialist," yet he ate the cheese steak and I was acting like the real hippie.
>
> When I moved into a vegetarian co-op in the fall of 2000, a shocked housemate exclaimed, "A vegan libertarian!?" It's different now. People might be surprised to learn that I'm vegan, or that I'm a libertarian, but it's not the combination of the two that surprises them. It usually works out either way, because it makes me seem more complex and harder to pigeonhole. Liberals can't completely hate me, because with my veganism, I'm as holy as them, or holier. Some right-wingers may be suspicious of my diet, but they're heartened to learn I don't want to take their property.

Similarly, libertarian and home schooling advocate Cathy Cuthbert, who describes herself as a raw food vegan, tells her experiences on LewRockwell.com:

> I cannot without derision expose myself as a vegan to libertarians. Similarly, I cannot reveal my libertarian politics to vegans and escape with my life. What's a vegan libertarian to do? Whenever I go to a vegan potluck, I'm forced to listen to stories of greedy capitalists committing

horrors that only tougher government regulation can dispel. I have to keep my mouth full of kale and carrots for fear that a libertarian sentiment may escape my lips. Only my favorite soup—an amazingly flavorful tomato avocado chowder that I invented myself, e-mail for recipe—prevented the murder of Terry when she said, "I like paying taxes. The more I pay, the more money I get back."

The frustration is different although equally acute with my libertarian friends. When they comment on my habit of eating salad for dinner, I hide behind the excuse of having to watch my weight, adding, "Wow, that steak looks great." I suffer in silence as they hoot and laugh at the crazy "granola crunchers" who are so stupid to think that organic matters. And I'm itching to break it to them that wisecracks about coffee enemas do not demonstrate even the slightest comedic genius. If only I had the courage to wear my "Thomas Jefferson was a vegetarian" sweatshirt—but alas, I don't. . . . I know one thing I absolutely can't do, and that is approach vegans for understanding. To confess my libertarianism would be tantamount to proclaiming myself the devil incarnate.

Varied images of vegetarianism, prejudice against vegetarians, cognitive dissonance thwarting vegetarians' efforts to teach the benefits of a plant-based diet—these are small potholes on the path in comparison to the earthshaking troubles that beset other members of the meat-free U.S. population.

8

LIFE, LIBERTY, AND THE PURSUIT OF VEGETARIAN RIGHTS

We hold these truths to be self-evident, that all men are created equal, that they are endowed by their Creator with certain inalienable Rights, that among these are Life, Liberty, and the pursuit of Happiness.

The Declaration of Independence, July 4, 1776

Prejudice from meat eaters toward vegetarians may be a miniscule problem, or a behemoth that harms their lives. Evidence suggests that vegetarians who work to change society's use of animals, or who just want to exercise their right to refuse vaccination, or who want to raise their children without meat may experience grave trouble.

In today's paranoid political climate of fear of terrorism and controversial laws that undermine the Bill of Rights under the guise of protecting the populace, people who engage in constitutionally protected activities for particular causes—including promoting vegetarianism or working for animal rights—have come under suspicion, scrutiny, and even arrest.

Millions of Americans are vegetarians, but most are not activists. Those who are engage in educational or legislative activities such as letter writing, lecturing, leafleting, or lobbying. Some "veggies" take to the airwaves with their own radio broadcasts, and still others campaign against specific companies that produce paté or chicken cutlets. Vegetarians are among activists campaigning against vivisection (animal experimentation). The American branch of Stop Huntingdon

Animal Cruelty (SHAC) is an organization that critics claim stretches or even surpasses the limits of the First Amendment.

SHAC's Web site features footage of horrifying experiments on frightened beagles and statements like the following: "Currently there are over 15 countries world-wide fighting to shut down Huntingdon Life Sciences forever. Through a well thought out, tactical campaign, these activists have dismantled HLS's financial structure (by getting some of the world's largest financial institutions to drop their support for HLS)."

Vegans in their twenties, the "SHAC 7," Kevin Kjonaas, Lauren Gazzola, Joshua Harper, Jacob Conroy, Darius Fulmer, Andrew Stepanian, and John McGee, are charged in New Jersey under the Animal Enterprise Protection Act. The U.S. Department of Justice in a news release stated:

> Among SHAC's "top 20 terror tactics" recommended and publicized on its websites: invading offices, vandalizing property and stealing documents; physical assault, including spraying cleaning fluid into someone's eyes; smashing windows of a target's home or flooding the home while the individual was away; vandalizing or firebombing cars and bomb hoaxes; and threatening telephone calls or letters, including threats to kill or injure someone's partner or children. The five-count indictment charges SHAC and seven of its members with animal enterprise terrorism.

However, one journalist on the case reported that SHAC's Web site offers "careful advice on what are legally permitted forms of protest and what are not. They only advocate that legal methods be used. They do have articles and reports on other activities, just like any activist Web site that reports information or that publishes articles. This is clearly a First Amendment case."

The outcome of the SHAC 7 trial could affect the future of activism. "The federal indictment against the SHAC 7 is a potential watershed in the history of the animal rights movement, for it represents the boldest governmental attack on activists to date, and it likely augurs a new wave of political repression in response to the growing effectiveness of militant animal liberation politics," writes Steven Best, PhD, chair of philosophy at the University of Texas at El Paso, and coeditor of *Terrorists or Freedom Fighters: Reflections on the Liberation of Animals*, and Richard Kahn, publisher of *Vegan Blog: The (Eco)Logical Weblog*, whose motto is "Don't get mad, get vegan!"

Most vegetarians will not push the limits of the law and face arrest, and the actions of the SHAC 7—legal or not—spark controversy even within the vegetarian world. The efforts of the SHAC 7 fall at the opposite end of the spectrum from leafleting and lobbying for animal rights or to promote vegetarianism. Other activists have exposed factory farming by filming it with hidden cameras or by spiriting away animals. These acts, which might be construed as acts of civil disobedience or compassionate rescue, are increasingly met with draconian responses by government and industry. In recent years, several states have passed animal rights and ecological terrorism laws. Investigative journalist and nationally syndicated radio talk show host Alex Jones, who has made twelve documentaries on the state of America's freedoms, wrote on Infowars.com: "The fake right will support this kind of legislation under the naive belief that it will curtail the extreme left. The legislation is then used to target U.S. citizens. It is important for us to protect the freedoms of both the right and left otherwise we'll be caught in a police state vice which will crush us from both sides."

Attorney Lee Hall, legal director of Friends of Animals, a nationwide animal rights group located in Connecticut that advocates veganism, thinks the rights of law-abiding vegetarians are not threatened, and that vegetarianism is a potent act of protest against the dominant meat-eating culture:

> Minorities' rights are constantly at risk, particularly in a political atmosphere such as we have today, which is so strongly influenced by people who believe their ends justify their means. Vegetarians have a lot going for us, however, because eating plants is perfectly legal. And yet, being a pure vegetarian is a powerfully subversive undertaking. It seeks to change a blood-letting paradigm with a respectful, gentle worldview. That's revolutionary—and it's not repressible in the way illegal activism is. Go out and cheerlead for illegal and violent acts and you become immediately controllable.

But what of most activists, who do not engage in illegal acts, but simply distribute information promoting vegetarianism at demonstrations on behalf of farm animals or for human health?

VEGANS UNDER ARREST

In late 2005, the American Civil Liberties Union of Georgia filed a federal lawsuit on behalf of two vegans who were arrested, Caitlin Childs and Christopher Freeman, who were "subjected to false imprisonment, false arrest, and harassment" by officials of the Homeland Security Division of Dekalb County and the local police department.

A few days before Christmas 2003, Childs and Freeman were standing on public property in front of a Honey Baked Ham store, passing out pamphlets about alternatives to pork. After the protest, the pair noted that they were being watched and photographed by a man in an unmarked car. They walked over to the car and wrote down the license number, make, and model of the car. When Childs and Freeman drove away, they noticed that they were being followed, so they pulled over in a parking lot.

A police officer and a detective with Homeland Security ordered them out of the car and demanded that they hand over the piece of paper with the license number. Childs refused and was searched, and her house keys and the slip of paper were confiscated. Both Childs and Freeman were arrested and charged with disorderly conduct and later released from custody.

By stopping and detaining the activists and refusing to tell them the reason why, Homeland Security and the Dekalb County Police "deprived them of their right to be secure in their person and to be free from unreasonable search and seizure," argues the ACLU.

Vegetarians were shocked by the incident. Talk host Meria Heller says she was horrified. "Homeland security has been set up the same as FEMA, to protect the government from its citizens. I think the work of the protesters at Honey Baked Ham deserves a medal, not an arrest. With obesity, heart diseases, etc. rampant in our country (don't forget Mama Cass died by choking on a ham sandwich), they were doing the right thing. We pay for Homeland Security, thus we pay to have them harass and menace us."

Caitlin Childs told the press, "I hope to send a strong message that activists will not be intimidated by bullying, harassment, and illegal arrests. We will fight back and continue to utilize the rights we are guaranteed by the constitution.... They're using security and the idea of terrorism, which is such a hot word and scares people, to silence people who have unpopular beliefs." Freeman also had a few words to say: "People of this country need to realize that our basic human rights are being whittled away on a daily basis. I hope this case brings to light the fact that anyone can come under government scrutiny."

Other activists echo these sentiments. Chris DeRose, author of *In Your Face: From Actor to Animal Activist*, and founder of Last Chance for Animals, a nationwide animal rights organization based in California, believes that the labeling of certain forms of activism as "domestic terrorism," and in particular legislation that restricts First Amendment freedoms, poses a threat to the promotion of vegetarianism and advocacy for farm animals. "This is an issue very close to my heart because I am seeing where we as activists are rapidly becoming more and more limited on what we will be able to do to help farm [or any other] animals. Already in many states it is now a felony to enter a barn where animals are being held even if it's just for recording the violations and suffering." Despite such threats, DeRose, like other activists, remains undaunted.

It is like a "chilling effect" that is set up to stop people who care about the exploiting of these animals. Once we give up or are too afraid of taking risks these animals won't have a chance in hell and that is where they are—hell! We are all they have and we better do something about it. I would like to see the larger organizations with the millions of dollars to watch what laws are being passed to prohibit activists from doing their job. As primarily an [investigative] organization I feel more and more the restraint of video taping and entering facilities that were once either a misdemeanor or a low grade felony to much more serious violations. We must reverse this and bring it back to the status quo. Either way we must never stop or even slow down our efforts. Never!

Ingrid Newkirk, cofounder and president of PETA, an international organization with headquarters in Virginia, says laws or harassment of activists won't slow them down. "I can't imagine anyone is frightened away from activism by idiotic and repressive laws and attempts to pass them. If anything I think such abuse of power incenses the social activist and makes them all the more determined. The government has been in bed with the meat and dairy industry since the inception of the

Vegan Chris DeRose. Courtesy Chris DeRose.

USDA, certainly, and yet it has had to face facts and make changes in its wretched food pyramid to accommodate and recognize the fact that a vegetarian diet is superior."

In the October 2005 issue of *Satya*, Newkirk wrote a commentary on civil rights detailing how authorities have harassed members of PETA: "Key PETA staffers are met at the plane on our return from every trip abroad and taken into a back room so that everything can be searched while we miss our flight connections. Eighty percent of our staff taking a group trip to Los Angeles to help with our gala in September were searched along with their luggage."

VEGETARIAN SCHOOL

It isn't only activist vegetarians who come up against the law. Those who own a school for young children, or adopt children, or object to vaccinations that contain ingredients derived from animals all claim to have been punished for their beliefs and actions. Challenges posed by the dominant meat-eating culture against vegetarians date back to at least the 1830s, when vegetarian A. Bronson Alcott's Temple School in Boston, Massachusetts, praised by other progressive educators and by Alcott's students and their parents, was admonished by the press and then society. Alcott's use of the Socratic method, his invitation of Sylvester Graham—the leading advocate of vegetarianism—into his classroom, and the fact that he allowed a black child to enroll in the school caused preachers and the press to balk, and parents to yank their youngsters out of the school. One politician called for Alcott's arrest for corrupting youngsters. The school closed. Today Alcott receives accolades from some as a great teacher and a leading Transcendentalist philosopher.

About a century and a half later, in 1983, another educator founded an innovative and vegetarian school that met a fate similar to that of Alcott's. Ellouise Carroll, PhD, says she attracted attention when she switched to serving vegetarian food at her school, the Early Education Center in Puyallup, Washington. "I couldn't, in good conscience, feed the children in my care in a way that I now knew was not healthy for them," she says. The state prohibited the school from going further down the plant-based path. "We were not allowed to be vegan (in order to be licensed in the State of Washington, you *must* serve dairy products and, if you don't serve meat, you actually have to serve twice as many dairy products: one as a liquid dairy and one as a substitute for the meat)."

The school was unique. The children put on shows, singing and dancing in English, sign language, and Spanish. Carroll provided or

taught environmental education, conflict resolution skills, appreciation of culture, cognitive development skills, organic gardening, and
moral values, and held summer day camps. But the school, which drew
favorable media attention, was forced to close after the state revoked
her license. According to state officials, the school was closed in 2003
after a settlement agreement was reached for failure to resolve several
licensing violations. However, Carroll claims,

> [The] stated reason for closing me down was that a child had gotten
> out of the room but the real reason, I believe, was because we were
> vegetarian. Let me explain. We took many [problem] behavior children
> and some of them were runners. We were not allowed to put slider locks
> on the doors to keep these little ones in the rooms so we put locks on all
> the gates so that they couldn't get out even if they got out of the room.
> A child, whose mother was changing another child's diaper, ran out of
> the room. The licensor was told that a child had gotten out of the facility
> (not the room). . . . My parents were aghast and wrote over 100 letters of
> anger to the licensing department, all to no avail. I hired an attorney and
> tried to fight it but, because my $12,000 a month mortgage could not be
> paid with no income, I finally had to say that I accepted them closing me
> down.
>
> I do not believe that most people in the U.S. understand vegetarian-
> ism and veganism, and school administrators are among those with
> misunderstandings.

The *Seattle Times* favorably reported on the bill of fare at Carroll's
ECE Academy by stating that students "get used to homemade bread
with freshly ground wheat, big salads and foods sweetened with
honey instead of sugar" and that the children hardly noticed that their
teacher substituted soy for beef in recipes.

The Notmilk Man, vegan Robert Cohen, who, on syndicated radio
shows like Howard Stern's, promulgates the message that cow's milk is
hazardous to human health, and who has testified before the FDA,
discussed Carroll's case on his Web site Notmilk.com, "Ms. Carroll has
70 children in her school, and she is suing the state and the United
States Department of Agriculture because she does not want to serve
milk to her children. Ellouise has discovered, through a lifetime of
teaching, that milk makes kids wild and creates runny noses, conges-
tion, and asthma attacks. Many years ago, she eliminated milk from
her schools and found the instant cure to many of these children's ills
while improving their ability to learn. Now the state of Washington is
demanding that she give the children milk, and her case is in the
courts."

BETRAYED BELIEFS

Like other people whose philosophies, beliefs, or lifestyles are uncommon, vegetarians often draw disrespect, which for some vegetarians is an almost daily reality. Disrespectful people have been known to teasingly elaborate on the details of a meat meal ("it was so *juicy*") in front of ethical vegetarians; meat eaters have insisted on questioning vegetarians about nutrition, and hosts have purposely excluded vegetarians from social events because meat was served, or invited vegetarians but offered no suitable food.

People who eat no meat are often singled out for their dietary choices or values, sometimes out of ignorance or misunderstanding, or a host of other reasons. In the 1980s, vegetarian Jennifer Graham challenged a high school class rule by refusing on ethical grounds to dissect an animal in science class, but offered to do any alternate assignment. Graham was punished with a low grade for challenging the teacher's law that all students must cut up an animal.

Graham's exercise of her right to refuse to commit an act she believed unconscionable helped spark a social revolution. A few years after her story was publicized, states began enacting laws to protect students' rights to refuse to dissect for ethical reasons, and in some cases to refuse to vivisect (experiment on living animals). By 2005, most medical schools had abolished vivisection laboratory class.

But acceptance of vegetarians and their values rarely moves forward in a linear fashion. Several years ago, John Ouimette, a teen attending a Utah high school was suspended for wearing a T-shirt displaying the word Vegan, apparently because other students calling themselves straight edge and vegan had been involved in trouble at the school. In protest, the sixteen-year-old vegan returned to school wearing a T-shirt that bore a different slogan: "Vegans Have First Amendment Rights." At a rally, Ouimette stated: "Veganism is not gang-related any more than Mormonism or Christianity. Veganism is about compassion and justice for all living beings. Veganism is about promoting nonviolence."

Like Ouimette, others are taking on the system and standing up for their rights as vegetarians—and as Americans. But like Graham, who received a lower grade than she might have, they are not always victorious in their attempts, at least not on the first try. Yet there have been notable exceptions.

When California bus driver and vegan Bruce Anderson was told to distribute coupons for free hamburgers to passengers, he refused on the grounds that promoting meat violated his spiritual beliefs. Instead, Anderson offered to either place coupons in a basket for passengers to help themselves, or to work in the office on days when the coupons were scheduled to be distributed. Anderson, characterized by one magazine as "gaunt, dyspeptic, and amazingly argumentative," was fired from his job. But he took legal action against his boss, the Orange County Transportation Authority. The press reported that Anderson's famous attorney, Gloria Allred, said his beliefs were just "as valid as any religious or political beliefs." He won his case brought before the Equal Employment Opportunity Commission and a $50,000 settlement from OCTA.

Anderson's case made headlines, but not nearly as much as did another victory for the rights of vegetarians: the McDonald's french fries lawsuit. In the early 1990s, the fast-food company announced that their french fries and hash browns were vegetarian since they were cooked in vegetable oil and not beef tallow. But some beef flavoring was added at their potato processing plants. Harish Bharti, Seattle lawyer and Hindu, filed legal action, which soon developed into a class-action suit. McDonald's said it was not required by the U.S. Food and Drug Administration to reveal the use of beef flavoring. In 2002, McDonald's agreed to apologize and to pay out $10 million in settlement money to Hindu groups, and to vegetarian organizations.

Bharti told the press: "Ten years down the road, no one will remember the money. But this apology and disclosure will change the way the food industry treats its customers because McDonald's is the leader in the industry and everyone else will have to follow."

Washington, DC, attorney and vegetarian James J. Pizzirusso "laid the groundwork for the McDonald's class action suit, petitioned the Food and Drug Administration back in 1999, asking it to require that food labels indicate the source of natural flavorings in a product's ingredients," reported *Forward*, a newspaper, in 2002.

REFUSING VACCINATIONS

Like Jennifer Graham, another vegetarian who took a stand lost his case. Jerald Friedman, a vegan, challenged a mandatory vaccination rule at his workplace. Vegetarians who challenge entrenched medical practices that most Americans agree with or erroneously accept as mandatory are modern-day versions of the biblical boy David against the giant Goliath. Thus far, Goliath is winning.

In a statement, Friedman said,

> Ultimately, I was fired from Kaiser Permanente for not complying with an arbitrary policy. I have found no medical or legal reason to be required to take the mumps vaccine. Kaiser claimed to CBS news that the law requires them to vaccinate their employees, but the law does not

(governing law, Title 22, requires a health screening and TB test, no mention of vaccines).

Whenever someone has profoundly held moral values, employers must not force their staff to comply with an arbitrary policy in conflict. Policies should allow for exceptions, just as the law does, because every circumstance cannot be predicted. Ethical Veganism clearly fits into the State definition of religion, generally "one's profoundly held moral values that take the place of traditionally held religions." Ethical Veganism is my guiding principle. Therefore, the purpose of my lawsuit, apart from recovery for injuries I suffered, is to allow other people with profoundly held moral values, vegans or not, to use laws that are already in effect to protect them from arbitrary discrimination even if their morality is not traditional, for I am against discrimination, not just the discrimination against traditional religions. The question should be, "is the policy arbitrary," not "does the person believe like I do."

Friedman lost his case against vaccination. Friedman's attorney, Scott D. Meyer, told the press: "The effect of the ruling would allow courts, and not the believers, to determine what is a 'religion.' Allowing only traditional religions to be protected could lead to the persecution of nontraditional religions, just as Protestants were persecuted in the Dark Ages."

On his Web site, VeganValues.org, Professor Stanley M. Sapon warns, "If Veganism is to attain the respectful recognition that Mr. Friedman and other Vegans believe it merits, Vegans must first insist on plainly labeling the motivations that distinguish Veganism. Then they must earnestly strive to cultivate a climate of understanding and appreciation of Veganism as a universal philosophy, a lifestyle of mindful, nonviolent, gentle, compassionate and unconditional beneficence."

Although no law compels people to be vaccinated, those who dissent might end up in court, or turning to an advocacy group for assistance. Dewey Ross Duffel, a vegetarian for more than thirty years who lives in Montana and works for Vaccination Liberation (VacLib.org), explains the vegetarian perspective on the issue:

> The main reasons for being a vegetarian are religion, health, compassion for animals and to minimize one's impact on the earth. These motives are interrelated, although individuals resonate more to one motive than another. Vaccination is a procedure which violates all four of these motives for being a vegetarian.... A religious person may be allowed to eat flesh but will still abhor the blood pollution of vaccination (religious prohibition and violation of spiritual science) as well as the cruelty to animals (compassion) involved with vaccine creation. Today of course, the ethical questions surrounding the use of cells from aborted babies to culture vaccine virus adds to this situation. Even if one is not

opposed to abortion, the taking of human cells into one's body is akin to cannibalism, a practice which I assume is even more abhorrent to most vegetarians than the killing and eating of animals.... Anyone grounded in the fundamentals of health will naturally not want to take vaccine ingredients into their body. These ingredients include heavy metals like mercury as well as aluminum, which is light in weight but very difficult to eliminate from the body. Other chemical ingredients include formalde-hyde, phenoxyethanol (a component of antifreeze) and antibiotics. Animal ingredients include monkey cells, eggs, chick embryos, pig pan-creatic cells, sheep red blood cells, gelatin from cow and pork sources. This list should not be considered complete. Also, I look at immunity as the natural result of health, that is, immunity is created by a clean bloodstream that is well nourished. Where there is health, there is no need to stimulate the immune system with concoctions made of waste matter and poisons. Besides, the procedure is ineffective. Pediatricians who have both vaccinated and unvaccinated children in their practice know firsthand that unvaccinated children are healthier. A proper vegetarian diet promotes health and thus is of benefit to one desiring immunity. Health is the only real immunity.

Are American rights and the freedoms of vegetarians that are pro-tected by the Constitution threatened or under attack? Attorney James J. Pizzirusso of Cohen, Milstein, Hausfeld & Toll, PLLC—a pioneering and powerhouse plaintif class-action law firm—told us,

> It's not necessarily that vegetarians' Constitutional rights are at risk—they don't even really exist insofar as they relate to veganism. What Mr. Anderson and Mr. Friedman (as well as others) have been attempting to do is to get courts to recognize that vegans can hold deep moral beliefs which are similar enough to other religions that those views should be given some protection under the Constitution. Courts have been reluc-tant to recognize such a holding, although Mr. Anderson was successful in his petition to the EEOC in California....
>
> I wish there were more of a movement towards vegetarian legal rights. We attempted to start such a movement back in 1999 with the first lawsuit against a corporation for misleading vegetarians. As a result of that effort, I cofounded VLAN (the Vegetarian Legal Action Network) with several other law students. Unfortunately, after we graduated from law school in 2001 and we all went our separate ways, there was no one available to carry the torch and lead the effort.

However, Pizzirusso seems optimistic. He writes, "We have seen more of a movement to ensure that companies are disclosing their ingredients in better ways. For example, on many food labels, you now see words to the effect of 'contains milk ingredients' even if the dairy product is not commonly known, such as whey. This is more due to concerns of food allergies, but better disclosure is good for all consumers—especially vegetarians."

Noah Lewis, 2005 Harvard Law School graduate from Pittsburgh, Pennsylvania, explains that the law and the courts lag behind social change. "On paper, vegans have the same rights as everyone else regarding freedom of speech and religion (reverence for life can, in theory, be regarded as a religion), but the practical implications of those rights are still going to be determined by administrators and judges who will simply follow the prevailing societal views regarding the relative importance of veganism. The law cannot be relied upon to create social change and until society begins to take seriously both vegans and, by extension, nonhuman animals, the law cannot even be relied upon to protect the existing rights of vegans." Lewis founded the Liberation Project, an animal rights organization.

DENIED ADOPTIONS AND ACCUSATIONS OF CHILD ABUSE

Unlike Friedman, who directly challenged the system, other vegetarians may be perceived as offering a challenge by feeding their families a diet devoid of meat or all animal products. This may have dire consequences.

Scientists Sterling D. Allan, whose Web site bears his name, and Thomas D. Rodgers of VeganCowboy.org, both residing in Utah, and working separately, are two among a number of vegetarians who are standing up for a family who experienced a tragedy and then a nightmare. The family's baby died, and then their other children were temporarily taken away by the state. The state claimed the baby's vegan diet led to his demise, but Allan and Rodgers, who claim to have investigated the circumstances, state the baby died and other members of the family were made ill due to faulty ventilation in their house, which caused the family to suffer the carbon monoxide poisoning that killed the youngest.

In another case, a couple from Indiana, James and Shirley Dumas, claim on the Internet that they were denied adoption of a child they love because of their frankness in advocating a whole foods, no-additives, organic, vegetarian diet that they learned was beneficial to youngsters' physical and mental health.

Shirley Dumas says she and her husband even had to change their residence because of irreparable harm to their reputation when they were denied the child. She says vegetarians from across the nation have offered her support, including well-known figures, and also that people are reporting to her similar stories, or that they fear their meat-free families might be next to be torn apart. Lige Weill of Knoxville, Tennessee, president of Vegetarian Awareness Network USA, who tried to help the couple, confirms that similar cases exist. Shirley Dumas tells her story of the lost adoption on VegetariansinParadise.com.

The late Charles Attwood, MD, author of *Dr. Attwood's Low-Fat Prescription for Kids*, was a pediatrician with experience in child abuse cases and an advocate of vegetarianism, who wrote an account of the Dumas case that we quote from the Internet:

> [Shirley Dumas] was confronted by two members of Child Protective Services (CPS), a social welfare agency of the State of Indiana, and two armed policemen. They insisted, she said, that she strip the clothing from Jeremiah, the seventeen-month-old son she and James had adopted eight months earlier. They inspected the child for bruises and then asked if they could look in the refrigerator. Shirley reports that when she said "no," and demanded to know what this was all about, it was opened anyway. She was told that their son was being taken into state custody because she and James were not feeding him proper food. The refrigerator search was done to confirm that there was no meat in the house. It was known at CPS that Shirley and James were vegetarians.
>
> The child was small for his age, but Shirley, who has a degree in early childhood education, had known at the time of the adoption that Jeremiah likely had fetal alcohol effects and would grow more slowly than a normal infant. To assure that Jeremiah was properly fed, she had regularly read about nutrition and sought advice from health food stores. His meals consisted of a varied diet of vegetables, fruits, legumes, and goat's milk. He especially likes lentils. When she explained this to the agents from CPS, their only response was that they were only doing their job. It's been three months since Jeremiah was taken, and all efforts to get him back have failed.

Families raising their children without meat on the table, and particularly without cow's milk in the refrigerator, were demonized a few years ago when newspaper headlines and television newscasters proclaimed that a "vegan" family was accused of child abuse because their daughter was malnourished. That the Swintons of New York, whom attorneys argued were loving but misinformed parents, were apparently not even raising their youngster as a vegan since one of the items in her diet was an oil derived from fish, and that the child's diet seems to have been woefully inadequate did not stop reporters from repeatedly mislabeling the diet as vegan.

Physicians Committee for Responsible Medicine attempted to set the record straight. "Vegan diets provide excellent nutrition for all stages of childhood, from birth through adolescence," PCRM president

Neal Barnard, MD, said in a press release. "In fact, vegetarian children grow up to be slimmer, healthier, and live longer than their meat-eating friends. Raising your children on a well-balanced plant-based diet is one of the best gifts you can ever give them." PCRM even pointed out that famous pediatrician Dr. Benjamin Spock "embraced the use of vegan diets in the seventh edition of *Baby and Child Care*."

Yet even after the Swintons' case was tried and appealed, and the couple imprisoned, the press continued to label the diet as vegan. Undoubtedly, the negative publicity directed at the supposedly vegan family cast suspicion on all parents actually raising their children as vegetarians or vegans. A few who believe that posted their opinions on the Internet, including at Vegan Represent Forums.

> My child is on a strict vegan diet too. I wonder when the child welfare people are going to come knocking.

> Frankly, in my opinion, this is bad journalism. So these parents were vegan. There are bad parents all around. We should have a vegan newspaper with headlines that say "Meat eater kills his wife," "Meat eater cited for driving drunk," "Meat eater jailed for prostitution," "Meat eaters declare war on Iraq," and so on.

> Why is it that the only things in "mainstream" media about vegans or veganism are always negative? Why? Oh but let there be one bad or misguided vegan parent, unhealthy or ill vegan out there and the news is all over that like flies on crap!! Grrr!!

Coming on the heels of the tsunami of Swinton trial publicity was a volcano that erupted on the vegetarian world. This time, all parents raising their children as vegans were virtually accused of child abuse, partly because of a study conducted in Africa on malnourished children. "There's absolutely no question that it's unethical for parents to bring up their children as strict vegans," Professor Lindsay Allen of the U.S. Agricultural Research Service stated at an annual meeting of the prestigious American Association for the Advancement of Science.

Jeff Nelson of VegSource.com, whose ancestors founded the giant Armour meat company, was not about to keep silent. He questioned Professor Allen's study.

> Was this based on carefully conducted research? No. Was it based on a structured study with control groups and meticulous monitoring of what children ate? No. Was it perhaps based on a large number of children eating a normal vegan diet who were found to have a greater than usual risk for illness? No. Her basis for this bizarre and completely unfounded declaration was her experience in Africa. Children who had been eating

nothing but corn and beans were given a little meat and their health improved. Not children on a normal, healthy vegan diet—children who had been eating *nothing but corn and beans*. Adding almost *anything* to their diet would have caused improvement.

Two respected experts on vegan diet, both dietitians and authors of *Being Vegan*, Vesanto Melina, RD, and Brenda Davis, RD, also weighed in on VegSource.com with assessments of Allen's study. Melina wrote in part, "Professor Allen's assertion that feeding children a vegan diet was unethical is unfounded, and reflects the fact that Professor Allen does not know how to create a nutritionally adequate vegan diet." Davis stated, "A standard North American diet of cheeseburgers and fries, presweetened cereals, potato chips and soda pop is a far greater threat to health than a well-planned vegan diet will ever be."

We asked attorney Lee Hall about potential threats to vegetarian families.

> Threatening to remove children from parents who are raising them as vegans has some characteristics in common with challenging Christian Scientist families. These families wish to raise their children according to their ethical beliefs about health. Those who oppose their right to do so may have a motivation that's completely benign: People are earnestly concerned that the children's health is at risk. . . . And sometimes there are strong vested interests motivating the attacks on vegan parents. Lindsay Allen, a scientist with the U.S. Agricultural Research Service, recently lashed out at parents who feed their children vegan diets, going so far as to call such parents "unethical" if the children are very young. The study was partially supported by the National Cattleman's Beef Association. And it was conducted in an African community where children were malnourished, so the subjects naturally responded well to any food, including dried meat. Professor Montague Demment, from the University of California at Davis, was quoted in relation to this study, saying that more emphasis should be placed on animal source food to combat global malnutrition. Plainly there are some political interests here into which the flourishing of vegan children does not fit.

Are vegetarian families at risk from well-meaning but improperly educated social workers and judges—even scientists and physicians? These experts have enormous power, but, in most cases, is their knowledge of vegetarian and vegan nutrition lacking? These are questions raised in the vegetarian world.

Dr. Attwood offered a warning. "Since I've become involved in the . . . Dumas cases, several other vegetarian families have contacted me concerning state threats of taking their children and court orders to feed them meat and milk. Unfortunately, social workers and judges learned about food in grade school—just like the rest of us—from materials and advertising supplied by the National Dairy Council and the National Beef Industry Council. If this must be accepted in order to live in a free country, then we must also accept the possibility that innocent parents are sometimes fallaciously accused of child neglect."

As interest in vegetarianism and veganism rises, and more families raise their children on plants rather than animal products, could meat-eating and milk-drinking politicians, health experts, and child welfare workers pose a threat to those families? Despite the traditional American image of rugged individualism, meaning that the worth and freedom of the individual outweigh the demands of the group or state, the United States today greatly differs from the days when patriots Thomas Paine, Thomas Jefferson, and Patrick Henry forged a nation. The people of that era would have grabbed their pitchforks in protest of freedom-restricting laws and excessive taxation, enacted under the guise of protection or helping the greater good. Whether the collective wants to place a sin tax on fatty foods, prohibit sales of snack foods in public schools, restrict a restaurant's right to allow patrons to smoke cigarettes, arrest a pub owner for a drunken patron who causes an automobile accident, or force parents to feed children cow's milk and animal flesh, no doubt the attacks on freedom, including that of vegetarian families, alarm today's civil libertarians.

Vegetarians are becoming vigilant about their life, liberty, and the pursuit of happiness, as is required of every person in a constitutional republic. In some cases, vegetarians are not even aware that their values may be on the brink of being violated by scientific creations—or, rather, are these creations beneficial to people who do not eat meat?

PART
III

THE FUTURE OF VEGETARIANISM
IN THE UNITED STATES

9

BRAVE NEW WORLD: GENETICALLY ENGINEERED VEGETABLES, LABORATORY-GROWN MEAT, HUMANE SLAUGHTER, AND "VEGETARIANS" WHO EAT MEAT

When I found so astonishing a power placed within my hands, I hesitated a long time concerning the manner in which I should employ it. No one can conceive the variety of feelings which bore me onwards, like a hurricane, in the first enthusiasm of success. Life and death appeared to me ideal bounds, which I should first break through, and pour a torrent of light into our dark world. A new species would bless me as its creator and source; many happy and excellent natures would owe their being to me.

Vegetarian Mary Shelley, *Frankenstein;*
or, the Modern Prometheus (1818)

DR. FRANKENSTEIN OR FUTURE FOOD?

Can Johnny still claim the title of vegetarian if he eats cucumbers containing codfish genes? Plants containing genetically modified organisms (GMOs) have passed from science fiction into reality as scientists have inserted animal genes into some varieties of fruits and vegetables. In the 1990s, scientists created the Flavr Savr tomato by inserting Alaskan flounder genes into a tomato to prolong its shelf life and to reduce the risk of freezer damage. The Food and Drug Administration approved the creation, but the makers pulled it from the market in 1997 after tests showed a likelihood of detrimental health effects from eating the tomato.

Vegetarians have long sounded warnings about animal-plant hybrids and the likelihood that they will show up on supermarket shelves. The technology might usher in a *Soylent Green* movie scenario, suggested San Francisco State University Professor Ronald Epstein, PhD, an expert on Buddhism and vegetarianism. "The types of these genetically engineered 'vegetables' are sure to increase and may very possibly also include human genes. If you are a vegetarian, do you want to be in the position of inadvertently eating vegetables that are part meat?"

Microbiologist Emanuel Goldman, PhD, of the New Jersey Medical School, lauds biotechnology as a great breakthrough for vegetarians. He apparently does not want the International Vegetarian Union to accept any policy against the manipulation of plant and animal DNA. "In my view, the 'fish gene' is simply a sequence of chemical information specifying a protein, which in nature happens to be found in a fish. No fish is killed to get the protein," says Goldman, a vegetarian for ethical reasons for more than three decades. Vegetarians have already benefited from genetic engineering because the FDA more than a decade ago approved a "biotech version of chymosin"—a yeast and bacteria spliced with a gene from a cow—used to make "vegetarian" cheese, says Goldman.

On the other side of the debate, ethicists, environmentalists, religious leaders, health professionals, and citizens are trying to alert the public to what they call Frankenfood—a takeoff on the mad scientist of vegetarian Mary Shelley's novel *Frankenstein*. Jeremy Rifkin, perhaps the leading figure sounding the alarm for more than two decades against genetic engineering, says scientists have already created chimeras with the bodies of goats and the heads of sheep, goats who produce spider silk in milk, mice engineered with human brain tissue, and rabbits that glow in the dark (with a jellyfish gene). He calls the fact that the rabbits have been exhibited as art "high-tech eugenics." Rifkin, director of the Foundation on Economic Trends, warns, "They may be less a harbinger of a second renaissance and more a reflection of the 'brave new world' that Aldous Huxley warned of more than seventy years ago."

Jeffrey Smith, in his book *Seeds of Deception*, lists cases where animals with ready access to both GMO food and non-GMO food always chose the latter. Smith says scientists trying to warn the public about the immediate and long-term effects of genetically modified food are subject to "suppression and vilification" by government and industry, and therefore American consumers aren't fully alerted to these dangers. Dr. Arpad Pusztai, considered a father of GMO technology, lost his job after warning the British public that scientists were introducing genetically modifed food without long-term studies of the possible effects.

Craig Winters, director of the Campaign to Label Genetically Engineered Foods, and a vegetarian, would like see GMO food labeled so people can choose for themselves. At least 90 percent of Americans agree that foods with GMOs should be labeled, he says. Winters's campaign focuses on labeling because it would be "virtually impossible to get an outright ban through Congress."

New York City writer and blogger Mickey Zezima (a.k.a. Mickey Z.), author of *50 American Revolutions You're Not Supposed to Know: Reclaiming American Patriotism* backs labeling efforts but believes people are complacent about the issue of genetically engineered food. "Within the commodity culture we live in, I'd say, yes, we need GMO labels. The longer answer would address how we've reached a point where vegetables contain DNA from a pig and why humanity isn't in an uproar about it."

Raw food advocate David Wolfe, author of *Eating for Beauty*, would like Americans to take more personal responsibility for what they eat, but warns that the giant food manufacturers, the government, the pharmaceutical industry, the chemical conglomerates, and the mass media "have proved over and over again that they cannot be trusted to tell the truth. There is too much money at stake. How can a giant agricultural food company come forward with evidence that a pesticide they have been using for fifty years is actually carcinogenic? They can't. They don't want to open themselves to the negative publicity and the litigation. The media does not report anything that is important—they believe that only spiritually vacant sensationalism sells. The pharmaceutical industry has made doctors vastly more dangerous than gun owners (actually hundreds of times more dangerous). We have to take personal responsibility for our own destiny."

Howard Lyman, author of *Mad Cowboy* and perhaps the most prolific advocate of veganism, calls genetically engineered food the "largest experiment ever conducted on homo sapiens." According to the former cattle rancher, "We are going to find out the cost of this somewhere down the line." Lyman agrees that GMO food should be labeled.

Americans are largely unaware that, as of 2006, about one-third of agricultural land was planted with GMO crops, a number said to be increasing annually at double-digit rates, and about 75 percent of processed foods now contain GMOs—unlabeled.

People interviewed for this book were asked if they have concerns regarding GMO technology, and if a carrot contained DNA from a pig, would that carrot still be a vegan food and would the respondent eat it? Their answers show no clear consensus, but a majority was against the technology.

- Alaskan Delisa Renedio: "I am concerned (about genetic engineering of vegetarian food), but not enough to be working on the issue. I don't know of any other vegetarians working on it either. Are these fruits and veggies still vegetarian? Good question. But I guess I would still consider them vegetarian."
- Science fiction author Piers Anthony would eat such a food "because it doesn't kill an animal."
- Mark Eisenberg from Massachusetts would also eat the food "presuming nutritional and taste merit." He believes it is still a vegetarian food because, "No animal need have died to produce it."
- "It's still vegan," states Bruce Friedrich of PETA. "Veganism isn't a dogma; it's an ethic of compassion. But for an array of reasons (all well covered by others), yes, this is a concern."
- Gerry Coffey of Alabama, who was arrested for trespassing outside of a supermarket while participating in a campaign to alert consumers to the fact that much of the food they are buying contains GMOs, says Americans are being used as "guinea pigs without their knowledge and consent." The charges against Coffey were dropped after headlines like "Grandmoms Arrested at Supermarket" appeared in the national press.
- Will Tuttle says, "It's repulsive to me and I hope I never eat any! Very strange and unethical practices by a food industry that has completely lost all moorings in ethical, harmonious, respectful awareness."
- Libertarian writer Cathy Cuthbert believes that "GMO foods are a potential problem, maybe more politically than health wise."
- Eric Markus, author of *Meat Market*: "From an ethical basis, this is not a concern to me, since there is no evidence that lab-cultured meat would have the capacity to feel either pain or fear."
- Jinjee Talifero of California calls the technology "science gone completely mad."
- Savvyvegetarian.com's Judy Kingsbury answers the question, "Is the vegetable still vegetarian?" by replying, "I don't think so. I can't see GE food as anything but science gone mad and performing dangerous illegal experiments on the population at large without their knowledge or consent."
- Melanie Burtt, vegan restaurateur in Rhode Island: "I think GMOs are disgusting and repulsive. Furthermore, the fact that they are not labeled as such is exasperating. There are an infinite amount of alternative solutions to anything that GMOs would be used for. Sixteen pounds of grain and soybean are fed to a cow for every pound of beef produced. That is a lot of land being wasted to feed a cow that is taking up more land just to be eaten when the grains and soybeans could have been eaten in the first place—not to mention the water used to produce beef. If abundance of food is a concern, I think I might know where to start looking for a solution. If nutrition value is a rationalization,

GMOs are only going to lower that. Variety in the diet can also remedy this. If hardiness is a justification, I hardly doubt that strawberries lasting an extra week, but [that] are stripped of nutritional value because they are spliced with a gene from a fish, are worth any of that. I can live without strawberries for a few months, thanks.

- David Curry of Indiana says, "I do not consume animal products. Mainly [due] to the embodied energy associated with producing that as well as [that] the way it was raised is very cruel for the most part. I do not agree with genetic engineering of life."
- Author Gail Davis of Indiana replies, "No, a genetically modified tomato containing DNA from fish is not any longer a vegan food. Genetic modification of foods is the worst kind of mad science run amok. It has led to something that most people will find even more horrifying. The genetic modification of animals, not just for purposes of more expedient food production, but for medical purposes and who knows what other purposes?"
- Jim Taylor, National Humane Society: "In my mind, genetically engineered vegetables that contain DNA from animals are not, by definition, vegetables, and I would not knowingly eat them. In my mind, once again, a carrot containing pig genes would not, by definition, be a vegetable, and I would not knowingly eat it."
- Delaware's Diana Payne: "I think science is entering a territory that should be left to the way of natural. I do not eat genetically engineered vegetables. A vegetable containing DNA from an animal is not a vegetarian food. I grow as many of my own vegetables as possible to avoid what is on the market."

ABATTOIR TO LABORATORY: DINNER FROM A PETRI DISH

Genetically modified organisms are not the only creation creeping up on vegetarians. A new technology could someday make vegetarian arguments against meat obsolete, such as the argument that raising animals for food involves cruelty, and perhaps the "Thou shalt not kill" ethic. The technology exists to use cells taken from cows, chickens, fish, and other animals to manufacture processed meats, according to researchers from the United States and Britain. Jason Matheny, a University of Maryland doctoral student and coauthor of a paper on in vitro meat techniques, told the press "science is still far from reproducing artificially an entire natural meat, such as a steak or a chicken breast. But the technology is there to produce something like a processed meat, such as a chicken nugget."

Vegetarian Professor Stevan Harnad of the University of Southampton in England in a letter to *Guardian Unlimited* claimed that any meat abstainer who refuses cultured meat because it was "seeded" from an animal "will have lost sight entirely of the moral reason for vegetarianism in the first place—not to do needless harm to feeling creatures."

Like their fellow Americans, most vegetarians are oblivious to the introduction of cultured meat into the local grocery store, which seems imminent. However, some leaders of large vegetarian or animal rights advocacy organizations are already in support of the bizarre biotechnology, as *Satya* magazine reported in 2005.

PETA's Ingrid Newkirk told us the time for cultured meat has arrived. "Cultured meat (meat from cultured cells) is a big hope of ours, and something we've helped fund, so that compulsive meat eaters without the discipline to quit will one day be able to satisfy their urges without hurting animals."

Krissi Vandenberg, executive director of Vegan Action, seems reluctantly like-minded. "I think the creation of 'grown' animal parts is a great idea. If there is a way to satiate the meat eaters without causing suffering and death to farm animals then I support it all the way. I'm not sure about the health issues with this kind of product but decreasing the slaughter and suffering of millions of animals would be well worth it."

Opinions of other vegetarians on the subject of cultured meat are split.

- Bestselling author Piers Anthony is not sure he would eat cultured meat. "Ideologically I could eat it, but my stomach might balk." Mark Eisenberg believes laboratory-created meat "definitely addresses the cruelty issue" and would eat it if the meat is tasty and nutritious.
- Susan Branford: "In the attempt to end animal cruelty, I would hesitantly support cultured meats grown in a lab. YUK!!"
- Kaz Sephton of San Antonio says she wouldn't "touch it with a pitchfork."

SLAUGHTERED WITH HUMANE STANDARDS

People loathe learning how food companies turn animals into chops, cold cuts, and rump roast. A large percentage of Americans do know that factory farms aren't exactly the family farm of yesteryear—an awareness that people have worked for decades to bring about. People want both meat and a clear conscience. Several nationwide animal advocacy organizations and an apparently sizable number of food companies are working to make that happen.

In the 1990s, animal welfare organizations popular with middle America like the Humane Society of the United States appeared to be moving toward promoting vegetarianism and maybe even veganism. However, by 2005, the trend seemed to have screeched to a halt, and even reversed, back toward animal welfare and away from the liberation of animals used for food. Michael Appleby, vice president of the Farm Animals and Sustainable Agriculture Unit of the Humane Society, believes that "most people who are actively concerned about the treatment of animals will continue to eat meat nevertheless." Today, even some of the animal *rights* groups are campaigning for humane standards, while simultaneously campaigning for veganism.

Compassion Over Killing founder Paul Shapiro told the *Washington Post* in 2003 that the animal rights and vegetarian activists need to "stop looking at this as all or nothing, black or white. What if we convert two people to be vegetarian half the time? That's the same as converting one person to be vegetarian all the time, and it's probably easier."

Jim Mackey, CEO and cofounder of Whole Foods, the world's leading natural foods grocery store chain, has become the driving force for the enactment of humane regulations for the treatment of animals raised and slaughtered for food. He founded Animal Compassion Foundation, an independent, nonprofit organization that will educate, assist, and offer research services to inspire ranchers and meat producers to "achieve a higher standard of animal welfare excellence while still maintaining economic viability."

Mackey, a vegan, says, "By creating the foundation, Whole Foods Market is pioneering an entirely new way for people to relate to farm animals—with the animals' welfare becoming the most important goal. There are many universities and organizations out there doing research making production systems more productive and profitable, but there is no one place where meat producers can go to learn about making their processes more compassionate. We are out to change that with this foundation."

Groups such as PETA and VIVA!, which successfully campaigned against what they claimed was cruel treatment of ducks and other animals sold as meat at Whole Foods, now work with the company, as do other animal rights organizations. *USA Today* reported that Mackey says activists did not sway him: "I came across an argument I could not refuse: Eating animals causes pain and suffering to the animals."

In a press release, Viva!USA director Lauren Ornelas stated, "My conversations with Mr. Mackey have convinced me that he is sincerely interested in improving conditions for farmed animals."

If the work of Mackey and VIVA! for humane standards, as well as the work of others such as United Poultry Concerns, Humane Farming

Association, and Farm Sanctuary, results in the abolition of factory farming, would vegetarians forsake abstinence and join the ranks of meat-eating Americans? Or would they remain vegetarians? Most people interviewed for this book would remain vegetarians, but there were exceptions.

- Indiana's David Curry replies, "Yes. I would probably hunt and raise my own if I ever chose to eat animal products again."
- Mark Eisenberg replies that he would not be a vegetarian if factory farming was abolished.
- West Virginia's Jim Taylor: "Yes, I would still be a vegetarian even if factory farming ceased to exist."
- Susan Branford of Las Vegas: "There is no humane way to raise and slaughter animals for food. Laws cannot make what is murder right, moral or legal. I would still be vegan."
- Chris Heinrich, Idaho: "Humane standards for slaughtering animals have been in practice for quite a while. Even though this is in practice, I still don't deem it necessary for animals to be murdered just for a BLT or a leather belt."

Humane Standards don't exactly thrill the Connecticut-based Friends of Animals, which held vigils at Whole Foods Markets in 2005 in protest. "An interest in other animals' welfare doesn't mean paying hundreds of thousands of dollars to concoct new ways of relating to them on farms before baking, broiling, stir-frying or sautéing them. A day of 5% discounts on the store's vegan products would be far more appropriate," FOA founder Priscalla Feral stated in a press release.

It appears that most vegetarians aren't buying the welfare argument.

CARNISM AND FLEXITARIANS

Like meat grown in a laboratory, genetically engineered vegetables are tangible. Words, although intangible, have as much or more power than the material world to change the way people think of vegetarianism. A story in the *Washington Post* says, "What exactly is a vegetarian? The term is so liberally applied that it can describe a wide variety of eating patterns, from semi-vegetarians or occasional meat eaters to hardcore vegans who won't let any type of animal product cross their lips. Some vegans (pronounced vee-gans) are so strict that they won't eat honey."

Vegetarians know the importance of language in their daily interactions with meat eaters and in advocating vegetarianism. Melanie Joy, PhD, EdM, professor of psychology and sociology at UMass,

Boston, and author of *Strategic Action for Animals*, says people generally use defense mechanisms that distance themselves from the reality of meat eating. "This is because people typically need to maintain a positive moral sense of themselves; in other words, everyone needs to believe that she or he is living a moral life."

Most people do not consider themselves to be violent, and yet eating the bodies of animals is clearly an act that is based on violence. When our actions and practices are incompatible, we experience an internal dissonance or incongruence. People typically respond to this inner conflict in one of two ways: They change their behaviors to coincide with their beliefs (e.g., stop eating animals), or they change their *perception* of their behaviors to coincide with their beliefs. The latter relies on a variety of defense mechanisms that serve to distance one from the reality of one's actions. Such defenses depend on language to sustain them. For instance, by referring to a nonhuman animal as *it* rather than *she* or *he*, we are better able to treat her or him as the object suggested by our language. Accordingly, when we refer to meat as having been some*thing*, rather than some*one*, we increase rather than decrease the distance between the reality of meat and the misrepresented end product of slaughter.

> *Carnism* is the word I coined to refer to the ideology of meat production and consumption, with *carnists* being those who choose to eat animals. I created this word because, contrary to popular belief, meat consumption is not an ideologically neutral practice. Like other dominant practices, meat consumption is a social norm whose prevalence conceals its ideological foundation. Meat eating is therefore seen as a given, rather than a choice that is based on the belief in human superiority and that it is ethical and appropriate to eat nonhuman animals. Yet, eating meat, though the norm, is reflective of nothing more than a widely held opinion that is not espoused by everybody.
>
> Typically, it is only those beliefs which run counter to the dominant culture that are labeled. For instance, rather than name those who do not eat meat "plant eaters" or "herbivores," we have labeled the ideology beneath these practices because it is understood that vegetarianism is not merely a dietary practice, but a philosophy in which the consumption of nonhuman animals is seen as unethical, unjust, and unnecessary.
>
> By naming vegetarianism but not its opposite, we reinforce the assumption that eating animals is an ideologically neutral and inevitable practice. When we label the beliefs beneath the behavior, however, we are in a much better position to raise awareness of individuals' choices as consumers, and to challenge the foundation upon which meat consumption stands. This restructuring of language can help illuminate the reality that corpses are not necessarily synonymous with cuisine, and that the

focus of the vegetarian movement is not merely the elimination of meat consumption, but the abolition of carnism.

Some vegetarians would like to eliminate the latest word appearing on the cultural landscape: Flexitarian.

Flexitarian was voted Most Useful Word in 2003 by the American Dialect Society, a fact widely publicized in the press. The society defines it as "a vegetarian who occasionally eats meat."

Grant Barrett, Web master for the American Dialect Society, and whose point of view is his owns, thinks "flexitarian seemed to embody the problems of personal will vs. practicality. On one hand, a vegetarian tries to keep to the plan of excluding meat from the diet. But what about when visiting a foreign country where vegetarianism is a foreign concept? When an unwitting host offers a much-labored-over roast? When grandma and grandpa spring for dinner at the House of Meat?...In those cases, for many people, politeness wins out over vegetarianism: you eat what's on the table and return to vegetarianism as soon as you can."

What is more, writes Barrett, flexitarian has a second meaning: "It's a pejorative use and it tends to denote people who are not truly committed to vegetarianism: those who don't try too hard (who are more than willing to have a steak or beef-fat-fried doughnut at the first opportunity) or those who take on vegetarianism only as an emblem of their peer group, as a way of belonging but not as a way of living."

Barrett received a letter by e-mail from one vegetarian Web master for several vegetarian and vegan Web sites, and whose opinion he believes typical of "die-hard vegetarians and vegans": "A vegetarian does not include meat in their diet. A person who eats mostly vegetarian food is still an omnivore if they eat the flesh of an animal, which includes fish. Trying to put forward a replacement for a word that already exists only serves to inconvenience vegetarians and vegans more than they already are in a world that is largely intolerant to their chosen diet. Flexitarian, defined as a vegetarian who eats meat, is an oxymoron. Meat is not a vegetable. These people are omnivores."

The word *flexitarian* may be embraced by vegetarians, but it has been shown that many do not like it. The survey we conducted for this book reveals a nearly even split in opinion, with the majority disapproving of the new word.

Flexitarian is similar to terms such as the older *semi-vegetarian*, and nonsensical terms *pollo-vegetarian*, meaning a "vegetarian" who eats chicken, and *pesco-vegetarian*, a "vegetarian" who eats fish.

Such words are problematic to vegetarianism as a social movement in the United States. For one, these terms cause a miscomprehension: Does "vegetarian" soup contain ingredients from a chicken or fish?

The loose "flexible" supposed form of vegetarianism deemed "flexitarian," recently touted by the press, and apparently increasingly accepted in society, is diametrically opposite to vegetarianism, which is not ethically vacillating, not a temporary health measure or weight loss technique, but an enduring value not bent upon inconvenience or by a loved one who wants the vegetarian to eat meat.

- PETA's Bruce Friedrich: "I think it's great. The animals don't care if ten people eat one-tenth fewer of them or one person eats no more animals. And so many of these people will slowly go all the way."
- New York City's Heather Wise says, "That person is not a vegetarian. There really isn't a gray area in this."
- "I hate it," says Lisa Herzstein of California. "While I'm happy that those people apparently see something positive in being vegetarian, I hate all those terms such as pesco vegetarian, etc. The reason why—one of our local restaurants in small print at the bottom of the menu says 'vegetarian includes fish.' I think the terms vegan, vegetarian, etc. should be used per their true definitions. If people eat mostly vegetarian but occasionally eat fish or chicken that's what they should say. Ditto for people who are mostly vegan but occasionally eat honey, dairy, egg. [They] can say they're vegetarian, most of the time vegan."
- "I feel that this is a harmful term, which would give one the 'excuse' to eat animal flesh," states Rob Colletti of Louisiana.
- "I think that they are doing far more than most to help the animals. While ideally I'd like everyone to be completely veg, I think that realistically a flexitarian is doing more for animals than 95 percent of the rest of the world," explains Mary Margison of Rhode Island.
- "I think that omnivores are omnivores," states Dash Dennis of Oklahoma. "'Flexitarian' is just another example of spin, tailoring language to reframe issues."
- "The more people who are making choices not to eat animals, the better!" writes Vegan Outreach's Matt Ball.
- "I think they are meat eaters!" says Gloria Weers of Texas.
- Brenda Davis says, "I don't mind it, although I haven't heard it used much, other than in the written form. There are so many people who are largely vegetarian, social meat eaters that I think it makes sense to have a word for them. If they want the world to know that they are almost vegetarian, to me that says they are viewing vegetarian as a good thing."
- Erik Marcus: "I love it. I am all in favor of stepping stones."
- Judy Carman: "Anything that helps people think about the possibility of cutting down on their consumption of meat is beautiful. The more

well-known such terms become, the more people will feel empowered to discuss the idea of eliminating animal products altogether. Such a radical idea takes time for a culture to process. If someone tells me they are a flexitarian, I see a great opportunity there."

- Brian Duprey, New York: "As a vegan I think one who eats meat once in a while should be called a meat eater."
- Sukie Sargent from Texas: "I read somewhere that a part-time vegetarian is 100 percent better than a full-time meat eater. As long as they don't claim to be vegetarians, it's a step in the right direction. 'Flexitarian' could mean anything. This is the first time I heard this expression."
- "I recently bought a tee-shirt for a friend of mine whose last name is 'Flexer' that reads: 'Flexitarianism works for me!'" I thought the coincidence was hilarious and had no idea of the actual meaning of this word. One either eats meat or does not, and cannot be half-vegetarian and half-meat eater," writes Roslyn "Roz" Abramovitch Smith of North Dakota.
- Alaskan Delisa Renideo: "Flexitarian? I think it is ridiculous. However, I guess if it helps reduce the amount of meat eaten, and if it means people are wanting to be associated with vegetarianism, it is a sign of progress, I guess."
- Dilip Barman, North Carolina: "I sympathize with people who are trying to make a change. I am not one to point fingers and tell people what to do, so any change in reducing animal product consumption is a win in my book. I try to be a resource for folks through my talks, classes, publishing, and active vegetarian group that I lead to help them in any way when they are interested in vegetarianism."
- Will Tuttle: "I understand that any move toward veganism is to be applauded. However, a flexitarian typically lacks the ethical component (as often do raw fooders) to stick by any program of sustained animal-free eating. If a flexitarian hears that they need to eat beef for their blood type or astrological sign or whatever, there's nothing to prevent them from doing so."
- Matt and Mary Kelly, Massachusetts: "Although it would be a massively tremendous benefit to the planet if people even cut down on their consumption of animal products, we cannot define the concept of 'flexitarian' as vegetarian. Society is constantly bombarded by media message persuasion, and you will rarely find it in the economic interest of large industry to promote healthy and natural living. We urge people to keep moving in the plant-based direction, for every little bite helps."
- Judy Kingsbury shares he thoughts on "flexitarian": "It's catchy, but wouldn't mean anything to a nonvegetarian. I prefer the word semi-vegetarian."

- Rachel Mertz: "I think that anyone who is consciously avoiding meat is making an effort to better the world, the animals and their health and it is a step in the right direction."
- Matt Ball of Vegan Outreach: "The more people who are making choices not to eat animals, the better!"
- Iowa's Alyson Powers: "This concept seems to appeal to an audience of people who may not be ready to 'go all the way' as a vegan or vegetarian, but can consider 'cutting back' as a more realistic option for them. This flexible approach may also be a nice surprise for people who feel that animal activists work from an extreme 'all or nothing' viewpoint. It is also an effective message for caring people to hear who want to make a difference but feel like they can't change *any* of their eating habits until they are ready to make a complete shift to veganism. Like many things in life, changes sometimes require a gradual transition and for some people, simply reducing their use of animal products might be the step towards a decision to be vegetarian down the road. People who consider themselves 'mostly vegetarians' but who occasionally eat meat—'flexitarians'—are of course contributing to much less animal suffering than others who eat the standard American diet which is heavy in animal products. That being said, I feel that if people's decisions to stop eating meat are based on an ethical objection to animals being killed for the brief taste of their flesh, occasionally eating meat will not even be an option."
- Bill Shurtleff, soy foods historian and founder of the Soy Foods Center, says, "You can't be pregnant some of the time."
- Charles Stahler: "The word flexitarian is totally irritating and at the same time can be positive. In the movement, I think the battle we've always had has been that the movement's view of vegetarianism has often been different than the general public's view. Generally, veggie groups have defined a vegetarian as a person who does not consume meat, fish, or fowl. A challenge 'true vegetarians' often have is when others believe vegetarians eat fish, or a little meat or chicken, etc. So all the terms that waffle on vegetarianism make the problem larger and reinforce that vegetarians aren't really vegetarians. On the other hand, flexitarian is probably better than pollo or pesco vegetarian, which is a term that doesn't make sense to people in the movement, since you can't be a vegetarian and eat chicken or fish, just as you can't keep kosher and eat pig. So at least flexitarian is not using vegetarian in the name."
- Stacy Rice of Pennsylvania: "I have also heard the term 'freetarian,' meaning they will eat vegetarian if they are paying but if something is free at a party or somewhere they will eat it. I think that it's a start. I wouldn't be that way but I figure at least it gets people used to being vegetarian and also gets them eating more meals without meat, which

everyone should do more of! I don't know if these people should be considered vegetarian though. I think that it must be harder for some people than it was for me. For example, a group of my friends went out for dinner together a couple nights ago to a vegan-friendly restaurant (my boyfriend and I were the only vegans) and knowing that one of the girls who was with us had been trying to go vegetarian on and off the past few years, I asked her how it was going. She told me she was trying to go vegan now but it was hard. Later in the meal she ate broccoli off of another girl's plate that had been cooked with shrimp and the fried noodles that I told her had egg in them and she ate anyway."

- Psycholinguist Stan Sapon, PhD, said before the World Vegetarian Congress, "It makes a difference whether vegetarianism is a 'diet' or a 'philosophy.' A diet is a list of the foods you choose—a philosophy is a set of coherent *reasons* for making those choices. You cannot build a movement around a 'diet.' To have a movement you have to have people believing, living and working in concert to realize an ideal."

GOVERNMENT POLICIES AND GLOBALIZATION

Some politicians and vegetarians want meat taxed. They argue that people who don't eat meat should not have to pay the bill for the health and environmental costs of meat consumption. After all, federal and state governments levy excise taxes on alcohol and tobacco products, so why not meat?

On their Web site taxmeat.com, PETA outlines a proposal for taxing meat at a rate of 10 cents per pound. "The companies that raise and kill animals for food represent a multibillion-dollar industry, and the U.S. government has been giving them tens of billions of dollars in price supports and subsidies every year. It is unfair and un-American that the 26 percent of the population who are decreasing their meat intake, and the 6 to 7 percent who identify themselves as vegetarians, are forced to pay the costs attributable to other people's behavior."

However, most vegetarians would rather end subsidies to the animal agriculture industry than lobby for taxes. "Taxing is not the solution. My tendency is to favor less government over more government," says David Kidd, author of *Growing America*.

William Harris, MD, writes: "If we could abolish the CCC of the USDA and put agriculture on the free market, the cost of animal source food would go up and in a couple of generations most people would discover that plant foods are way cheaper and a whole lot healthier. We wouldn't need fat, sugar, tobacco, and alcohol taxes. The USDA/CCC has distorted the agricultural market and this in turn has created our huge and

William Harris, MD, lecturing. Courtesy
William Harris.

largely avoidable trillion dollar medical budget. We also need to abolish
tax deductions for health sensitive business advertising which would
make the media less beholden to the fast food, meat, and dairy misinformation campaigns." The doctor also notes that federal agriculture
policy squanders billions of dollars a year, and gives congressmen and
bureaucrats vast arbitrary powers over American citizens.

"I personally would not support a 'fat tax' or a tax on meat. The 'fat
tax' seems too intrusive. I believe in personal choice not coercion or
more government taxes. However, I would like to see less subsidies for
cattle and dairy," says San Francisco's Dixie Mahy.

Some threats to vegetarianism remain somewhat hidden from the
public. In the summer of 2005, despite widespread opposition, Congress passed the Central American Free Trade Agreement, a pact that
contains a provision requiring the United States and participating
nations to adopt the Codex Alimentarius, an international set of rules
regulating vitamins and food supplements. The Codex, enforced by the
World Trade Organization, slaps severe limitations on the variety of
vitamin supplements available to the public and limits dosages that
can be purchased without a doctor's prescription. It would not be farfetched for the WTO to override domestic laws dealing with GMO
foods and other issues important to vegetarians.

Though the Codex won't initially affect vegetarians, it would not be
farfetched for the WTO to override domestic laws dealing with GMO
foods and other issues important to vegetarians. Author Jeffrey Smith
believes that the Codex and other globalization policies like free trade
agreements give international corporations and governments "pieces
of ammunition [to] governments use to promote their agendas." Renowned vegetarian advocate Michael Greger warns that people "who

care deeply about animal issues . . . should be concerned with corporate globalization."

Judy Kingsbury, a lifestyle coach and founder of www.savvyvegeta rian.com, discusses the ramifications: "U.S. regulations conforming to the Codex will make it more difficult and expensive to obtain supplements, and will have a negative effect on the alternative health industry. Many small businesses will be forced to go under, or sell out to larger companies. Control of food supplements will become concentrated in the pharmaceutical industry, and in conventional medicine. That is the whole point of such regulations, of course, under the guise of protecting the public."

Former cowboy Tom Rodgers says that vegetarians need to watch issues like globalization. "Many vegans live in a closet. But they better pay attention. The freedom to live in a closet is in jeopardy."

Ingrid Newkirk sees an emerging threat to vegetarianism. "The media shrinking to a few stations owned by a few corporations mostly concerned with big business could be a problem for any social cause organization trying to get out a positive message on a limited budget."

"Frankenfood," hamburger grown in a laboratory, the extinction of the word *vegetarian* and with it the practice and philosophy—these are perhaps bizarre possibilities for the future, or very near future in the United States. This scenario is acceptable to some vegetarians and an abomination to others. Potential threats aside, vegetarians are hopeful that the future will only be better than today.

10

HOPE SPRINGS ETERNAL

Whatever my own practice may be, I have no doubt that it is a part
of the destiny of the human race, in its gradual improvement, to
leave off eating animals, as surely as the savage tribes have left off
eating each other when they came into contact with the more
civilized.

Henry David Thoreau, *Walden* (1854)

What does the future hold for vegetarianism in the United States?
Valerie Weaver, editor-in-chief of *Vegetarian Times* magazine, predicts
that the best years lie ahead.

I actually think it's about five to ten years from becoming the strongest
it has ever been. The need for—and it's a tired but true phrase—a kinder,
gentler way of eating is becoming as critical as the need for many more
hybrid cars. Americans (and the world) can be slow to change, but the
combination of obesity's health problems, the toxic (and unconscionable) damage factory farming does and the slowly swinging pendulum
that is finally moving away from the super-size-it culture . . . well, I think
vegetarianism will not explode so much as truly, consistently expand.
And what do you want to bet that flexitarians lead the way?

Like Weaver, Chris Beckley, chairman of the Vegetarian Society of
Colorado, believes vegetarianism will continue on an upward curve:
"Vegetarianism and veganism . . . have a very long way to go to become

mainstream however. But I think as the baby boomers grow older, we all want to live longer and healthier, so slowly the demographics are changing. As for what should be done, well . . . watch our model and see how we will increase our VSC membership dramatically in the next few years."

Stewart Rose, as codirector of the Vegetarians of Washington, has insight into what seems to work in attracting the meat-eating public, and what seems to impede the spread of vegetarianism:

> The vegetarian movement needs to learn that the vast majority of vegetarians are everyday people and come from all walks of life. It needs to represent their interests and also to realize that the majority of new vegetarians will likely come from the same mainstream demographics. Right now I don't see that understanding in many cases. Too many organizations are dominated by individuals who see themselves locked in a battle with "the other side." I believe that this adversarial attitude has not served the movement well. There also seems to be a lack of focus on the part of some groups who delve into issues not really related to vegetarianism. I believe that the vegetarian movement has far too little in the way of resources to engage in issues not very directly related to vegetarianism.

However, Rhys Southan believes that vegetarianism will ultimately prevail.

> I think American Exceptionalism is ahead of the curve on vegetarian-ism. Just like some Americans rejected Old World religions with religions like the Church of Latter-Day Saints and Christian Science, Americans have been relatively good about rejecting old, traditional diets in favor of strange new concoctions like analog meats, nutritional yeast, and wheat gluten. The world, including the United States, is becoming more and more vegan. I think the high-protein diet fad has basically been exposed as such. Most people aren't eating steaks because they think they're healthy. They just think they'll lose weight that way. It's pretty evident that a vegan diet can be healthy; anyone who is at all interested in animal rights won't be dissuaded by the diet plan of a man who died after aging terribly, bloating, and slipping on some ice. Unlike Atkins, a vegan diet potentially has the advantage of being healthy, and a good way to lose weight. Also, you can have a high-protein vegan diet. The "where do you get your protein?" question is still obnoxious, but ever easier to answer.

While Southan gives an optimistic view, Mark Matthew Braunstein, author of *Radical Vegetarianism* and an advocate of medical marijuana, predicts a less-than-rosy future: "While our numbers flourish, that's only alongside the nation's increase in population, as our proportion to the population hardly seems [to be] growing. Despite all our thoughts and wishes and efforts, the death march to the slaughterhouse continues. Will that change? Not in the farm animals' lifetimes, and not in mine. We remain a society of the flock and the herd."

Rod Colletti of Baton Rouge, Louisiana, predicts that the growth of vegetarianism will plod along on a slight upward curve. "Unless an outbreak of mad cow disease doesn't force people to become vegetarian, the present course of the veggie lifestyle will continue at a very slow pace."

Meanwhile, other factors might cause meat consumption to climb. PETA's Bruce Friedrich believes that "neocolonialism (called 'free trade,' but that's a misnomer, since labor can't travel across borders and environmental and labor laws vary so wildly between countries) is certainly going to hurt farmed animals by pushing meat prices down further still and increasing consumption in the developing world."

Perhaps vegetarianism lacks a robust growth curve because of the medical establishment's reluctance to advocate nonmeat diets. Or can it be a lack of knowledge? Michael Greger, author of *Carbophobia*, takes the latter view: "It's mostly ignorance. Medical education tends to center around the more profitable interventions—namely, drugs and surgery—not prevention or lifestyle treatments. Unfortunately, there is also a patronizing attitude that patients just wouldn't be willing or interested in changing their eating habits, so patients may not even be given the choice."

Medical schools flunk when it comes to nutrition. "Forget vegetarianism, what about just nutrition?" says Greger, noting that less than a quarter of all medical schools have a single course on nutrition. "In fact, there was even a head-to-head test of doctors versus patients on nutrition knowledge published in the *American Journal of Clinical Nutrition*. Guess who won? Patients. People off the street know more about nutrition than their physicians. Yet, people still go to their doctors for advice on healthy eating habits, and what their doctors are telling them is killing them. It was not too long ago that physicians advised their pregnant patients to smoke cigarettes to deal with morning sickness. Until doctors learn more about nutrition, their dietary advice can be considered physician-assisted suicide."

People are also seeking dietary information outside traditional channels. Author and lecturer David Wolfe attributes this to two conditions:

> Pain: People are more sick, tired and obese than ever. Everyone is looking for alternatives. Vegetarianism represents a peaceful and viable

choice with a tremendous history stretching back to the beginning
of recorded history. The Internet: The Internet is allowing formerly
controlled and suppressed information about pharmaceutical scams and
toxic animal-food production to reach vast amounts of people. I am
seeing that in the big metropolis on each coast more and more people are
seeking vegetarian options. In the middle of the country (in cattle
country) huge awakenings are occurring. I remember giving a lecture in
Wichita, Kansas and 150 people showed up. Upon talking with people
after the presentation, some of these individuals had never been to any
kind of seminar ever on anything! Again, we are seeing that pain is
motivating people to seek a better, cleaner, more karma-free way of life.

Some vegetarians believe that the environmental and health ramifications of a meat-centered diet will propel vegetarianism. Up in
Alaska, Delisa Renideo believes that Americans "will have to begin
considering the impact of our lifestyles and making more sustainable
choices." She also points to the health crisis as an impetus for a diet
switch. "Until we begin taking responsibility for our own health—and
that includes a whole foods, plant-based diet—we will continue being a
nation of sick and fat people."

New Yorker Pamela Rice argues that people won't give up eating
meat "no matter how logical the arguments for abstinence we throw at
them." But Rice predicts that "external forces will continue to chip
away at meat consumption. For instance, forces such as a bird-flu
pandemic could become a big factor in this sense almost overnight and
even any day now. An E. coli epidemic or mad cow disease outbreak
could make some people animal-flesh shy. Mercury in fish is already
putting a damper on seafood consumption. Dead zones around the
globe are worrying many; as are overgrazing and species implosions
due to ranching and the overcultivation of feed grains. Topsoil erosion
is certainly causing concern at the USDA. Ultimately, the depletion
and destruction cannot go on forever. Yet human evolution has not
wired enough of us to worry about problems further into the future
than the next planting season. Unraveling trends that take decades
or even centuries seem impossible for our species to comprehend.
And on that note, could you please pass the broccoli rabe and bean
salad?"

Connie Salamone, also of New York, who is a grassroots leader in
advocating the cause since the seventies, wrote an essay, "Future
Warning Times." Here is an excerpt:

> She was a small Scottish woman, age 25, with two children under four.
> Grandmother! I never knew you. The 1918 Avian Bird Flu struck you
> down. Your son survived, I was born. I see the red flags everywhere of the

determined will of microbes, bacteria, and viruses . . . in live bird markets, non-hygienic small or factory farms, and in rural villages, humans rip open the guts of those fowl who will be eaten. . . . China will have the audacity to VACCINATE 14 billion birds to "solve the problem." These, the descendents of dinosaurs! . . . Overhead migratory birds travel. . . . No world authority cuts to the raw root. IT'S EATING DEAD BIRDS, STUPID! The meateaters give not an inch in their denial. In their gluttony, millions of vegans and vegetarians could die! The mutated virus will proliferate because of flesheating.

Despite sensational mainstream media news accounts, on March 6, 2006, on ThePowerHour.com's radio show, Lorraine Day, MD, stated the disease of "bird flu" has not been verified, and that if a person has a healthy immune system, such a disease would have no effect.

On the other side of the country from New York, Lisa Herzstein, a lifelong resident of San Francisco, has mixed feelings concerning the future of vegetarianism. "I think that more and more vegetarians are going vegan, but don't see huge numbers of omnivores going vegetarian. I notice that more young people are identifying themselves as vegetarian and hope that it's a lifelong lifestyle change and not a rebellious phase for them. I'm rather pessimistic generally: I'm afraid there will be a huge movement to vegetarianism only when our soil, population, etc. make it the only feasible way of sustaining human life. But I do have hope for one individual/family at a time making changes and becoming vegetarian."

Chef Elaine Cwyner of Massachusetts predicts an "upsurge" as consumers become more educated about nutrition and demand that chefs honor their requests for healthier food. "Veganism will be hard to sell to the masses only because it is so easy to eat meat. Once the population understands how detrimental meat production is to the earth and how a diet with excessive meat is so harmful, they may choose to slowly include a vegetarian meal, once or twice a week for economical reasons and then shift their diet over a little more. The crucial element is time."

Bill Shurtleff, vegetarian and author of the *Book of Tofu*, who helped make soy foods popular, believes that an upsurge or explosion in the per capita number of vegetarians lies far in the future. "Of all the reform movements of the 1800s, vegetarianism has been the slowest to succeed," he says. Reformers of the 1890s believed that by 1990 most people in the world would be vegetarians.

SavvyVegetarian.com's Judy Kingsbury believes that the future growth of vegetarianism lies with the youth. "Most new vegetarians . . . are teens, and that could help bring about more change, although a lot of teens just continue their usual diet, minus the meat."

THE YOUNG VEGETARIANS

The younger generation of vegetarians has various concerns about the future. What they experience today might determine their actions tomorrow.

Amy Blizzard, who resides in a small farming town in Indiana, writes, "Most people in their early twenties are pretty laid back about it, after all, what I eat doesn't affect them. But of course you will come across someone that might roll their eyes or ask a load of questions, and then go into a tangent about how they could never give up meat and can't understand how anyone could." Generally, people are becoming more understanding of vegetarianism, she says. "It's evident in the smallest ways, seeing vegetarian options on dinner menus and in restaurants and special sections in grocery stores."

Small towns in the Midwest are gradually accommodating vegetarianism, but progress seems further along on the West Coast. Karaena McCormack, a young woman from Seattle, Washington, explains her perspective: "Most college campuses have vegan food and I feel that there is a major shift towards veganism as people are discovering the cruelties inherent in meat production and also with animal by-products. There is also so much evidence between animal-based food and human disease. People, especially young people, are discovering how great vegan food tastes." McCormack, daughter of Marcia Pearson, predicts that "vegetarianism is here to stay."

Young vegetarians, too, work to help their fellow citizens change their diets, or at least consider the option. Kim Zagorsky, manager of Foodworks, a health food store in Rhode Island, says:

> I think the bottom line is that a decent number of people really do want to help animals; they just think they could never go vegan because what would they eat? Salad? I can't tell you how many times people ask me what I eat. They think all I do is eat a big pile of fruits and veggies and tofu everyday. Lots of people come into the store to try tofu, but then have no idea what to do with it. They eat it straight from the carton and then never want to touch it again. I think a lot of people are concerned about what a vegan diet tastes like. In my experience, people are more open when you present them with something good to eat along with information. I think people are getting used to gory pictures on fliers. I think last year's vegetarian Thanksgiving was a great idea since people got to taste how great vegan food can be. I wish we had more restaurants here in Providence that were veg.

Similarly, Rachel Mertz of North Dakota works for a bright future for vegetarianism. "In my lifetime I can only hope that I can educate as

many people about vegetarianism, factory farming, and compassionate living as possible. Only with an educated mind can educated
choices evolve."

Meanwhile, some young vegetarians encounter resistance from
family, friends, and fellow students. Scott Ziegler, a philosophy major
at the University of Louisiana, tells of his experience: "The reaction of
family, friends, etc. was at first skeptical. After all, it is one thing to say
one is ready for a life-changing decision, and quite another to live the
change for an extended duration. The attitude on campus is often one
of benign ignorance. Though there are some who seem offended when
they think they are being judged (go figure), most people are curious
and interested. The school as a whole seems to overlook the untapped
resources vegetarians/vegans offer. This, however, is due more to misunderstanding than to malice, and we are always working to remedy
this."

Likewise, high school senior Jasmin Rhiannon Baker-Kinney of
Redmond, Washington, experiences some resistance from her peers.
"When I was little, kids thought it was weird that I was vegetarian....
Now, I'm not the only vegetarian at school and a lot more people are
deciding to stray from the way they've been raised and try to become
vegetarian for various reasons. Some kids don't understand and even
when I explain my reasoning, they think I'm nuts and they want me to
eat meat."

Baker-Kinney, who plans to attend college and major in theater or
film and media studies and minor in journalism, frequently hears
comments like "get a life" or "get a job." "Little do these people know,
but I ride my bike, ski, play soccer and softball, hang out with my
friends, I have *two* jobs, I will be a graduating senior from the class of
'06, I sing, and I act. So, when I get those comments I have to laugh."

Sometimes, Baker-Kinney told us, even adults do not understand
vegetarianism. "Doctors usually say that it's unhealthy to be vegetarian, but what do they know? I don't even have a family doctor because
it's unneeded. I'm never sick because I *am* healthy. Some of my coworkers know that I'm vegetarian and some of them think it's cool and
others think I'm nuts. My immediate family is vegetarian, too, but the
rest of my family doesn't really say much of anything about us being
vegetarian."

Nevertheless, Baker-Kinney believes people should be educated
about animal issues but finds that PETA's activism doesn't always
resonate with people. "A lot of people don't like PETA because they're
too forward and up-front about things, but they make controversy and
get noticed, so people start thinking. In my opinion, the best way to get
people informed is to work it into a movie, or to hear their favorite
band say something about it at a concert or an actor talk about it in an

interview. Most people aren't going to be interested in a subject like that, unless you involve it with something they are interested in."

Vegetarianism, according to Baker-Kinney, "has increased greatly since I was born. I used to be the only one in my school who was vegetarian." During her last year of school, she knew of about ten others. "I attribute it to the spread of knowledge, kids experimenting and the easy access to vegetarian/vegan food. You can go almost anywhere and find something to eat, even if it is only salad," she explains.

Melanie Wilson, founder of *Vegetarian Baby and Child Online Magazine* (www.vegetarianbaby.com) and *Vegetarianteen.com Online Magazine*, shares her insight:

> Whether or not a teen has a hard time being veg really depends on a number of factors, foremost being family support. We really see for most teens that that's the deciding factor. Though a few stay veg no matter what their parents say or do, a number of them find it difficult to stay veg in a family that doesn't support them. For one thing, adults hold the buying power, so especially for tweens (ten-twelve-year-olds) and young teens who don't have jobs yet, they really must depend on their parents to buy healthful vegetarian foods for them; some refuse. Also important is the child's personality and why they decided to go veg in the first place. Many indicate that it's something they read that makes them go veg. Those are the ones who are most likely to stick with it, in my experience. The ones who learn about vegetarianism from peers and never research it are often the ones who go back to eating meat. For them it's a fad. We're seeing the words "vegetarian" and "vegan" in the news so much these days that kids know it's cool to be veg.
>
> Veg teens today face a lot of pressures from all sides: family, friends, school. The stories we've heard have been unbelievable! Of course there are the heartwarming stories of kids who influence their parents and grandparents to go veg, but more often we hear from kids whose teachers and parents are downright hostile when it comes to vegetarianism (and even more so for veganism). I know that this stems from many different issues, but mainly it's a concern for the welfare of the child. Many parents first try the "You'll either eat what I fix or you won't eat anything" tactic, which works in some cases, but to the detriment of the parent-child relationship. For many kids vegetarianism is a serious issue, and it's the first time in their lives that they've chosen to believe in something and stand up for something that is different from what their families have taught them. Parents can handle it wisely, or they can break the bond of loving trust by handling it in a negative way. After awhile, when this tactic isn't working, you would think parents would back down and say to themselves, OK, I need to come at this from a different angle, or even,

hopefully, try to learn more about why the child is going down this road. Sadly, it doesn't always work that way, and some teens have to wait until they grow up and leave home to go veg.

Wilson thinks parents need to know that plant-based diets are safe and "normal." "It's not unusual for a child to independently make the connection between animals they love and the meat on their plate," she says, noting that the majority of teens cut meat from their diets out of concern for the well-being of animals.

> As omnivorous adults we've been desensitized to that whole issue, and we don't even like to think about animal agriculture. I can't tell you the number of times someone has said to me, "I know it's bad, but I don't want to hear about it." They don't want to change, because, let's face it, change is hard. But it's not so hard for a child or teen to change their mindset, because they are in a time of life when so much is new; their main job in life is to form opinions. It's our job as parents to pass on to our children the values we believe to be right, but then someday we have to set them free in the world, and like it or not they will be influenced and develop thoughts and opinions that differ from what we've taught them.

If teens have support, even just parents who say, "Yeah, whatever, eat healthy, OK?," their lives open up to a whole new way of being, reveals Wilson. "I've talked to parents who've developed a tremendous respect for their children, sticking to a lifestyle that the parent was sure was a passing fad. Kids who've been encouraged go on to be positive activists, getting veg food in the school cafeteria, working on state campaigns for better animal treatment, teaching others about the health benefits of vegetarianism. For those kids, being veg is really special and adds an important dimension to their lives. They are rewarded for being compassionate and for sticking to their beliefs. That's a good thing!"

Often, parents who are vegetarian and raise their children not to eat meat face alienation, at least initially. Mary Finch and her young family live near Fayetteville, Arkansas, in a small town of 4,000. "I have never met another vegan," states Finch, who with her husband is raising their children as vegans.

> Sometimes people will say a few negative words but after answering their concerns in a polite manner they seem to accept it, for the most part. I am asked a lot where my children are getting their protein and calcium. I live in the middle of cattle country, so I do get the old farmers who object quite a bit. Once I was told that my kids would grow up to be "really stupid and sickly" if I didn't feed them meat, which, of course, is

Mary Finch, vegan mother. Courtesy Mary Finch.

far from how they turned out. They are both are very bright and the healthiest children around. And people are always amazed because my children eat so many fresh veggies. At potlucks and buffets they always walk right past everything and head straight to the salad.

Like an increasing number of vegetarians, Finch and her spouse homeschool their children. The children's diet was factored into that decision. "They wouldn't get healthy vegan food from the school system. My husband and I were both homeschooled so it's what we are comfortable with. We like to do everything from home: homeschooling, home birthing, and home cooking," explains Finch.

Although those uninformed on the facts of the vegan diet might imagine children raised this way lead an austere existence or must eat bland food, this is untrue; for example, celebrations such as birthdays and holiday traditions in the Finch household are filled with Mary's creative desserts, which were published on VegFamily.com.

[Vegan] holidays are every bit as easy as ones given by meat eaters. There are many vegan cake recipes online that are very simple to make and most health food stores carry soy ice cream. For Thanksgiving and Christmas there are meatless "turkeys" you can purchase or you can start your own tradition. I make a tamale pie every year for Thanksgiving and last year for Christmas I made enchiladas. I used to make little vegan cakes for my children to take when they attended birthday parties but now I have to bake large cakes because everyone always wants a piece. At the parties I give, no one can ever tell that the food is meat, dairy, egg and sugar free and I get lots of requests for recipes.

Does the young mother encourage other parents to raise their children without meat on the table? "I think each family has to find what works out best for them. Would I like the whole world to be vegan? Sure I would, but I'm not going to demand that every parent I meet make their kids stop eating meat. If I'm asked for information about my diet I'm always happy to enlighten, but I'm not pushy about it. I've done a couple of articles about my daughter and the effect veganism has had on her.

Finch's children know they eat differently than others, and therefore they are more accepting of differences in others, explains their mother. "Today as I was taking my daughter to her karate lessons I asked her if she would like to get some flip-flops like the ones most of the other students wore to class and she replied, "No, I don't have to be like everyone else, mom. It's OK to be my own person. I like my pink sandals just fine."

Jasmin Rhiannon Baker-Kinney's mother, Karen Baker, told us about raising her vegetarian child: "We were solidly vegetarian and animal rights years before our daughter was born. She's been raised in a house full of animals and we taught her to respect them." In elementary school and middle school, Jasmin was the only vegetarian, explains her mother. "Because she is a vegetarian, she is recipient of teasing at school. Most is good-natured teasing by friends, and not nasty comments from people who are not friends. . . . Things have gotten better as we've gone along."

However, Baker concedes, "Vegetarianism is still very much a subculture." Three years ago, when Jasmine was in ninth grade, Baker was on the food committee for a school dinner event to ensure her daughter would have vegan food to eat. Baker did not want her daughter to be an outsider, or pay a fee for food she would not eat and have to bring her own meal to the event. "It was the principle of the thing," she says.

Asking that a vegan entrée be made available to her daughter created "turmoil," says Baker, although she carefully explained what that meant and even offered to provide for free the "meatlike" vegan food from a local gourmet company.

Although a vegetarian entrée was deemed acceptable, at first a vegan option was out of the question. Eventually, Baker was heard, but not until after she experienced conflict and the feeling of not having been heard. Turns out vegetarianism was practically unknown, and veganism was not known at all to the person initially resistant to offering a vegan option, says Baker. Jasmin did get to have a vegan meal, but her mother recalls that getting to that point was difficult.

MOVING INTO THE FUTURE

Vegetarianism and veganism in the United States continue to grow. Reasons for optimism aside, the very nature of vegetarianism is rapidly changing as biotechnologists take over from gardeners, and globalism trumps American food laws.

The mainstreaming of vegetarian and vegan products—that is, the enculturation and perhaps co-opting of vegetarianism by multinational corporations—might mean the dominant culture is moving away from meat, or might that have other implications? As Americans continue to incorrectly use the word *vegetarian*, believing a vegetarian eats chicken or fish, will the dictionary definition change?

As this book has shown, people who do not eat dead animals are part of the great tradition of American individualism, and that inherently means they have their own thoughts and opinions on everything and will not be of one groupmind. This strength helps vegetarianism as a social cause, as does devotion to the philosophy and practice.

Stanley M. Sapon, who as an elder vegan has wisdom and experience and as a psycholinguist has insight into aspects of vegetarianism others may not see (or may not agree with, vegetarians being vegetarians), writes,

> Without doubt the most pressing challenge facing "vegetarianism" in the USA is the dilution of energy and focus resulting from a crippling ambiguity in the meaning of the word, and the fading of its perception as a moral statement. It can be said that there are as many definitions of "vegetarian" as there are people who call themselves "vegetarians."
>
> When I reject a restaurant dish because it is made with chicken broth, I am often confronted by a server who informs me, "I have lots of patrons who are vegetarian, and *they* have no objection to chicken." When I ask for dishes that are free of dairy or eggs because I follow a Vegan lifestyle, I am sometimes chided, reproached or mocked for being too fussy, a fanatic beyond the fringe of vegetarianism, or carrying the notion of "vegetarianism" to extremely impractical and unreasonable lengths.
>
> And if I reach for some authoritative source to validate my values and my practices—say, get on the Web and "Google" the words "vegetarian" and "Vegan," I am overwhelmed by the number of differing and conflicting definitions, and confounded by a flood of "hyphenated vegetarians." The list includes: ovo-vegetarian, lacto-vegetarian, ovo-lacto-vegetarian, pisco-vegetarian, pollo-vegetarian, pisco-pollo vegetarian, complete vegetarian, semi-vegetarian, part-time vegetarian, ethical vegetarian, eco-vegetarian, animal rights vegetarian, raw foods-vegetarian, "flexitarian," and even a newly minted outrage, "Freegan." There are fewer ambiguities and contradictions under "Veganism," but while there are differences in

motivation, rationale or strategy, Veganism seems primarily concerned with ending the cruel treatment of animals through the widespread adoption of a plant-based diet.

In simplest terms, the word "vegetarian" has become a lexicographer's nightmare, a modern-day, real life situation presciently brought to life as Humpty Dumpty, in *Through the Looking Glass*, proclaims absolute semantic liberty. "A word," he declares, "must mean exactly what I want it to mean. No more, no less."

When the meaning of "vegetarian" includes all the "hyphenated vegetarians" it becomes impossible to know with certainty what are the missions, methods, rationales or philosophies that support the practice of every different kind of "vegetarian." It is not possible to know whether the word "vegetarian" refers only to a *diet* or to a guiding *philosophy* that incorporates some special restrictions on acceptable foods.

The lumping together of individuals whose primary motivations may be widely divergent is exacerbated by the introduction of other terms now current: veg, veg*n or veg'n, et al. This is obviously a convenient and economical sort of editorial shorthand, or "catch-all" that avoids the need to identify—and label—a cumbersome list of "varieties." There is a vast and growing assortment of beliefs, goals, practices and philosophies that have in common only the management of diets that reject or qualify the consumption of meat. Although obviously convenient, this "lumping" unfortunately results in blurring, ignoring, minimizing—essentially trivializing differences that are literally vital. These new terms erroneously presume that people whose lifestyles represent a "broad spectrum" of ideologies, values, motives, and practices would all feel comfortable and well-served in one common basket labeled veg, veg*n or veg'n. My wife and I have dedicated ourselves and our work for a quarter of a century to *expanding* our comrades' "circle of compassion," and teaching the Vegan values of unconditional benevolence. It is less than comfortable . . . or comforting . . . to be considered part of a "veg" community that encompasses people who conscientiously promote the exclusion of specified animals from their *narrowed* circle of compassion.

This kind of linguistic chaos—anarchy, more exactly—is what follows when a class of behaviors that reflects a glow or aura considered by many to represent admirable virtue, good judgement, and a sign of rational self-discipline may be independently and personally awarded to oneself. To be seen as a vegetarian bestows a special prestige on the bearer of that label, with more than a hint of nobility. The countless self-declared, self-anointed "vegetarians" often impress observers who conclude that vegetarianism has become a thriving "movement." The dictionary explains the word "movement" in terms of "an organized effort by supporters of a common goal. . . . A series of actions and events taking place over a period of time and working to foster a principle or policy."

If the vision of a "movement" is to have any validity, there must be some unifying community of *purpose*. The *practice* of abstaining from the consumption of flesh, or the adoption of some kind of diet—for any of dozens of reasons—does little to evoke an image of a *purpose*.

America in the twenty-first century has become obsessed with diet...all kinds of diets, literally, hundreds of diets, ranging from the logical through the ludicrous, and ending with the absurdly lunatic "freegan." It would take days...and pages...to keep current the growing a list of "diets" that include high protein, low carbohydrate, "caveman," "Archeological," blood-type, raw foods, road-kill, flexitarian, et al. Once upon a time we could only note the differences between omnivores, vegetarians, and vegans. Now there are dozens of diets that involve some degree of restriction of animal foods.

It is more than the words "vegetarian" or "vegan" that are endangered. The endangerment goes far beyond the meaning or definitions of the words. To be exact, vegetarianism is not simply a *diet*—it is an *idea*.

A long time ago there emerged the idea that it was wrong for humans to sustain their lives by taking the lives of animals. What is in dire jeopardy is the fundamental and unifying concept of compassion for the suffering that humans commonly impose upon sentient creatures.

Perhaps the simplest definition of vegetarian diet—the way it was meant by the earliest American advocates of vegetarianism—is the definition from the Bible book of Genesis mandating a frugivorous diet (fruits, nuts, vegetables): "God also said: 'See, I give you every seed-bearing plant all over the earth and every tree that has seed-bearing fruit on it to be your food; and to all the animals of the land, all the birds of the air, and all the living creatures that crawl on the ground, I give all the green plants for food'" (New American Bible).

Today's population abstaining from meat holds a mixture of beliefs, both secular and religious. Nineteenth-century Christian pioneers such as Rev. Sylvester Graham, Dr. William Andrus Alcott, A. Bronson Alcott, and Dr. Mary Gove Nichols were sovereign sons and daughters of the American Revolution who spread a vegetarian message of hope: health, self-sufficiency, and the dream of peaceful coexistence between human beings and animals, a dream that has not died.

On her Web site DietfortheNewAge.com, author Jody Patton paraphrases the late vegetarian singer-songwriter-peace activist John Lennon's "Imagine": "I imagine all the people living in the light of eternity. I imagine a New World Order, but not the 'New World Order' of the political insiders who are in charge of the United Nations. I imagine the establishment of the Kingdom of God on earth. I imagine a New Age where all of the people really do live in peace, sharing the

Marcia Pearson with daughter Karaena McCormack. Courtesy Marcia Pearson.

world in all of its beauty and abundance, an age where there is nothing to kill or die for. I imagine the restoration of all things."

Marcia Pearson, known as the Godmother of Vegetarianism of the Seattle area, warns about the future while offering hope for a meat-free future. Pearson writes:

> Vigilance, vigilance, vigilance! We must never rest on our laurels and assume that we have completed our task, even when it appears that vegetarianism has truly come of age. The best example I can think of, as founder of Fashion with Compassion, is the example of furs. We all assumed that the consciousness was raised because of the drastic drop in sales. The industry, caring only about profits, obviously was planning on resurfacing in a big way and it has reared its ugly head once more. . . . This very thing could happen with vegetarianism/veganism. And when it seemed like all of the "humane" groups were serving vegetarian meals and there were more vegetarian cookbooks than ever before in print, some people even within the grassroots movement assumed that "the work" was being done for us. Supermarkets had many products with the word "vegan" on the label. One of our own officers in the Seattle Vegetarian Society said that our "work was over," while another wise activist from England who was in her eighties protested and said that until every slaughterhouse was closed we still had our work to do.

Dick Gregory would always warn audiences at his lectures that we have to think for ourselves, do our own research, keep ourselves healthy and never let our guard down. He would end every lecture by telling the audience that we needed to confront the lies and act for justice and health freedoms, especially with regard to food—prophetically one of his biggest concerns. Apparently many of those 1970s and early 80s audiences did not heed Mr. Gregory's warnings because some of the biggest myths began to reappear about fifteen years later. While it presently seems to be fading, as the lawsuits against the Atkins "plan" and products are rising in number, it is still amazing that these "high protein" books that had been collecting dust at garage sales in the late 60s, resurfaced as if no one remembered that the whole concept didn't work back then. We must get the information out to the mainstream American public. We must reach those who are so caught up in a fast lifestyle that they cannot imagine anything better than a fast-food drive-through to feed a car of hungry kids. We must counter the dairy industry's myths.

Pearson looks at the cultural landscape and sees the forces threatening freedom when it comes to food choices:

More scary trends are on the horizon and they always involve the corporations we've learned to distrust as grassroots activists, yet mainstream America looks to them with trust and allegiance . . . as GMOs and spy chips (RFID [radio frequency identification] tags) will infiltrate all of the mainstream stores (exposed recently by authors Catherine Albright and Liz McIntyre of SPY CHIPS, as well as the Web sites of investigative reporters John Rappaport and Doctor Leonard Horowitz plus the "100 news stories" which are rejected by mainstream media each year). We must educate ourselves. . . . Vegetarian and animal rights activists need to go out and challenge the standing myths about animal-based nutrition [such as] the myth that hamburgers grow on trees and farms are happy places as seen in children's books. We need then to present the real facts and a realistic true picture of where our food comes from, what is being done to our food, and how it affects us and the planet and the animals' lives. We then need to motivate social action and have consumers take back control of their food supply, be it organics, local small farms, etc. We must tell the dairy industry that our tax dollars do not need to be spent on Milk Moustache ads that run into the millions for each celebrity endorsement. We must support those who speak out. Most importantly, we must show that it's not fleeting pop culture which stands on vegetarian roots but the founder of modern math (Pythagoras) to the inventor of the scissors (da Vinci). We must get vegetarianism's history incorporated into textbooks just as women's and African Americans and other formerly ignored ethnic groups' history and cultures are now included in most history books for school-aged children.

NOTES

INTRODUCTION

Karen Iacobbo and Michael Iacobbo, *Vegetarian America: A History* (Westport, CT: Praeger, 2004), 122.

Vegetarian Resource Group, "How Many Vegetarians Are There?" press release, July 1, 2003.

CHAPTER 1

Thomas Rodgers, "Nothing Needs Die for Me to Live," http://www.tomrodgers.org/MyStoryTLR.htm.

Earl Killian, "Why I Am Vegetarian," http://www.killian.com/earl/WhyVegetarian.html.

Anna Briggs, "Pledging Compassion: An Ethical Basis for Vegetarianism,"*National Humane Education Society Quarterly Journal* (Winter 1997), http://www.atbeach.com/veggie/articles/pledging.html.

Rachel M. MacNair, "Commentary," *Society and Animals Journal of Human-Animal Studies* 9, no. 1 (2001), http://www.psyeta.org/sa/sa9.1/mcnair.shtml.

Hope Tinsley, comment on "Meet Your Meat," http://www.seabury.edu/mt/voss/archives/000861.html.

CHAPTER 2

Mark Tatge, "Vegetarian Foods Plant Stronger Sales," Forbes.com, posted on MSNBC.com, http://www.msnbc.msn.com/id/6008949/, September 17, 2004.

Aramark, "Vegan Options More Popular Than Ever on College Campuses," press release, June 21, 2005.

Ellen Sweets, "Adherents Offer Raw Food for Thought," *Denver Post*, March 9, 2005, F1.

Ken White, "Appetizers: Go Raw Cafe Serves Organic 'Living' Dishes," *Las Vegas Review Journal*, February 25, 2004, http://www.gorawcafe.com/press .html.

CHAPTER 3

Hughes, Zondra, "Should You Become a Vegetarian?," *Ebony*, July 2003, available at www.Vegforlife.com, http://www.vegforlife.org/resources_ebony .htm.

The Veg Blog, "An Interview with Sage Francis," December 12, 2003, http:// www.vegblog.org/archive/2003/12/12/an_interview_with_sage_francis.php.

CHAPTER 4

"Life: Vegetarianism Hard to Define," *Atlanta Journal and Constitution*, September 18, 1992, D3.

Rachel M. MacNair, "Commentary."

John McDougall, letter to the editor, *San Francisco Chronicle*, March 26, 2003, 3WB.

Milton R. Mills, *The Comparative Anatomy of Eating*, http://www.vegsource .com/veg_faq/comparative.htm.

Jody Warrick, "They Die Piece by Piece," *Washington Post*, April 10, 2001, A1.

"The Vegetarian," *Food, Home, and Garden*, January 15, 1898, 2.

Heidrich, Ruth, *A Race for Life: A Diet and Exercise Program for Superfitness and Reversing the Aging Process* (New York: Lantern Books, 2000).

"McDougall Interview with Dr. Roy Swank, MD, Founder of the Low Fat Diet Treatment for Multiple Sclerosis," McDougall Wellness Center, http:// www.drmcdougall.com/swank_interview.html.

"Ruth Heidrich—Defeats Cancer and Osteoporosis," McDougall Wellness Center, http://www.drmcdougall.com/stars/star07_ruth-heidrich.html.

William Harris, *The Scientific Basis of Vegetarianism* (Hawaii Health Publishers, 1995).

Gina Kolata, "Scientist at Work: Dean Ornish," *New York Times*, December 29, 1998, F6.

Judith Blake, "A Whole-Hearted Effort," *Seattle Times*, August 9, 2000, C1.

Dean Ornish, *Dr. Dean Ornish's Program for Reversing Heart Disease* (New York: Random House, 1990).

"Ornish Plan May Help Battle Prostate Cancer: A New Study Indicates That a Very Low-Fat Diet and Lifestyle Changes Might Keep the Disease from Getting Worse," *Omaha World-Herald* (Nebraska) August 11, 2005, A9.

"Diet/Drug Combo Rescues High-Risk Heart Patients," http://www.pcrm
.org/magazine/GM99Autumn/GM99Autumn4.html.

C. B. Esselstyn Jr., "Updating a 12-Year Experience with Arrest and Reversal Therapy for Coronary Heart Disease (An Overdue Requiem for Palliative Cardiology)," *American Journal of Cardiology* 84 (1999), 339–341.

Feminists for Animal Rights: An EcoFeminist Alliance, http://www.farinc
.org/about.html.

Hank Pellissier, "Is Eating Meat a Catholic Sin?" SFGate.com, February 2, 2004.

"Didn't Jesus Eat Meat?" Christian Vegetarian Association Web site, http://
www.christianveg.com/wwje.htm.

VegWeb, Surveys, http://vegweb.com/cgi/survey/survey.cgi?action=view&
survey=Veg_Survey.

CHAPTER 5

Trulie Ankerberg-Nobis, "A Feminist Animal Rights Activist Tells Her Story," *Animal Writes*, February 1, 2004.

CHAPTER 7

John McDougall, "Vegan Diet Damages Baby's Brain—Sensationalism!" McDougall Wellness Center, http://www.drmcdougall.com/news/brain_dam age.html.

Stanley M. Sapon, "When Is a Question?" Vegan Values, http://www.vegan values.org/when_question.htm.

Carol J. Adams, "Carol Explains the Absent Referent," 2004, http://www
.triroc.com/caroladams/absent.htmlCarol.

Paul Amato and Sonia A. Partridge, *The New Vegetarians: Promoting Health and Protecting Life* (New York: Plenum Press, 1989).

Cathy Cuthbert, "Confessions of a Vegan Libertarian," http://www.lew rockwell.com/cuthbert/cuthbert11.html.

CHAPTER 8

Stop Huntingdon Animal Cruelty, http://www.insidehls.com/events.htm.

U.S. Department of Justice, press release, http://www.usdoj.gov/usao/nj/
publicaffairs/NJ_Press/files/shac0526_r.htm.

David Sugar, "America's War on Speech and the Shac 7 Trial," http://
www.dissidentvoice.org/June05/Sugar0606.htm.

Steven Best and Richard Kahn, "Trial by Fire: The SHAC 7 and the Future of Democracy," http://www.indybay.org/news/2004/08/1692517.php, August 20, 2004.

Alex Jones, "New 'Eco-Terrorist' Legislation a Hidden Assault on All Americans," www.prisonplanet.com, March 30, 2005.

American Civil Liberties Union, "Homeland Security Officials Wrongly Arrested Peaceful Protesters in Georgia, Charges ACLU," press release, September 22, 2005.

Ingrid Newkirk, "Remembering Our Rights," *Satya* (October 2005), http://www.satyamag.com/oct05/newkirk.html.

Stephanie Dunnewind, "Happier Meals," *Seattle Times*, January 30, 2002, C1.

Ketrina Hoskin, "Good Ol' Boy," *USA Today*, June 19, 1996, A3.

Harish Bharti, http://www.pressreleasenetwork.com/pr-2002/mar/mainpr 1097.htm, March 11, 2002.

Jerry Friedman, http://www.vegparadise.com/news1.html, June 26, 2001.

Scott D. Meyer, "Appeal Filed on 'Ethical Veganism' Religion Lawsuit Against Kaiser Permanente," http://www.myerlawfirm.com/pr06.htm, May 10, 2001.

Neal Barnard, "Reporters Misusing 'V' Word in Undernourished Baby Story," press release, Physicians Committee for Responsible Medicine, May 4, 2002.

Lindsay Allen, annual meeting, American Association for the Advancement of Science.

Michelle Roberts, "Children 'Harmed' by Vegan Diets," BBC News, http://news.bbc.co.uk/2/hi/health/4282257.stm.

Jeff Nelson, "National Cattlemen's Beef Association Pays for Sadistic Anti-Vegan 'Study,'" VegSource.com, http://www.vegsource.com/articles2/ncbs_vegan_study.htm, February 22, 2005.

Vesanto Melina and Brenda Davis, VegSource.com.

CHAPTER 9

Ronald Bailey, Veggie Tales, Reason Online, November 27, 2002, http://www.reason.com/rb/rb112702.shtml.

Ronald Epstein, "Genetic Engineering: A Major Threat to Vegetarians," *Vajra Bodhi Sea: A Monthly Journal of Orthodox Buddhism* 23, series 55 (February 1993), 44–45.

Claude Pasquini, "Genetic Engineering: Can It Be All That Bad? Ask the Animals!" *IVU News* (August 1999), http://www.ivu.org/news/aug99/genetic .html.

Rupert Cornwell, "Why Meat May Not Be Murder for Vegetarians," *The Independent* (London), August 13, 2005, 11.

Stevan Harnad, "Few Beefs Over Laboratory-Grown Meat," August 16, 2005, *The Guardian*, http://www.guardian.co.uk/letters/story/0,1549781,00.html.

Dennis Rodkin, "Vegetarianism vs. Mindful Meat Eating: What's Better for the World?" November 2002, Conscious Choice.com.

"Whole Foods Market Establishes Foundation to Help Achieve More Compassionate Treatment of Farm Animals," Austin, Texas, December 14, 2004. http://www.wholefoodsmarket.com/company/pr_12-14-04.html.

Bruce Horovitz, "Whole Foods Pledges to Be More Humane," *USA Today*, http://www.usatoday.com/money/industries/food/2003-10-21-wholefood_x.htm.

"Whole Foods Market to Create Humane Farming Standards: Viva! Declares Campaign Moratorium," October 21, 2003, http://www.vivausa.org/newsreleases/10-02.htm.

Friends of Animals, "Whole Foods Promotes 'Responsible' and 'Compassionate' Flesh Foods," press release, January 19, 2005, http://www.friendsof animals.org/news/2005/january/whole-foods.html.

http://www.peta.org/feat/proggy/2004/winners.html.

Sally Squires, "Eat Your Veggies!" *Washington Post*, http://www.newveg.av .org/Eat-your-veggies.htm.

David Montgomery, "Animal Pragmatism," *Washington Post*, September 8, 2003, C1.

People for the Ethical Treatment of Animals, www.taxmeat.com.

Michael Greger, "FTAA: Trading Away Our Right to Protect Animals," *Satya*, www.satyamag.com/jan04/greger.html.

CHAPTER 10

Stanley M. Sapon, "When Is a Question?" http://www.veganvalues.org/when_question.htm.

SELECTED RESOURCES

BOOKS

Amato, Paul, and Sonia Partridge. *The New Vegetarians: Promoting Health and Protecting Life* (New York: Plenum Press, 1989).

Iacobbo, Karen and Michael Iacobbo. *Vegetarian America: A History* (Westport, CT: Praeger, 2004).

Maurer, Donna. *Vegetarianism: Movement or Moment* (Philadelphia: Temple University Press, 2002).

Masson, Jeffrey. *The Pig Who Sang to the Moon* (New York: Ballantine, 2003).

Smith, Jeffrey. *Seeds of Deception* (Fairfield, IO: Yes! Books, 2004).

WEB SITES

General

Judy Kingsbury, http://www.savvyvegetarian.com/
Stanley Sapon, www.veganvalues.org/
Jeffrey Smith, http://www.seedsofdeception.com/
Jenna and Bob Torres, http://www.veganfreak.com/
Vegetarians of Washington, http://www.vegofwa.org/
Craig Winters, www.thecampaign.org

Politics and Blogs Pertaining to Vegetarianism

www.erikmarcus.com
www.erinpavlina.com/blog/
www.meria.net

www.notmilk.com
www.rense.com
Vaccination Liberation, www.vaclib.org/
www.vegancowboy.org/

Business

All Vegan (Joy Zakarian), www.allveganshopping.com
Duprey Cosmetics, www.dupreycosmetics.com
Eccobella, www.eccobella.com
Pangea, www.veganstore.com
Savvy Vegetarian (Judy Kingsbury), www.savvyvegetarian.com
Soyfoods Center (Bill Shurtleff), www.thesoyfanclub.com/SoyaScandatabase/
    soyfoodscenter.asp
Snooty Jewelry www.snootyjewelry.com
The Veg Advantage, www.vegadvantage.com
Vegepet, www.vegepet.com
Whole Foods, www.wholefoods.com

Religious, Spiritual, Peace/Nonviolence

Catholic Concern for Animals-USA, http://www.catholic-animals.org/
Keith Akers, www.compassionatespirit.com
http://www.allcreatures.org
Hallelujah Diet, www.hacres.com
Richard Schwartz, www.jewishveg.com
Jody Patton, www.dietforanewage.com
Humane Religion (Christianity and vegetarianism, etc.), humanereligion.org
Father John Dear, www.fatherjohndear.org
Center for Teaching Peace (Colman McCarthy), 4501 Van Ness Street, N.W.,
    Washington, DC 20016, (202) 537–1372 (no Web site)

Health and Diet

The Campaign (for labeling genetically engineered organisms), www.the
    campaign.org
Brenda Davis, www.brendadavisrd.com
Lorraine Day, www.drday.com
Get Well Stay Well, America!, www.getwellstaywellamerica.com
Doug Graham, DC www.foodnsport.com
Michael Greger, www.drgreger.org
William Harris, http://www.vegsource.com/harris/
Healthful Living International, www.healthfullivingintl.org
Ruth Heidrich, www.ruthheidrich.com
Hippocrates Health Institute (Brian Clement), www.hippocratesinst.com
Suzanne Havala Hobbs, http://www.onthetable.net/bio.html
Last Chance for Animals (Chris DeRose), http://www.lcanimal.org/

John McDougall, www.drmcdougall.com
Models (Heather Chase), www.modelswc.com
National Health Association (formerly American Natural Hygiene Society), www.healthscience.org
Not Milk (Robert Cohen), www.notmilk.com
People for the Ethical Treatment of Animals (Ingrid Newkirk, Bruce Friedrich), www.peta.org
Physicians Committee for Responsible Medicine, www.pcrm.org
Kerrie Saunders, www.drfood.org
Seventh-Day Adventist, http://www.llu.edu/llu/vegetarian/
Vaccination Liberation, www.vaclib.org
David Wolfe, www.davidwolfe.com

Food: Culinary, Hunger

Chef Beverly Lynn Bennett, www.veganchef.com
Chef Al Chase, www.chefal.org
Food for Life (Hare Krishna), www.ffl.org
Food Not Bombs, www.foodnotbombs.net
Chef Ron Picarski, www.ecocuisine.com

Vegetarian Organizations

Miriam Cocoran, veg dating, http://www.veggiesinmotion.org/
Great American Meatout, www.meatout.org
International Vegetarian Union, www.ivu.org
Soy Happy, www.soyhappy.org
Vegan Cowboy (Thomas Rodgers), www.vegancowboy.org
Vegan Values (Stanley Sapon), www.veganvalues.org/
Vegetarian Resource Group, www.vrg.org

Multimedia

http://www.goveganradio.com/
http://www.vegtv.com/

Vegetarian Publications on the Web

Herbivore, http://herbivoremagazine.com/
Satya, www.satya.com
Vegetarian Baby and Child, www.vegetarianbaby.com
Vegetarian Journal, www.vrg.org
Vegetarian Teen, www.vegetarianteen.com
Vegetarian Times, www.vegetariantimes.com
Vegetarian Voice, www.navs-online.org
Veg Family, www.vegfamily.com
VegNews, www.vegnews.com

Animal Rights or Welfare: Groups or Publications

Animal People, www.animalpeoplenews.org
Animal Rights Online (Susan Roghair), www.geocities.com/RainForest/1395/
Farm Sanctuary, www.farmsanctuary.com
Friends of Animals, www.friendsofanimals.org
Last Chance for Animals (Chris DeRose), http://www.lcanimal.org/
Models with Compassion (Heather Chase), www.modelswc.com
People for the Ethical Treatment of Animals (Ingrid Newkirk, Bruce Frie-
   drich), www.peta.org
United Poultry Concerns, www.upc.org

INDEX

ABOUT THE AUTHOR

KAREN IACOBBO is a journalist, researcher, and Adjunct Professor of Freshman Studies at Johnson & Wales University. She and Michael Iacobbo are the authors of *Vegetarian America: A History* (Praeger, 2004).

MICHAEL IACOBBO is a journalist who has worked for the Associated Press, the Providence *Phoenix*, and other publications. He and Karen Iacobbo are the authors of *Vegetarian America: A History* (Praeger, 2004).

For further information contact Karen and Michael Iacobbo at the Vegetarian Museum, P.O. Box 334, Greenville, RI 02828; e-mail: reg usa@cox.net. Their Web site is www.vegusa@info.